Grandparents/
Grandchildren

Billy's drawing.

Grandparents/ Grandchildren

The Vital Connection

**Arthur Kornhaber, M.D.
and Kenneth L. Woodward**

With a New Introduction by the Authors

Transaction Publishers
New Brunswick (U.S.A.) and London (U.K.)

Second printing 1991
New material this edition copyright © 1985 by Transaction
Publishers, New Brunswick, New Jersey 08903. Original edition
copyright © 1981 by Arthur Kornhaber and Kenneth L.
Woodward.

Library of Congress Catalog Number: 84-28034
ISBN: 0-87855-994-9 (paper)
Printed in the United States of America

Library of Congress Cataloging in Publication Data

Kornhaber, Arthur.
    Grandparents/grandchildren.

    Bibliography: p.
    Includes index.
    1. Grandparent and child—United States.
2. Grandparents—United States—Interviews. 3. Children
—United States—Interviews. 4. Conflict of generations.
I. Woodward, Kenneth L. II. Title.
HQ759.9.K67   1985   306.8'7   84-28034
ISBN 0-87855-994-9 (pbk.)

TO:

Chantal
David
Jeff
Kyle
Mila
Sabra
Todd
their Mothers
and their Grandparents

AND TO

Maryasha and Mordecai Vinocur, Great-Grandparents
in loving memory

Acknowledgments

We wish it were possible to acknowledge the contributions of all those people who helped us in this work. It is truly the sum of the emotional and intellectual contributions of hundreds of people; those who worked as investigators, and those who shared their life experiences with us.

We thank the institutional administrators, teachers, caretakers, therapists, writers, scientists, and consultants, working in schools, offices, day-care centers, old folks' homes, and social agencies who have assisted us in our investigation.

The format for the clinical investigation was designed and conceived by Arthur Kornhaber, M.D. Several people were instrumental in this process, supplying encouragement and inspiration. Among them are Mr. Shamus Culhane, Mrs. Ruby Houlihan, Eugene Kornhaber, M.D., Mr. Stuart Ostrow, and Mr. Eugene Wolkoff. Our colleagues were especially helpful in exchanging ideas and helping to refine the research questionnaire. Among them are Linda Seaver, A.T.R., John Stanley, A.C.S.W., and Susan Cook, A.C.S.W. Our research efforts were assisted by Kate Johnson, Chantal Kornhaber, and Evie Wissner. Emanuel Hammer, Ph.D. gave us helpful advice concerning the interpretation of the children's drawings.

The clinical interviews were done by Arthur Kornhaber, M.D. and Carol Kornhaber. The latter participated in all phases of the investigation and helped to refine the questionnaire used in the study. She interviewed grandparents "in place" and made many new friends in the process. Her gift of compassion enabled children and grandparents to express themselves freely to her in a short period of time. The invaluable information that she helped us to obtain is the basis for our "emotional history."

Most of all we thank the people who shared their life experiences with us, as grandchildren, parents and grandparents, and who taught us that whether or not we acknowledge it, we are all connected to a grandparent somewhere.

Introduction to the Transaction Edition

Arthur Kornhaber and Kenneth L. Woodward

Ten years ago, we began the first in-depth study of the relationship between grandparents and grandchildren. That study produced an extensive body of research; that research eventually turned into a book; that book led to the creation of a foundation—the Foundation for Grandparenting—and all this helped fuel a national movement.

The goal of that movement is to create a truly intergenerational society. Put another way, the movement aims to reverse the current trend in America toward an age-divergent society, a society in which grandparents, parents, and grandchildren have become increasingly segregated and emotionally alienated from each other. In a divergent society, each generation suffers from the loss of those emotional bonds—what we call "vital connections"—which history and human experience tell us ought to bind them together. We are convinced that the old and the young have great need of each other, and that the burdens of being a parent are considerably reduced when children have regular and intimate contact with their grandparents. But the sad truth is that in most American families, relations between grandparents and grandchildren have become increasingly formal, strained, and devoid of emotional substance. Our ongoing research indicates that no more than 15 percent of

American children enjoy regular and intimate contact with at least one grandparent.

The good news is that families can recover their natural, intergenerational ties. When we began our study, our aim was to analyze and describe the power of the grandparent-grandchild bond. We discovered that this bond is second in emotional power and influence only to the relationship between parents and children. Moreover, we discovered that no matter how grandparents act, they affect the emotional well-being of their grandchildren, for better or worse, simply because they exist. By listening to what grandchildren and grandparents revealed about their need for each other, we were able to draw up an agenda which families can use to assess their intergenerational ties and strengthen their vital connections.

Thousands of Americans who have read this book have discovered themselves in it. Grandparents, in particular, have recognized that something is missing in their lives—their own grandchildren. And many have resolved to do something about that loss. We know because in the past five years more than 10,000 people have written to us, pouring out their stories of severed relations with children and grandchildren. To cite one recent example: a woman from Texas wrote to tell us of her grandson, partially retarded, whose parents had placed him in a public institution for the mentally handicapped. This grandmother brings the boy to her home whenever possible, and each time the boy cries when he has to return to the institution: "Grandma, why can't I live with you?" he asks. The grandmother, still in her midfifties, has repeatedly offered to raise the child herself, but her daughter and son-in-law refuse permission. "There's bad blood between my daughter and me," the grandmother admits.

The Foundation for Grandparents (Mt. Kisco, New York) was created in part to help untangle such family problems.

Organized in 1982, it now has hundreds of members in every state. One purpose of the foundation is to galvanize support for the Grandparents' Rights Movement. As matters now stand, parents can—for whatever reasons—prevent their children from having any contact whatsoever with their children's grandparents. But, as our research shows, the natural and inevitable emotional conflicts between parents and children often triggered by divorce need not and should not vitiate the unique emotional bond between grandparents and grandchildren. One of our most important psychological findings is that conflict between parents and children are not passed along to those parents' grandchildren. In other words, no matter what kind of parents we are or were, all of us can be wonderful grandparents.

Through the Grandparents' Rights Movement, this message from the book is getting across to lawyers and judges. As of this writing, 49 states have passed Grandparents Visitation laws; and a model for a uniform law for all states, which grandparents can use to secure their right to see their own grandchildren, is now pending in the U.S. Congress. Congressmen Mario Biaggi (Democrat, New York), sponsor of the bill, has spoken eloquently of the plight of the disconnected grandparent and grandchild—and of the delicacy needed when families resort to the courts to help preserve intergenerational bonds. Said Biaggi: "Visitation should only be awarded when it is in the best interests of the child. Yet the vital connection between grandparents and grandchildren should be given full consideration by judges when making this determination."

Inevitably, the movement to protect the grandparent-grandchild bond has led to a wider social concern: the development of a truly intergenerational society. It is within this larger movement that this book rightly finds its roots and rationale. We do not regard the modern nuclear family as a natural or sufficient environment for raising children, especially when both parents are working outside the home. Viewed historically, the nuclear family is a human aberration. For the 4,000 years humankind has been known to exist, children have been typically raised by tribes, clans, and variously extended networks of kin. America itself was settled by extended immigrant families. These families did not always share the same house—they usually did not—but they lived near each other, supported each other, loved and fought for each other, and enriched each other's lives through emotional attachments.

Through their own experience of trying to raise children, parents are discovering that the truncated nuclear family is not enough. That is why we are witnessing a national movement to bring the generations back together. Evidence of this movement can be found in scores of programs that have lately sprung up in cities and towns across the United States. In some of these programs, elders of the community take their lunch with children in school cafeterias; some become class grandparents; in others, children visit nursing homes. Some colleges are providing intergenerational housing where retirees cut off from their own families live with students who are away from home for the first time. And in countless churches, synagogues, and temples, each generation is learning to minister, in the fundamental meaning of that word, to those who have preceded and followed them in life.

Sensing a trend, academicians are holding intergenerational conferences and workshops. They are exploring the dynamics of the trigenerational family and reexamining the meaning of old age in light of the opportunities for nurture which being a grandparent, aunt or uncle, or even a godparent provides. To cite but two examples since this book was first published: the 1981 National Forum on Inter-generational Relationships, sponsored by the Federal Council on Aging, and a similar conference in 1982 jointly sponsored by the National Institute for the Family and the American Jewish Committee.

The media, too, have lately gotten the message. Notice how many more grandparent figures are appearing in television commercials and print advertising. Grandparents Day, designated for the second Sunday in September, has become a national observance. And to augment this trend, publishers are putting out how-to books for elders who have forgotten how to be grandparents.

The irony is that being a grandparent is not a learned experience. As this book amply demonstrates, grandparenting is something that comes naturally to people if they are at all sensitive to vital connections. All they need to *know* is how much their grandchildren need them. And all they need to *do* is spend time with their grandchildren. Human nature does the rest. But today's grandparents, it seems, need to be told they are needed. That is why we wrote this book.

This is a book for both parents and grandparents. Open its pages and find yourself in it. It is also a book for students of psychology, sociology, gerontology, intergenerational studies, and social work. Teachers and professors will find in the book's appendixes the same questionnaires we used in our field work. Using those questions, they can test our results against those of their own students. We are confident that they, too, will discover the meaning and value of vital connections.

Contents

List of Illustrations

Introduction

A. *Human Connections*

Every time a child is born, a grandparent is born too. Society records the child's birth, and its parents, but not its grandparents. Grandparents do not belong among our vital statistics. One reason why this is so is that a child is born only once, while a grandparent is reborn with each new grandchild. Another reason, perhaps, is that people do not have to *do* anything in order to become grandparents. Parents cannot choose to be grandparents any more than children can choose to be born. In both cases, it is something that happens to them, a gift. For children, it is the gift of life. For grandparents, it is a gift of a new connection between all who have preceded them and all who proceed from them.

To exist is to be connected. In the natural order of things, the generations emerge telescopically, one out of the other. Genetically, every child is the sum of two parents and four grandparents and so on past the borders where memory keeps watch. The child in the womb already possesses instincts, temperament, and emotions that are not his or hers alone. Psychologically, every child develops not only within the world of its parents but also within the larger world of its grandparents, of "our fathers' fathers." Thus, there is a natural, organic relationship between the generations that is based on biology, verifiable psychologically and experienced as feelings through emotional attachments.

This book is about the emotional attachments between grandparents and grandchildren. More precisely, it is about the *loss* of these attachments and the effects of this loss on children, on older people and, to a more limited extent, on the generation in between. Our conviction, borne out by more than three years of lengthy, in-depth personal interviews with some three hundred children and as many grandparents, is that the bond between grandparents and grandchildren is second in emotional power and influence only to the relationship between children and parents.

This is also a book about the family. Specifically, it is about the three-generational family—grandparents, parents, and children—which experts assure us no longer exists. But it exists to children. Sociologically, the experts may be right; psychologically, they are most assuredly wrong. All children know that they are grandchildren. All grandparents know that they are grandparents. When grandparents fulfill their role, as some still do, they create the three-generational family. When they do not, they become, at best, mere figureheads to a two-generational "nuclear" family. But no matter how grandparents act, they affect the emotional well-being of their grandchildren, for better or worse, simply because they exist.

Finally, this is a book about human emotions. Emotions never change. People change; their bodies change with age; their ideas and attitudes change; cultures evolve and societies change. But emotions remain the same. Through emotions we join and respond to others; they become a part of us and we a part of them. Emotional attachments, therefore, are the cement of human connections. Without emotional attachments, we can know *about* each other but we cannot *know* each other. Emotional attachments cannot be measured, they can only be experienced.

Emotional attachments between grandparents and grandchildren are unique. The normal conflicts that occur between children and parents simply do not exist between grandchildren and grandparents. This is because grandparents, no matter what they were like as parents, are exempt from the emotional intensity that characterizes parent-child relationships. The common view that grandparents have all the fun of being a parent and none of the responsibility is based upon a profound psychological truth that has become evident in our research: neuroses are passed on between consecutive generations but are not transmitted to alternate generations. Therefore, grandparents and grandchildren are naturally at ease with each other while both have intense emotional relationships with the middle generation. In short, grandparents and grandchildren do not have to *do* anything to make each other happy. Their happiness comes from *being* together.

With grandparents, grandchildren do not have to perform as they must for parents, peers, and teachers. With grandchildren, grandparents are removed from the ranks of the "Aged"; to grandchildren, close grandparents are ageless. The emotional attachment between grandparents and grandchildren, in sum, confers a natural form of social immunity on children that they cannot get from any other person or institution. The attachment is, in itself, an emotional sanctuary from the pressures of the outside world.

B. "Billy"

This book was conceived and written because a young boy named Billy loves—and is loved by—his grandparents. Had we never met Billy, we might never have come to understand what a grandparent really is and what grandparents are really for. We are all grandchildren, but only children like Billy understand what grandparents are all about.

Billy was brought to see us because he was having great difficulty adapting to a world which understandably wanted him to sit still, behave, and learn. He was a nervous, sensitive eight-year-old, constantly in motion. Much as his mind wanted him to comply with what his parents and teachers asked of him, his body and emotions just wouldn't follow orders. He was constantly being criticized and chastized by people in a busy, hurry-up world. Like other adults in his life we were concerned with what was "wrong" with Billy, but he insisted upon telling us what was "right" with him. He wanted to talk only about his grandparents. Even though therapists are for listening, it took a good deal of stomping and stubbornness from Billy before he could make us pay attention to what he wanted to say.

Billy told us that his grandparents made him "feel good." Only with them could he find a refuge where he did not feel guilty or stupid or bad. With them he could feel relaxed, calm and accepted. We rarely heard a child laud his grandparents in the way Billy did in session after session. We talked with his grandmother and grandfather and learned that they were just as delighted with Billy as he was with them. Billy was someone special to them and only with them did Billy himself feel special.

During his treatment, we asked Billy to draw a picture of his family and tell us a story about the drawing—a routine procedure which enables therapists to gain a view of the child's inner life. We have reproduced this drawing as the frontispiece to this book because, from an emotional point of view, what Billy spontaneously produced is a universal image of the human family.

We were awed by Billy's drawing and by his brief but emotionally complete account of what was going on in his world. His picture is biologically accurate: it reveals the form of one generation's emergence out of the other and the emotional process that accompanies these biological connections. It is also, we believe, a psychologically accurate image of the way *all* young children experience themselves, their families and the world.

Billy sees and feels his world as a pyramid of family connections; children supported by parents who, in turn, are supported by grandparents. The entire family structure rests upon numerous faces representing the outside world of society. The child at the top of the pyramid, Billy said, is himself "playing football, being happy." Underneath him, he placed his parents, together, "watching how good I play." And below his parents, in the widest stratum of the pyramid, he placed his grandparents "watching me play and watching my parents watch me." Next to his grandparents, but on the same level, Billy drew himself playing cards with his grandfather. "That's what I plan to do," he told us, "after I finish playing." Billy explained the difference between his grandparents enjoying "watching" him play and how his parents were "judging" the quality of his play. He felt that the way that he played was important to his parents, but that his grandparents didn't care about things like that. "With them," he said, "whatever I do is fine." Billy finds a dimension of freedom and acceptance in his relationship with his grandparents that he does not feel with his parents who are concerned about the way that he "performs" and "develops."

In the picture Billy feels free to "play"—and therefore to "be"—because of the foundation of security he feels underneath him. He feels safe because all eyes in the family are on him, watching over him. But his grandparents have a double role: they are also watching over Billy's parents, thus supporting the "nuclear" family; at the same time, Billy has a direct connection to his grandparents which is independent of his parents. He sees them not only as his "parent's parents" but as his own grandparents. Because of this intimate knowledge of his grandparents, Billy doesn't experience them as "Aged." To be sure, their faces are wrinkled and they carry canes. But they are large figures— and this is not by accident. As we will shortly discuss, when a child draws a picture of a family member, the larger the figure, the more important that person is in the child's life.

Billy's picture reveals some relevant truths about the family and the grandparent's function within it. Despite their canes, his grandparent figures stand upright like pillars. They support his parents as well as Billy. Without them, the family would lack its proper foundation. In the three-generational family that Billy drew, his grandparents provide a buffer between Billy's two-generational "nuclear" family and the outside world. If his parents were to die, separate or divorce—if the second echelon of the pyramid were to split apart—Billy would, according to his image, fall into the lap of his grandparents.

Like other young children, particularly those who have not attained the "age of reason," Billy lives in an emo-

tional now. He knows people by the way that they make
him feel. In addition, his youth places him closer to nature
than the adults who govern his life. His emotional and biological knowledge, little affected by rationality, makes him
an accurate reporter of the emotional state of the world in
which he lives. His image of his family is organic. It is
based on his feelings about his biological connections
which have been reinforced by direct emotional attachments between the generations. In his view, his grandparents are indispensable both to himself and to his family.

We submit that Billy accurately reflects the view that
young children have of the nature of the family. It is not to
be found in textbooks. But then, children do not write
textbooks.

C. *The Disappearing Grandparent*

Billy's image dramatizes the way all children naturally
view their families, whether grandparents are present or
not. He differs from most other children only in the degree
of solidarity that he feels with his grandparents. According
to this view, the family is three-generational in form, organic in nature and emotional in substance. It is a structured, although flexible system, able to accommodate to
the changing needs of its members. Grandparents have a
distinct place in the family.

In all respects, this view contrasts sharply with contemporary adult concepts of the family as elastic in form, increasingly voluntary in nature, and emotionally imploded
in substance. In this open system, individual family
members look to society to accommodate their needs.
Grandparents have no place in these families.

According to children, grandparents are very important

people. They are, simply, a part of the "way things are." According to experts, grandparents have moved to the margins of family life; functionally, they have ceased to exist. As a consequence, they have all but been ignored in contemporary discussions of the family.

For example, few researchers have ever bothered to examine the meaning grandparents hold for grandchildren, and grandchildren for grandparents.[1] Their primary focus has been on the interactions between parents and children. Even Sigmund Freud, who devoted most of his life to describing and analyzing the life-long psychological impact of parents upon the young, never expanded his investigations to include relationships between grandchildren and grandparents. Yet there is a seldom discussed episode in Freud's life which suggests that what Freud ignored as a scientist he felt deeply as a grandfather. The only time Freud was known to have shed tears was upon the death of his beloved grandson, Heinerle Rudolph, who died of miliary tuberculosis at the age of four-and-a-half. The death of this grandson caused the first known depression in Freud's life. Three years later, in consoling a close friend upon the death of the latter's eldest son, Freud confessed that since the death of Heinerle, he had been unable to enjoy life. And then, in an oblique reference to his own developing cancer of the mouth, Freud added: "It is the secret of my indifference—people call it courage—toward the danger to my own life."[2]

Since Freud, theorists and practitioners of psychotherapy have been slow to expand Freud's original focus on the parent-child relationship to include other members of the child's world. Not only are families still conceptualized as two generational, they are treated, with rare exception, in the same fashion. Grandparents and their function within the family are ignored. When they are considered, it is only in relationship to their children, and not to their grand-children. To make matters worse, when grandparents are acknowledged by psychotherapists, they are often cast in pejorative roles as "meddlers" or "child spoilers." Only as a last resort are grandparents even considered as persons who could help their families.

The literature of social science treats the three-generational family as a myth. The nuclear family, social historians tell us, is the "norm" for American society and has been for two hundred years. But these experts fail to distinguish—often, it seems, for purely polemical purposes—between multigenerational *households*, in which grandparents cohabitate with their grandchildren and children, and extended family *networks* in which grandparents live nearby and take an active role in the nurture of the young. The multigenerational household may indeed be a historical anomaly, but the extended family network is not. It has supported American immigrants in every century. It has nurtured neighborhoods in every city and flavored the life of every Faulknerian hamlet.

Our quarrel is not with historians of the family, as such, whose academic discipline is still in the process of development. Nor do we have any argument with social programs and planners who stretch the definition of the family to cover those truncated family structures which desperately need help. Our concern is with academics and activists who advocate the nuclear family as both inevitable and desirable. The nuclear family, with grandparents sheared from its foundation, may indeed be a statistical norm in the United States and other "advanced" Western societies, but this sociological fact does not make the nuclear family either inevitable or desirable. For the 40,000 years that humankind has been known to exist, children have typically been raised in tribes, clans, and variously extended networks of

kin. In the long view of history, the isolation of grandparents from grandchildren is a recent event. It is also a biological, psychological, and emotional aberration. In short,
the "myth" of the extended family is itself a particularly
destructive myth, one which deliberately devalues the emotional needs and attachments of children in the name of
"individual autonomy," "freedom of choice," and other
slogans designed by and for a society of "adults only."

Grandparents are rarely considered in current discussions
of the problems and pressures besetting contemporary family life. Working mothers, now a majority among women
with children under age 18, are criticized for neglecting
their children. Fathers are censured for failing to share
equally in the rearing of children. But no one criticizes
grandparents for failing to help out with the raising of
their grandchildren. No one, it seems, expects them to.
Thus, in *All Our Children*, a ten-year study of "the way
children grow up" in America sponsored by the Carnegie
Council on Children, every social, economic, and political
resource affecting children is scrutinized except one: grandparents. Every facet of a child's life is discussed except one:
its relationship to grandparents.

Readers of *All Our Children* and numerous other studies
may well conclude that grandparents are no longer part of
"the family." In too many cases, unfortunately, this is literally true. As we will demonstrate later in these pages,
today's grandparents were the first members of the three-
generational family to abandon the young. As fathers, today's grandfathers typically spent most of their time, energy, and interest at work pursuing a better "living" for
themselves and their families. Later, they were joined—often reluctantly—by today's grandmothers, who followed
their husbands into "retirement" by retiring from their
own traditional functions in the wider family circle. To-

day's absentee parents are merely accelerating a trend set by their own parents. As a result, much of the care-taking responsibilities formerly exercised by grandparents as well as by parents have now been turned over to impersonal outsiders: day-care centers, schools, peers and the omnipresent television set. Ours is becoming a society of surrogates: surrogate families, surrogate parents, and surrogate grandparents.

Where have all the grandparents gone? If social theorists and government planners are to be believed, they have shed their identities as grandparents and joined the anonymous ranks of the "Aged." To be among the aged is to be an object of intense study. In 1979, there were over 1,300 educational programs on aging. To be among the aged is to be the object of public concern. The National Network on Aging currently coordinates the activities of some 1,400 public agencies. To be among the aged is to be the focus of a whole new industry involving retirement homes, medical specialties, land developers, pharmaceutical companies, and their attendant suppliers, research departments and sales forces. To be among the aged is to have a "gray lobby" in Washington, second in power only to those who represent gun-owners and munitions manufacturers. To be among the aged is to be part of a "movement" to combat the latest social sin: "Ageism."

To be among the aged, however, one need no longer be concerned about being a grandparent.

Who are the aged? The answer depends on who supplies the definition. By the most elastic of definitions, the aged include everyone fifty-five years of age or older or everyone who has retired. Until recently, one's sixty-fifth birthday generally marked one's entry into old age. But in recognition of the increased longevity that Americans now enjoy,

sociologist Bernice Neugarten has introduced a new concept of the aged which distinguishes between the "old-old"
and the "Young-Old" much as, a century ago, adolescents
were distinguished from children.[3] The old-old are those
men and women seventy-five years of age and above who,
because of infirmity, require the support and services of
others. The young-old are those between the ages of fifty-
five and seventy-four who, as a group, tend to be vigorous,
self-reliant, and unwilling to settle for a spectator's role in
society. Dr. Neugarten regards the emergence of the young-
old as a new division within the human life cycle, one that
more accurately reflects the lives, activities, and ambitions
of a new generation of older Americans who no longer
conform to negative stereotypes of "old Granny and
Grandpa." All this is for the good. But we seriously question the programmatic uses to which even the most "disinterested" research is put. For example, historian David
Hackett Fischer, a specialist on the history of aging in
America, links his vision of past family life—in which the
three-generational family does not exist—to a vision of the
future in which "adults of every age are recognized as autonomous individuals who have a right to *choose* their as-
sociative relations, and rarely wish to circumscribe them to
the narrow limits of consanguinity."[4] What is missing from
this brave new world of consenting adults is any sense of
prior emotional attachment to or responsibility for the
young. It is a vision which, unfortunately, is coming to
pass. The brutal fact is that more and more grandparents
are choosing to ignore their grandchildren. In turn, grandchildren are ignoring them. Where emotional bonds
existed, a "new social contract" is now in place, one which
proscribes meddling between families in the same bloodline and, like a decree of divorce, establishes "visiting
rights" between grandparents and grandchildren.

Ironically, the more the aged are studied, the less they are seen as grandparents. "Grandmothers are a little studied population," we read in a 1978 report on "The Older Woman: Continuities and Discontinuities" prepared jointly by the National Institute on Aging and the National Institute of Mental Health Workshop.[5] "We know little about their relationships with grandchildren. We need to know what older women offer and receive from their relationships with their grandchildren."

Indeed we do.

Presumably, grandparents and grandchildren are the best people to ask if experts want such information. But no one asks them. The Administration on Aging of the U. S. Department of Health and Welfare has been conducting and analyzing interviews with representative national samples of 1,000 50-year-olds and as many 70-year-olds with a view toward "Identifying Opportunities for Improving the Quality of Life of Older Age Groups."[6] The interviews, we are told, last up to four hours each and are aimed at eliciting individual responses relative to "fifteen empirically-developed quality of life dimensions." Among these dimensions are "material well-being and financial security," "health and personal safety," and various personal and social activities. Yet, not one of these "Quality of Life" dimensions concerns relationships with grandchildren. Not a single question permits participants to discuss whether or not emotional attachments to grandchildren are among the needs or satisfactions of old age.

Again, in *Why Survive?* psychiatrist Robert N. Butler's Pulitzer Prize-winning study on "being old in America," the distinguished head of the National Council on Aging writes eloquently of the plight and the promise of the aged. But his only reference to the importance of grandparents occurs, revealingly enough, in a "personal note" appended

to his main text. There, Dr. Butler movingly describes how
he was raised from infancy by his grandparents; how the
love of his grandfather inspired him to become a physician,
and how "the strength and endurance" of his widowed
grandmother enabled them both to survive the lean years
of the Great Depression.[7]

Grandparents exist only in relation to grandchildren.
Anything said about grandparents is always "personal." To
ask an adult about a grandparent is to evoke memories.
When adults want to tell us about grandparents they invariably resort to autobiography, which is the only mode
into which emotional attachments can be translated. For
anthropologist Margaret Mead, her paternal grandmother
was "the most decisive influence on my life." Dr. Mead's
grandmother lived with her family all her life. In her nineties, Grandmother Fogg escaped from an old-folks' home
with the aid of her son. In *Blackberry Winter*, an autobiography of her early years, Dr. Mead describes this extraordinary woman and, by implication, what a grandmother
means:

> She sat in the center of our household. Her room . . . was the
> place to which we immediately went when we came in from
> playing or home from school . . . The strength of my con-
> science came from Grandma, who meant what she said. Per-
> haps nothing is more valuable for a child than living with an
> adult who is firm and loving—and Grandma was loving. I
> loved the feel of her soft skin, but she would never let me give
> her an extra kiss when I said good night.[8]

And what is a grandfather like? In *The Words*, an autobiography of his youth, philosopher Jean-Paul Sartre describes in a luxury of detail the mutual joy that a grandfather and grandson can bring each other when their lives are
intertwined. Sartre's father had died when his son was only
seven. The boy and his mother moved in with his patriar-

chal grandfather who left retirement without hesitation to provide for his unexpected family:

> I was his wonder because he wanted to finish life as a wonder-struck old man. He chose to regard me as a singular favor of fate, as a gratuitous and always revocable gift. What could he have required of me? My mere presence filled him to overflowing. He was the God of love with the beard of the Father and the Sacred Heart of the Son. There was a laying on of hands, and I could feel the warmth of his palm on my skull. He would call me his "tiny little one," in a voice quavering with tenderness. His cold eyes would dim with tears. Everybody would exclaim 'That scamp has driven him crazy.' He worshipped me, that was manifest . . . I don't think he displayed much affection for his other grandchildren. It's true that he hardly ever saw them and that they had no need of him, whereas I depended upon him for everything: what he worshipped in me was his generosity.[9]

These different memories of different grandparents are each presented in a nexus of emotion-laden attachments, mental images, and shared experiences. Margaret Mead not only tells us what she thinks about grandparents, she also puts us together, in the same room, with the source of these thoughts—her own grandmother. Sartre gives us himself and his grandfather together, reveling in the bond between them that seems so fatuous to others. What is striking about these memories, and those of other adults who have had a close relationship with a grandparent, is the powerful emotions experienced by the story tellers when talking about beloved grandparents. Although they are relating the events of the past, feelings are experienced in the present, signaling the enduring nature of the grandparental bond.

Poets have a special purchase on emotion. They give it shape and meaning. In his *Life Studies*, a volume of his so-called "confessional" poetry, Robert Lowell dramatizes his preoccupation with his ancestors.[10] In "Grandparents" the poet moves about the old farm house, now his own, where his grandparents once lived. At first, he recalls them as rather distant, formal survivors out of the nineteenth century. But toward the poem's close, the sight of a single billiard ball evokes buried moments of communion between grandfather and grandson, producing an outrush of grief in mourning this lost attachment.

>   *. . . Five*
> *green shaded light bulbs spider the billiards-table;*
> *no field is greener than its cloth,*
> *where Grandpa, dipping sugar for us both,*
> *once spilled his demitasse.*
> *His favorite ball, the number three,*
> *still hides the coffee stain.*
>
> *Never again*
> *to walk there, chalk our cue,*
> *insist on shooting for us both.*
> *Grandpa! Have me, hold me, cherish me!*
> *Tears smut my fingers . . .*

To ask what a grandparent means to a grandchild is to inquire about an emotional attachment. Adults can relive their memories as grandchildren. But how do we learn about the feelings that a young child has for a grandparent? How can we learn what a close grandparent means to a child? What happens to children when they are abandoned by grandparents? Such an inquiry cannot proceed with the tools of science. Emotions do not translate into quantifiable data and they disappear altogether when filtered through intellectual abstractions. Emotions are only "felt." How then do we gain access to the emotional experience of young children?

Billy showed us the way.

1

What Grandparents Mean to Grandchildren

"(The Child) talks. She says things whose significance she does not understand. God, the good old Grandfather, listens, filled with wonder."

Victor Hugo, LES MISÉRABLES

A. *The Child as Oracle*

Children will reveal their world to us, but only if—like all oracles—they are properly consulted.[1] Children live in an emotional "now" but they have difficulty putting their feelings and emotional perceptions into words. However, they readily reveal what is inside them through drawings. This is not surprising since we all learn how to express ourselves through graphic images long before we learn how to master the symbols of speech. Indeed, in the process of growing up children recapitulate the historical experience of mankind. For millennia prior to the advent of recorded speech, primitive man re-presented the world to himself through cave drawings. Thus the adult who dismisses primitive art or the deceptively childlike forms of some modern painters, with the assurance that "my child could do as well"—is psychologically correct. For there is something universal in the need to give external form to what lies inside us. Like the primitive or modern artist, then, the child in the act of graphic composition expresses his/her fears, hopes and fantasies.[2]

Psychiatrists and psychologists have long recognized the value of "projective" drawings as a path into the child's world. Hand a child blank sheets of paper and a set of crayons and he will hunch over his work with all the intense concentration of a poet under the inspiration of his muse. Absorbed in his own world, the child is free to express those matters which most trouble him without fear of retribution from adults. "Next to dreams," Freud wrote in 1924,[3] art has become "the acknowledged *via regia* into the depths" of the human consciousness. Craftsmanship and accuracy of details are not important. What is important is that the child have the time and encouragement to find expressive form for his most problematic relationships and unresolved emotional experiences.

For example, if a small child is asked to draw a dog, he may, after considerable deliberation, sketch only a large set of teeth attached to the merest suggestion of a body, and then sit back with the satisfaction that what he feels about dogs is fully represented. And it is. To a small child a large dog is likely to be a fearsome monster capable of chewing him to pieces.

Even projective drawings which seem at first glance to be without meaning or movement often contain explosive feelings and intense drama. Asked to draw a house, a child may sketch a windowless jail which accurately reflects his feeling about his home life. Or, he may draw a gay, multicolored mansion even though his own home is a plain tract house. In his sovereignty as creator, a child may include members of his family in his picture—or eliminate a resented brother or sister. In this way, projective drawings provide clues to a child's entire life situation.

To a therapist or other interested observer, the child's behavior while drawing—and especially his comments—are important guides in interpreting more precisely a child's feelings about the subject of his work. The child may smile, frown, laugh, or grumble. In these moments of creative communion with their feelings, most children find it easier than at other times to talk about their relations to the subject they are struggling to depict. All these elements —graphic image, behavior, and running verbal commentary —are essential to the revelations children give us about the way they experience themselves, others and their cultures. Indeed, about the only limits on the amount of information obtainable from projective drawings, says psychologist Sidney Levy, are those imposed by the observer's "understanding, experience and skill."[4]

Suppose, now, that we ask a child to draw a picture of his mother or father and to talk about what that parent is doing in the picture. The actual figure may be unrecognizable—and usually is in drawings done by children (up to about age ten) who have not yet acquired the motor and other instrumental skills necessary to render the human body with some degree of accuracy. Or it may be an older child's surprisingly deft representation of his parent. In either case, there are certain characteristics common to all projective drawings, which even the lay person can recognize and interpret. (Figs. 1 and 2)

One is *size:* the larger the image, the more important that person is in the life of the child. Another is *placement* on the page: if a person absorbs a great deal of the child's time and emotional investment—that is, if the person is "central" to the child's life—the child will draw that person in the center or toward the bottom of the page. (By contrast, a person who was once central to a child's life but remains so now only in memory, will often be drawn to the left of the page.) A third characteristic is *view*: a child will draw a full, frontal view of a person whom he feels he knows intimately or "inside and out." A profile or partial view indicates that the child literally knows only one side of that person: how that person acts, perhaps, but not what that person feels or thinks. A fourth characteristic is activity: if the figure on the page is doing something, say, standing at the stove or mowing the lawn, this indicates a rich relationship between the person and the child. (Fig. 3) At this point, what a child says about his drawing becomes most important. The figure on the page, after all, cannot move. But in the mind of the child the real person is doing things which he will describe in great detail. Conversely, a person whom a child does not know well is vague and static in the child's mind, and thus the child will have little to say about that person.

In sum, when a child draws a picture of a person, he acts like a movie projector.[5] The drawing he produces is a mirror image of the internal "object" or representation of that person in the child's mind. The more familiar that person is to the child, the stronger is the mental image. Psychologists call this "object constancy," a rather technical label for what in reality is a very rich and universal human experience. If Romeo loves Juliet and the two are separated, each lives on in the other's mind and that mental object *is* the beloved until they are reunited. United, lovers make love and a life together. Separated, gifted lovers make poetry—or music or paintings, and their internalized images of the beloved live on as Dante's Beatrice, Gluck's Euridice and Botticelli's Venus.

Normally, the first person to become a strong internal object for a child is his mother. But even she must bide her time until the child is old enough to retain her within through an "internalized" mental image. Usually, a child must be at least ten months old before he begins to develop the capacity to form such images. Before this, if he doesn't see it, it isn't there. This is what the peek-a-boo game is all about. At the outset, the child really believes that his mother is no longer "there" when he covers his eyes with his hands. He has to peek through his fingers and see his mother to establish her presence. But, as the child develops his capacity for forming internal images, the game of peek-a-boo loses its savor. Mom is always there.

A child requires regular, intimate, and predictable contact with his mother up to the age of about thirty months in order to maintain a strong image of her in his mind when she is absent. When mother and child are separated a series of reactions are triggered off in the child. This is known as "Separation Anxiety."[6] At first, the child *protests* by kicking and screaming in the crib. After about a week, he will become relatively quiescent and lapse into a state of *despair* of ever seeing his mother again. If the separation continues, the child will become *detached* from his mother and will show little or no interest in her when she reappears. This phenomenon is well known to parents who leave their children for even a short period of time. The child often ignores the parent for a brief period of time after the parent has returned from a brief absence. Clinical studies of institutionalized children vividly demonstrate what can happen when maternal contact is withdrawn. Clinicians call this "hospitalism":[7] in severe cases, children afflicted with hospitalism never do renew their attachments to their mothers—or to a maternal substitute—and eventually they loose their will to live. In short, when the mental image of the mother dies, the child dies too. Such is the need for strong human attachments.

For all these reasons, then, every child is an oracle of the human condition, and what he reveals to us is as accurate, in its own way, as the work of our most profound artists. Since Freud, we have become deeply aware of the pervasive importance of mothers and fathers in the lives of children. But Freud and his followers never went beyond mother and father to probe the importance of those other parents —grandparents—in the lives of children. Yet, just as children enter the world as the genetic product of two parents, so they are also the product of four grandparents. And just as in the course of our lives we may find important parent substitutes, so, it seems, do we find grandparental substitutes—elders who embody for us the qualities of wisdom, compassion, patience, and disinterested love which even the most gifted mothers and fathers cannot provide. Is it possible, then, that something in a child dies, or at least fails to mature, without the intimate contact and love of grandparents?

B. The Method

This is the central question behind our study of children. We visited more than 300 youngsters ranging from five to eighteen years of age. We asked them to draw pictures of their grandparents and we listened while they chatted on about what grandparents do and mean to them. Most found the exercise fun, even absorbing. We saw some children in their homes; others were seen in schools, churches, community and day-care centers. Our "field trips" were mainly along the East Coast, though some children from other parts of the United States are included in our "sample." We did not establish a sociological model or quota system, so that every racial, ethnic, and religious swatch in America's patchwork culture would be proportionately represented.* Although the children you are about to meet come from all kinds of families and life situations, the connections we were looking for are universal. In other words, when a child is functioning as an oracle, what he reveals about grandchild-grandparent attachments transcends cultural differences.

After we had collected a substantial number of drawings, we noticed that children who were close to their grandparents produced drawings that were markedly different from those produced by children who had little or no contact with their grandparents. The differences were so extreme that, from looking at the drawings alone, we were able to ascertain the degree of intimacy between grandparent and child.

Intimacy, therefore, became the measure by which the children sorted themselves into three groups and allowed us to classify grandchild-grandchildren relationships along a continuum of shared time and experience:

Close Contact	Sporadic Contact	No Contact
Group I	Group II	Group III
Maximum Time	Irregular Time	No Time

* The study population was composed of the following groupings: Racial: White—80%; Black—10%; Hispanic—8%; Asian—2%; Socioeconomic: Upper—20%; Middle—40%; Lower—40%.

C. *Summary of Projected Drawings*

GROUP I (FIGS. 1–20)

These children are close to one or more grandparents. The grandparent lives either in the same house with the child or, as is more often the case, close enough for frequent contact. Just as important, the child often has free access to the grandparent. As a result of this mutual experience the child has a vibrant image or mental "object" of his grandparent, which is evident in his drawings. There the grandparent is portrayed as a large, active, fully viewed figure, dominating the page. The child knows his grandparent in many dimensions—including how he thinks and what he feels.

GROUP II (FIGS. 21–38)

These children have an irregular and intermittent relationship with their grandparents. Within this highly diverse group are children whose grandparents visit them sporadically. Some grandparents have moved away; more often, the children have been moved from them. In some cases, the children's parents are divorced and because of this family disconnection the grandparents seldom see the child. In their drawings, the children portray their grandparents as small, immobile, and lifeless. Frequently, only a profile of the grandparent appears and the relationship with the child turns out to be self-serving. Often, the image is placed on the left side of the page, hinting at a relationship that was intimate in the past but is no longer so. In other cases, the child's internal image of his grandparent is so vague that he recruits images from his own fantasy or from the media (television, comic books, movies) to fill the page.

GROUP III (FIGS. 39–49)

These children have minimal or no grandparent contact. In many cases, the grandparent has died or, what is worse, has walked out of the child's life. Usually, these children do not draw a person at all. Instead, they draw puppets, cartoon characters, shadowy figures or stereotypes inspired by movie or television personalities. The drawings are typically lifeless or even grotesque because the children have no image of a grandparent in their minds.

Taken altogether, these drawings demonstrate, if anything can, that every child has a place inside him for at least one grandparent. If this place is not filled by a living person, the child will fill his empty inner space with a grandparent drawn from his own fantasy or copied from the "entertainment" media. The continuum we have discovered demonstrates another, simple truth: the single necessary condition for ensuring a strong grandparent image within a child is actual time spent with a grandparent. This factor alone—*even apart from the quality of the relationship*—determines the "reality" of the grandparent within the child.

One final comment: only *five percent* of the children in this study had at least one intimate grandparent.

GROUP I: CLOSE CONTACT

Mary* is a six-year-old who persevered until she drew in all the stubble on her grandfather's chin. (Fig. 4) Mary laughed at the familiar drama unfolding in her head and mimicked her grandmother's voice as that drama took shape on paper.

> Grandma says, "Harry, you didn't shave clean again! I'm not going to let you near me with that sandpaper. I got a rash last time. No more kisses till that stubble is off."

Mary sat back and surveyed the pictures of her grandparents that she had just completed. "No more hugs till Granddad shaves," she chuckled. Mary's picture of her grandfather was a large, round face with eyes as big as fried eggs and a puckish curve of smile. Grandma's face was even larger, but her mouth exposed commanding teeth, as if she were accustomed to giving orders. (Fig. 5) Mary felt that she understood her grandparents very well, even to the nuances of their good-natured banter.

To younger children, a close grandparent is a familiar environment, full of emotional caves and crevices which a child comes to know by heart. Patty, seven, drew an idiosyncratic picture of "old Grandma" telling her a story about how it was when she herself was a small girl. In the picture, Grandma is standing on two straight pillars of legs and is supporting herself with a cane that flows from her left hand as if it were a natural extension of her arm. (Fig. 6) Patty knows her grandmother is old and hobbled but

---

* Because of confidentiality, we have changed all names. For the same reason we have not used our patients in this study except for a few children who, with their parents' permission, were eager and generous enough to share their drawings and thoughts with us.

that, to her, is an inconsequential fact, like Grandma's maiden name.

> Grandma has got a bad leg, so she can't walk around without her cane. I can sit on her lap, though, and she tells me stories about when she was young and I can cuddle up with her. It sounds weird, but I like to snuggle into her and smell her and rub her arm in my face. She is so cozy. She can't walk too well, but she can talk. And she is the best back-rubber in the world.

The older the children, the more details they were able to put into their pictures, and the more they could talk about what their grandparents mean to them. Myra, twelve, drew what she called "a family holiday," with grandfather serving drinks, grandmother cooking and the grandchildren playing. (Fig. 7) The drawing was crammed with activity, color, emotion. Myra's grandparents live two hours away by car and, from what she told us, Myra visits them often.

> Grandfather is so funny. He laughs a lot. He loves whiskey sours, makes 'em for everyone who comes into the house. He's so happy to be with us. He tells everyone how terrific I am. I can't stop him. I feel so good when he's there and the family is all together. He goes around playing the proud grandfather. He actually enjoys us. It's like he's saying, "Keep it up, kids, you're doing well." Sometimes he makes his arm muscles jump and wiggles his ears for us. We all laugh.
>
> Grandmother's easy to talk to about stuff in the past. She knows a lot about long-ago things that help me with the present. If I'm having a problem with my parents or something, she'll sit down and talk to me. She has time for me, that's important. She'll tell me about problems that she had with my mother and then I can understand my mother a little better— even though some of the things that my grandmother told me are pretty wild. I can't see my mother doing them, sometimes, but I believe my grandmother. I really know my grandmother well because we did so much together when I was younger. I

know what she likes to eat and her favorite perfume. She always smells so good . . . yes, that's important. Grandma
smells good, cozy.

When grandparents are that intimate, consistent, and
openly loving with their grandchildren, they become an ir-
replaceable presence within the child. Here's how Myra
put it:

> I think of my grandparents a lot. I talk to them in my head
> when I'm alone, especially when I have a problem. I think of
> what they would say to me. I really need them for reassurance.
> It's different from my parents. Weird. I feel guilty saying this,
> but they are so proud and enthusiastic about us. Not more
> than my parents, of course, but I guess they show it more. I'll
> tell you, I don't know what I did to have them love me and
> make such a fuss about me. It's almost embarrassing some-
> times. I mean, when I'm around my friends, but I really love
> it.

Children who live in the same house with grandparents
—a situation which adults often find trying—were eager to
draw and tell us about them.

Doreen, five, lives with her grandmother and her mother
because her parents are divorced. Her mother works to support the three of them, so grandmother is the adult whom
Doreen sees most often. Doreen was very happy and highly
animated while she drew her grandmother standing tall,
like a watchtower, amid hardy flowers in the family garden.
(Fig. 8)

> Grandma makes sure that everything grows good and noth-
> ing dies. Look how tall she is! She can see everything so noth-
> ing goes bad. Nothing bad can ever happen to me when she is
> looking. I look forward to coming home from school and
> Grandma's always there, with milk and cookies. Always
> there . . .

Indeed, many children we visited singled out "worry" as
the thing grandparents do most—perhaps because the chil-

dren are constantly moving in and out of their grandparents' lives. Joan, eleven, drew her grandmother with both arms open wide, waiting for a tardy school bus to arrive. (Fig. 9)

Not all of the children who had close relationships with their grandparents were uniformly fond of them. Michael, nine, drew large, centrally placed pictures of both his grandparents, indicating that they are major figures in his life. But he drew them in profile, showing only the "stern" sides of their personalities. (Figs. 10, 11)

> They're different, though. Grandma, I can't get away with anything with her. She bosses all of us around, except Grandpa, sometimes. When she says, "Do it!" I jump, you bet. But she is really nice and she is only after me when I do wrong—like when I lost her TV guide. Boy! Did she blow her top. That's when I disappear, too. Like Grandpa does sometimes.
>
> Grandpa teaches me a lot of stuff and we do a lot together. He only blows his top if I mess with his tools. One thing, though, Grandpa taught me how to fight. I can beat up anybody in my class if I want to, but Grandpa said I should never start a fight. My father doesn't have time to teach me things because he works long hours and is always tired. Grandpa takes his place, I guess.

Michael knows that his grandparents care very deeply for him. This caring is more important to him than the fact that they are also strict. He senses—rightly—that each grandparent is trying to teach him something no matter how much he might resent the way that the lesson is taught. Grandma, with her penetrating eyes and ample bosom is laying down the rules and regulations of life inside the home. Grandfather, who sometimes feels the wrath of Michael's grandmother too, is telling him how to get along in the outside world. Under the surface of the "games" his grandparents play, Michael has a deep sense of comfort in their "togetherness" and commitment to each other. It makes him feel secure.

Because of their close attachments to their grandparents, the Group I children gave us ample evidence of how grandparents function as "role models" for same-sex grandchildren. The boys invariably observed their grandfather's behavior carefully and drew their grandfathers as men of action or involvement and talked about them like grateful apprentices might about a revered mentor. Peter's grandfather lives just down the road and likes to garden. In his drawing, Peter, nine, projected a large foreground figure against brown fields that stretch off to a tree-lined horizon. (Fig. 12)

> My grandfather shows me how to garden and grow vegetables. I watch him carefully and I help him plant. When I grow up I'll show my children how to do it, too. My grandfather said that he learned gardening from his grandfather, so it's really like my grandfather's grandfather taught me, too.

Jeff's grandfather enjoys more sedentary pleasures—as the ten-year-old youngster reports in his drawing. (Fig. 13) When Jeff talked about what his grandfather was really "doing" in the picture, the powerful attachment between the two became apparent.

> I'm a Yankee fan just like my grandfather. It's a tradition in my family. We're all Yankee fans. My grandfather never misses a game. He drinks beer and watches the game and I have a soda and we root for the Yankees together. He says that I better marry someone who is a Yankee fan—not like my aunt who married someone who is a St. Louis fan—and my kids had better be Yankee fans, too.

To girls, a close and loving grandmother often takes on the dimensions of a primordial "Great Mother" who cradles the entire family within her body. In Gail's family, everyone calls grandmother "Big Ma." And the picture that

Gail, twelve, drew of her grandmother turned out to be a madonna. (Fig. 14)

> That's a pretty good picture of my grandmother. She's holding the baby over her heart, like the baby is part of her. That's where my grandmother is cuddling the baby—in her heart.
>
> Grandmother used to work in a foundling home, where the children have no mothers. She got the job because she loves babies and she is such a loving person. She always tilts her head like the picture when she holds babies and looks down on them. She adores them. In my picture she is humming to the baby and rocking it. The baby feels very secure and happy, right next to grandmother's heart. It makes me want to be a baby again.

Gail's grandmother is sixty-five years old, but notice that in the picture she appears to be a very young woman. That's because children like Gail who are close to their grandparents ignore signs of aging, obesity, deformity, and other surface appearances; such things are not part of the persons the children are in touch with, not relevant to how they feel about their grandparents.

For Carol, also twelve, grandmother is a kind of fairy godmother who dazzles ("when she gets dressed") with her resplendent clothes and bestows gifts from a family treasury which will someday belong to Carol herself.

> My grandma is old but she's gorgeous, a knockout. When she gets dressed she's sooo beautiful. She smells good, like heaven. And all those glittering jewels on her! Mmmmmmmm . . . I can smell her perfume now.

Carol herself was carefully dressed—much more elegantly than her classmates—and she played with her own necklaces, bracelets and rings while she talked about her drawing.

> My grandmother gave this little bracelet to keep for myself and to remember her by when she gets old and dies. I'm to give it to *my* children someday, she told me.

Carol's grandmother has given her something precious: not just a bracelet but an heirloom which allows her granddaughter to feel in her own fingers the emotional bonds that anchor her between those who preceded her in life and the eventual issue of her own body. Grandmother has also given Carol a vigorous model of an "elder" whom Carol can "be like" when she herself is beyond parenthood.

Among both boys and girls, the dominant image of grandmother is that of "Grand Nurturer." Grandfather may be an expert—the fixer, the teacher in the ways of the world—but his expertise is in matters that lie outside the family circle. What grandmother knows and does, is inside in the home, *whether or not she holds an outside job.* The home is the center of children's lives and there grandmother rules. Her kitchen is her command post and everyone—kids, parents, and grandfather—is dependent upon her table.

Manuel, eight, drew his grandmother waiting for him at a dinner table laden with goodies—including his favorite dish, barbecued spare ribs. (Fig. 15) The dining room takes up the entire picture of grandmother's house, which in reality is right across the street from Manuel's home. Manuel's family emigrated from Cuba to the United States in 1962. A handsome boy with large brown eyes and a pudgy face, Manuel explained how the family had roasted a pig the previous Sunday and that grandmother had saved the left-over ribs especially for him.

> I'll be a big fat pig before she is through with me. She has so much food in the house, her table is stacked with fruits and vegetables and she always has cakes and cookies and plenty of ice cream for me.
> I run across to visit her and the first thing she asks me is whether I had enough to eat today. And then she says, "Eat a little more." The food she has really tastes good. I'd rather eat

my grandmother's cooking than at MacDonald's—and I'd rather have a MacDonald's instead of what my mother cooks. Grandma's stuff really tastes good. But my mother is working and doesn't have the time my grandmother has to prepare the meals.

My friends say I'm so lucky to have a grandmother who stuffs me so much. My problem is that I can't say no. My grandmother says that in Cuba being chubby is a sign of beauty and good health. But in America people don't like to be fat.

She's always got something special *for me.* She says to me that cooking for people makes her happy and that she gets pleasure when she sees me eating and enjoying the food she cooks for me. I don't understand that because I'm the one who is eating it and not her. Maybe I'll know what she means when I grow up.

There is little doubt that Sunday (or, less often, a holiday) dinner at grandmother's house is still the central family experience for children with close attachments to their grandparents. Several recent studies indicate that the family dinner is a rapidly disappearing ritual in American homes. But when grandmother and grandfather are brought into the picture, the dinner table again resumes its centrality in the liturgy of family life.

Carmine, thirteen, used all his considerable artistic gifts to sketch the high point of his grandparents' day-long Sunday meal. He drew his grandmother cooking the meal and his grandfather trying to quiet the family as he prepares to open the wine. (Figs. 16, 17)

Every child's relationship with a close and loving grandparent is unique. Yet, there are certain fundamental modes of attachment between the generations which emerged after we had visited hundreds of children. We have categorized these "vital connections" but they are best understood, we think, by listening to Deborah, a lively and loquacious sixteen-year-old, who ranged over a rich emotional tapestry of family attachments during an extended visit with her and her family.

Deborah lives with her parents, a brother and a sister in the suburbs of a Midwestern city. Deborah's grandfather died when she was eight, but he remains a fixed and vital resource in her mind. Her grandmother lives in an apartment in the center of the city and continues to play a close, evolving role in Deborah's life. In the course of producing her drawings, Deborah laughed over family jokes, grew sad and reflective when recalling her grandfather's death, and was quite serious in discussing her grandmother's ability to live as "an independent person."

Sunday Dinner at Grandmother's: Nexus of Family Connections

For as long as she could remember, Deborah and her family have eaten most Sunday dinners with her grandparent(s). In her family drawing, she displays her grandparents sitting at either end of the table, presiding over the meal like elders of the tribe. (Fig. 18) Her parents are discussing family matters and the children are listening. Everyone feels contented, Deborah explained, because they have had so much to eat.

> Sundays, we'd usually all get together in my grandparents' apartment. My grandmother is a really great cook and she'd usually cook spaghetti and stuff like that. We just ate at the dinner table for hours. And I remember my cousins and I—all the little kids—we'd just sit there waiting for the adults, 'cause they'd talk and talk and talk for hours after dinner. That's what we used to do.
>
> I mean it's not like we don't do that anymore, it's just that we don't do it to the extent that we did then. Now that my grandfather's not alive, we go over to grandmother's sometimes during the week and she always fixes something good. But now we're on a different level. It's not the kids being rest-

less at the dinner table anymore. It's us being adults and talking to her.

The Grandparent as Constant Object: Knowing Grandfather Through Personal Experience

Deborah drew her deceased grandfather "watching young children play" because that is essentially how she remembers him. (Fig. 19) The image is large and full-faced indicating that the relationship he established with Deborah in life was many-sided and close. As she looked at her picture, Deborah described her grandfather as happy to see the children and pleased that they could continue his family. He wanted, she said, to have a good time kidding around with the children when they had finished playing games with each other.

> My grandfather was strict as anything but he was really a good guy. He had a nickname for all of us—he used to call me "Buttercup." I remember sitting on his knee and stuff. When we were little, he always let us climb all over him. We always had my birthday parties out on that patio and he'd just sit there in his chair. We'd have these family things and he'd sit there kind of looking over everything like he was in a powerful position. That's what I remember.
>
> And then I remember at the end, before he died, we went to see him at the hospital. He was really sick. Boy, was I a strange case because whenever something upset me I wouldn't show it as an upset. I would get a fever or something. The day after we went to see him in the hospital I got a really bad fever. That's how I knew that something was really wrong.

The Grandparent as Constant Object: Knowing Grandfather Through Stories

> You know, I think from what mother and grandmother have said it's helped me to remember him. Like I know him from before I ever met him, when he was just mother's father. The time he is in my mind the most is, well, like we'll be over at

my grandmother's and we'll talk about him and she'll tell me about him. Right after those conversations I'll think about him and I'll feel close to him even though I didn't know him that well. I'll feel close to him through my grandmother or through my mother.

My mother's told me so many funny stories about her bringing in dates and grandfather would just sit there with a newspaper and he wouldn't even look up at them. He was really strict. But you could kind of laugh at him and I think he could laugh at himself, too. I mean he wasn't close-minded. I looked up at him and almost idolized him. Like my grandmother was pretty cool and I looked up to her but with my grandfather it was different. He was a good guy.

Deborah drew her grandmother sitting in a chair feeling pleased and reminiscing about life in general. (Fig. 20) She said her grandmother was thinking about how nice it is to have a large family and hoping that everything would stay the same after she is gone. After completing the picture, Deborah talked at great length about the many different ways her grandmother was involved in her life.

The Grandparent as Teacher

I'm a terrible sewer, terrible. Grandmother always tries to teach me, but no one can teach me how to sew. One time, she stayed with me for a week when my parents went away and we'd whip up these really good dinners together and everything. She taught me how to cook.

The Grandparent as Caretaker

She's brought me up, too. It's not just my parents who have brought me up. She doesn't interfere. She seemed to agree with my mother on how to bring me up when I was little. Now, I can talk to her about things I talk to my mother about and she's not out of touch. I mean, she understands what is going on, which is good. You know, it surprises me how in touch she is with my generation. I guess it's because of my cousin and me.

The Grandparent as Negotiator Between Child and Parent

Well, sometimes she really bugs me. She is so agreeable. If my parents are telling me something, she'll just keep agreeing with it. It's nothing that bothers me seriously; I mean, sometimes I get mad at *my* grandmother for butting into my life. I'll just say, "Go on Granny." But then she'll take *my* side sometimes and my parents really *listen to her.*

The Same-Sex Grandparent as Role Model

It sounds corny but she's kind of an inspiration because I think of everything she's done for herself. You know, she works and everything. I don't know, we always have such a good time together. She's so cute. It's kind of an inspiration that someone can just pick themselves up like she does and have a good time.

I think my grandmother and I are alike. She always tells me that she's like me because I see her with her friends—she has her whole little group of friends—and she's very lively and she can be very funny sometimes. I'm usually pretty outgoing once I get going, so in that way I think we're pretty similar.

When I was little, I would look up to her. I didn't idolize her, but I looked up to her 'cause they spoiled us like all grandparents do. But now I look at her as my equal. It's not that I've lowered my standards of her. It's that I've gone up to her level. I've got two women to look up to, to see how they do things. My mother is different from my grandmother, but deep down we are all the same.

Grandparents as the Connections Between the Past and the Future

Grandmother and mother are always telling stories about my great-grandmother—that's my grandmother's mother. She was supposed to be really strict. She was a character. My mother kind of laughs about it now, but at the time she respected her so much and she still respects her. I didn't see much of her 'cause she was pretty senile the last ten years of her life. But I remember my great-grandparents from a picture of them around here somewhere. It's wonderful to be able to say I've met my great-grandparents. It's important—I don't know why—I just feel it. It's like an animal going extinct if you don't connect together. So many people don't even know their heritage that much. I mean my grandmother's Italian and just in little things like food I feel that I'm connected.

When I'm a grandparent I hope I'll have the energy that my grandmother does. I won't just sit around. I want to do a lot of stuff with my grandkids and not be a hindrance to them, like I'm sure some grandparents are. Just laugh together. I'm going to make a point of seeing my kids a lot, and hopefully my great-grandkids. I think it's such a good thing to be able to say you remember your great-grandparents because a lot of people can't say that. I will teach my children how to cook like my grandmother.

Grandparents as Determinants of How the Young Feel about the Old in Society

Old people are almost what they make of themselves. If they want to be old they make themselves that way. I don't think of my grandmother as being old at all, just 'cause the way she keeps going. My other grandmother just sits around the house. She doesn't get out and do anything and now it's almost too late to do anything because she's so used to depending on other people. And that kind of bothers me that she let herself get like that. I think you can prevent that if you really want to.

I think a large part of why I have such a good relationship with my grandparents is just the *time*, the *quantity* of time, we spent with them when we were little. They lived so *close*. I think that's the basic thing. Both my grandparents put a lot of time into the kids—you know, playing with the kids—and I think that's really important.

Grandparents as "Great Parents"

> Grandparents are so important. It's kind of like different
> kinds of parents to you. Like there's your parents and you live
> with them, but there aren't many other adults you can treat
> almost as your parents, that you know you're related to. I
> guess it's like being close to the boss's boss.

GROUP II: SPORADIC CONTACT

Children who enjoy close, regular relationships with
grandparents help us understand the feelings of the majority of children, who are not so fortunate. Most children,
we found, see their grandparents intermittently and ir-
regularly, usually because the families are physically or
emotionally apart. Indeed, numerous children, when asked
to draw their grandparents, pictured them waving goodbye,
as if leave-takings were the most emotionally significant
moments between grandchildren and grandparents. (Figs.
21–23) One eight-year-old girl, in fact, adroitly summarized her relationship to her grandmother in Florida by
drawing an airplane. (Fig. 24)

The children in Group II represent a very broad range of
actual life situations. Among them, for example, are children who can remember a time when their grandparents
were a central part of their lives as well as children who
never knew such intimacy. There are also children whose
grandparents still live close by but are not involved in their
grandchildren's lives. This situation is probably the hardest
for grandchildren to understand. But although the circumstances of their family life vary greatly, the children of
Group II are readily distinguishable from those who know
their grandparents intimately (Group I) and those who

have had little or no experience of grandparents (Group III). In a negative way, these children confirm by their sense of loss, deprivation, or abandonment, what the children in Group I taught us: namely, that time and place are indispensable for maintaining grandparent-grandchild attachments.

Sheila is a pretty eight-year-old whose grandparents had moved away from her eighteen months before our visit. The youngster smiled to herself as she drew a grinning grandmother leaning on a cane. (Fig. 25) "Grammy's watching children on a playground," Sheila explained. "She's saying, 'How cute the children are.'" The image, though large, hovers near the left side of the paper, indicating that Sheila already feels that her grandmother has slipped into the past.

Sheila stared a long time at the figure she had drawn. "'I wish I had someone to stroll with,' Grammy's saying." Gradually, Sheila's eyes began to tear as she talked about her feelings.

> I love my grandparents very much. They moved away when I was in the first grade. They had to because my grandpa didn't have to work anymore. I only get to see them summers and Christmas, now. They live so far away and it costs a lot of money to get there. I miss them a lot. Grandma always thinks that I'm such a good girl, better than I really am. She never changes her mind about that, even when Mom is mad at me. I like to cook and do housework with her.
>
> My grandfather used to cook with me, too. We fish and he taught me how to put a worm on a hook. Ugh! Grandpa never shaves when we go fishing. He says it's for good luck.
>
> Whenever I see my grandmother, I ask her if she got her mink coat yet because she really wants one. I feel really sad when I talk about them. I don't think they did such a good thing when they moved away. I'll never do that to my grandchildren when I grow up. I felt so bad when they did that, even though I was too young to tell them.

Sheila struggled, behind blurry eyes, for an explanation of the "why" of her grandparents' departure.

> They said that when Grandpa didn't have to work they would move to retire. I don't like it. When they lived close by I could walk over after school and when my parents went out they would babysit me. They tell me that they miss being with me, so I don't know why they stay away. Why don't they move back if they feel that way?
>
> Maybe they are just saying that. No, they wouldn't do that. But . . . it's terrible when I do see them because they leave so soon and I feel awful again. Sometimes I think that it would be easier if they didn't visit at all.

Children who have never known a grandparent intimately are at least fortunate in one respect: they will never know the pain of being abandoned or removed from a loving grandparent—a loss that is second only to losing a parent. Sheila is still suffering the pangs of separation from her grandparents. They still loom large in her mind (and therefore in her picture) and she feels sorry for them as well as for herself. She cannot, as yet, understand why they have abandoned her. But in time she will undoubtedly realize that her beloved grandparents moved away by choice and then her longing for them is likely to congeal into anger.

That is what happened to Elizabeth, fourteen, who was very close to her paternal grandmother before her parents' divorce. Her grandmother sided with her son in the marital battle and, after the divorce, rejected both her daughter-in-law and Elizabeth in one package. When we visited her, Elizabeth was still hurt and confused by her grandmother's rejection. The picture she drew captured her feelings precisely; in it, her grandmother's back is turned. (Fig. 26)

> She doesn't want to talk to me and she is not saying anything until I go away. She doesn't want to be reminded of the

problem. When I was younger, I always felt that she was so wise, you know, had all the answers. I was sure that when she gave me advice it was right. The bottom line, as they say, and now . . . she won't have anything to do with me since my parents have separated. She thinks that I side with my mother in the fights. But . . . she's my *grandmother*. How could she act this way to me?

Elizabeth looked away for a moment and began to sob. "I'm so hurt," she said at length. "She used to be so nice to me and now she is so mean." Later, when she had stopped crying, Elizabeth narrowed her eyes and added a final thought:

> Whenever I see an old person, I hate them now. I can't help it because they remind me of my grandmother. I get so upset I have crazy thoughts, like I'd like to kick them in their wrinkled faces.
>
> When I see old people hobbling along I think that I'll commit suicide before I become like that. My grandmother used to make me feel good, special, in a different way from my parents or friends. We used to just spend time together, without rushing around. I would like to talk with her like we used to because she's fun to talk to . . . at least she used to be. I think that she hates me now—and I didn't do anything to deserve it.

Elizabeth feels, rightly, that she is the innocent victim of her parents' divorce and is being unjustly punished by her grandmother. Tormented by her parents' situation, and refused succor by her grandmother, the girl's hurt is already turning into anger and evolving into a generalized derision of all "older" people. In time, the negative image of her own grandmother may fade and, if she is lucky, she may find a "substitute" grandparent. Or, as we will discuss later, she may come to hate all older people, including the "wrinkled, hobbling" person that she herself is destined to become.

To be sure, the internal image of every grandparent changes as the child matures. But a living grandparent who ceases to manifest regular interest in a grandchild undergoes a particularly negative transformation—especially if parents insist, as they frequently do, that the child continue to show affection toward that grandparent. Norma, twelve, helped us to understand the emotional turmoil that can plague children when a relationship with a beloved grandparent sours. For the first six years of Norma's life, her grandparents lived nearby and saw her often. Then they moved to Florida.

> I remember when they left. I told them, "Have a good time." Everyone was excited but crying, too. That was confusing. I thought they were just going away for a while. I had no idea that I would hardly ever see them again.

In fact, Norma continued to see her grandparents twice a year until her grandfather's death, which occurred ten months before we visited her. At our invitation Norma drew a picture of her grandmother, who had decided to remain in Florida where, she said, "Grandmother has her home and her friends." The figure is large and centrally placed, indicating that Norma still feels a strong emotional attachment to her grandmother. (Fig. 27) But the image is doll-like, a stylish granny that looks more like a fantasy out of an adolescent's imagination than a real grandmother. When she had finished her picture, Norma talked about what she imagined her real grandmother to be like.

> This is what she looks like to me now. She's pretty and having fun in Florida swimming and being with her friends. I remember her very well from when I was younger. We were close then. She played with me and we baked tons and tons of brownies together. Now, she really doesn't know me anymore. I mean really, she still thinks of me as in the past. I try to tell myself that we're close, but I really don't know her anymore.

It's hard to explain. I really feel uncomfortable around her, like I'm supposed to make believe that we're close and I don't feel it. To act fake . . . you know? I feel guilty sometimes that I don't like her as much as she says she loves me. Maybe I should love her more . . . I don't know. Do you think I'm bad because I don't feel that I love my grandmother?

Norma senses that despite what her grandmother says, she really has forgotten her granddaughter. The strong emotional attachment Norma feels is itself a product of happier days when grandmother was the woman with whom she shared time and space baking "tons and tons of brownies." Now that grandmother is a widow, Norma feels more than the usual parental pressure to "act" like a devoted grandchild. But without regular contact with her grandmother, Norma feels, the bonds between them are bogus. She is sad about the growing gulf that separates them and uncertain about how she should react to her grandmother's periodic displays of affection.

I feel that grandmother missed out on my growing up. She wasn't there when I needed her. Now, I don't know her. Sometimes, I want to visit her but it brings back pain, especially if I let myself enjoy myself. If I don't visit her when she invites me, then I feel guilty. And she does buy me presents. I don't know, I just go along with the whole thing.

Norma seems to recognize that her grandmother's gifts are meant to replace the "self" that grandmother once gave her. But Norma is also wary of showing too much gratitude, of allowing herself to get too close when the two of them are together. We asked her if she would like her grandmother to move back close to home.

I don't know. I guess it's too late because I don't need her too much now—at least not like I did. Grandmother tells me that maybe it's good that we are not too close because when we are together it makes it more special. That's a bunch of baloney. If she did come back there wouldn't be much to come back to anyway because I am close to my friend's grandmother and we do things together sometimes. She is a very funny person and nice. I guess I've kind of got another grandmother.

Norma is working her way out of an emotional bind experienced by many children whose grandparents are only intermittently present in their lives. Such grandparents—and they are the overwhelming majority in our study—expect to receive more affection from the grandchildren than they themselves are willing to give. "My dividends" is the way one grandparent described his grandchildren. But children, as we observed earlier, are emotional geniuses; they can readily sense a grandparent's pretense at love. Children are also more honest, emotionally, than most adults; therefore, they find it more difficult to uphold their end of an emotional charade. Often, if they are required under parental fiat to "fake it" the entire sham can easily collapse into hatred.

"There she is, you can have her," said Mark, shoving over to us his drawing of his grandmother, which he had sketched quickly in broad crayon strokes. (Fig. 28) Mark is ten years old. When he was a baby, his parents moved to New York from their native Boston and he rarely saw his grandparents. Mark particularly remembers his grandmother's birthday cards to him because after his grandfather died the cards started arriving on the wrong date. Several of them even bore the wrong name. Mark's picture of his grandmother is a fearsome profile: a large head with wide, heavy lips; a cleft and jutting jaw; an almost tribal ring hanging from the single visible ear and a bulging eyeball that seems to have permanently bent her glasses. If there is another, warmer side to grandmother, Mark has not felt it.

I see her just once in a while. It's no fun. When she sees me she looks at me and goes, "Oh, my little darling grandson, I miss you so much." And then she doesn't talk to me anymore. My parents get mad at me because I don't want to talk to her. I tell them that I don't like her. Then my parents say, "How can you feel like that about your grandmother?"

We went to her house once and her friends were there. She acted different towards me, made a fuss over me, to show her friends, I guess. To show off. If I ever touch anything in her house, forget it. She has a fit. My parents say that she is nervous. All I can say is I can't wait to get away from her. I hate it when she touches me.

Oh yes, when my grandfather died she said, "Do you miss your grandfather? He loved you very much." I told her yes but that was a lie. I felt sad because I saw my parents so sad, but I didn't even know my grandfather. I would be sadder if my Little League coach died. I did feel a little sad when I saw my grandfather in the coffin. I thought that it's too bad that I didn't know him better. Maybe we would have gotten along. If you want the truth—and it sounds terrible—it wouldn't bother me at all if I never saw my grandmother again. I get so mad when I think of the way she acts towards me alone, and then when she puts on this act in front of her friends . . . All I am to her is a prize on her charm bracelet.

The grandchild as mere *ornament*. Mark wasn't the only youngster to use this strikingly evocative image. Indeed, it might even be taken as a central metaphor for the emotional trauma expressed by most Group II children. They feel attached, but their sense of natural connection has been turned into bitter emotional bondage to a disinterested grandparent. And so in their words and drawings, these children protest against their emotionally detached grandparents for failing to show them that fullness of interest which we all expect from people who lay claim to our affections.

Marian, age twelve, drew a picture of herself doing carpentry with her grandfather. Marian sees her grandfather about once a month—more than most children we visited. But during these encounters her grandfather enacts only the "work" side of their relationship. In her picture, Marian and her grandfather appear as two profiles suspended on either end of a seesaw. (Fig. 29) Significantly, grandfather's image is a ghostly form without substance.

> I can't draw anymore, I'm getting too angry. Here I am working with my grandfather. He's teaching me how to use a plane. I've already got three splinters in my hand and he's being very bossy and telling me the "right" way to do it. I'm so angry that I can't even finish this picture.

Buddy, age nine, also sees his grandmother several times a month. But like Marian, he finds these meetings emotionally upsetting. His grandmother has a full-time job and hates to cook. Nonetheless, the kitchen is where Buddy most often sees his grandmother. Buddy remarked that he has the only grandmother among all his friends who doesn't like to cook, a fact which in his mind seems to color her relationship with him. Nor, as he explained, does she much like being a grandmother—a feeling which Buddy captured in his small, doll-like figure.

> She has no time for me. She's always busy working and running around with her friends. She really doesn't act like a grandmother. She says that she is too young to be one anyway.

Buddy's comments are significant in two respects. First, they demonstrate the importance of the grandmother's role as a provider of food—as a "Grand Nurturer." Secondly, it dramatizes how a grandmother's unwillingness to fulfill this simple but basic role function of providing food can damage a grandchild's sense of his own self-worth. Buddy's grandmother may have very good reasons for not liking to cook. *But these "adult" reasons are meaningless to a child.* All Buddy knows is that his grandmother will not do for him what other grandmothers do—what all grandmothers, he likely feels, do. And the only reason a child his age can supply for her behavior is that his *grandmother does not really "care that much" about him.* This leads Buddy to the devastating conclusion that he himself is not worthy of her love.

Up to this point, we have been discussing children who all have had some personal "first-hand" experience of their grandparents which serves as the basis of an emotional attachment. But many children—nearly a third of those we visited—knew only "about" their grandparents, either through stories told by their parents, through family albums, or through occasional "wish-you-were-here" postcards from the Sunbelt. Grandparents known only in this second-hand manner are easy to spot in projective drawings. Their images tend to be featureless specters, like the ghostly grandmother in Fig. 30, or childlike dolls or puppets, as in Figs. 31, 32, 33. Sometimes, children with no real grandparental relationship to draw upon will substitute a stereotype of an adult which looks as if it had been copied from a poster for The Future Farmers of America.

When we asked Mary, age ten, to draw a picture of her grandmother she responded by producing a stereotypical "Grammy" whom she obviously doesn't know or feel. (Fig. 34) There is no expression on her grandmother's face and her clothes are inappropriate for any contemporary woman, suggesting that Mary has seen her grandmother only about five times, she guessed. She called her grandmother "Mother's Mother," a term that succinctly sums up the hand-me-down nature of their relationship.

> The person in the picture is saying "What am I doing here?" I don't know what else to say. I don't know what she does during the day. I think maybe she has a job somewhere. I wish she were here so that I could get to know her. I have a

lot to tell her. But when I did see her, she talked mostly with my mother. She isn't too interested in me.

Children whose second-hand knowledge of their grandparents is very vague drew on every scrap of information—or fantasy—to come up with a picture of their functionally nonexistent grandparents. Sean, twelve, proudly displayed his drawing of two figures in full-length bathing suits of the sort adults wore in the Gay Nineties. (Fig. 35) "I guess that's what they look like," he shrugged. "I never see them and I don't care about them. Who needs grandparents?" Jerry, another twelve-year-old, accepted our challenge with considerable humor. He has seen his grandparents only once. All he knows about them is that they live somewhere "near Texas" and that grandfather was an accomplished tennis player when he was a young man. So that is what he drew: an athletic grandfather ready to serve the ball and a stereotypical "Granny" pestering her husband. (Figs. 36, 37)

> I guess this is what they look like now. I never see them. My grandfather is a tennis player, so I guess he looks like an old tennis player now . . . And here comes old Granny, saying, "Harry, get off the court and come on home." I don't know what they are really like. I just made up the pictures from what I guessed that they do where they live.

We asked Jerry to try to imagine what he would do with his grandparents. He protested again that he had no idea. But when we persisted, he drew a picture of himself sitting down with his grandparents to an empty dinner table. (Fig. 38) Jerry is neatly attired but a feeling of isolation and detachment dominates the scene. To fully appreciate the barren emotional tone of Jerry's picture compare it with the "table" pictures of Group I. (Fig. 7)

Melissa, fifteen, taxed her imagination to the fullest in

order to come up with a picture of her grandparents. All but one of them are dead. But she did not place her only living grandparent in her picture; nor did she talk about him—as if this real but absent grandfather would contaminate the ideal family scene she had constructed. (Fig. 39) The grandparental figures all have a frozen and stilted quality, like a diorama, and they are placed at the top of the page, indicating their dreamlike existence in Melissa's mind. But she talked about them as if they really did exist.

> Their lives are peaceful and harmonious. Grandparents take care of the family. They watch over the young. Grandfather is growing food for his family and Grandmother keeps her eyes on the young, preparing to call them to eat the dinner that she has prepared. They are happy and feel that their life is full because they are with their family and are needed. They're loved by everyone in the family.

Melissa's idealized family, guarded by grandparents, does not exist—not even in the deep reaches of her mind where emotional attachments, once formed, are cemented forever. Nonetheless, her fantasy family fills a real place in her mind, a place that exists inside everyone, regardless of age, and is reserved for grandparents only.

Like God, if grandparents did not exist, children would inevitably invent them, particularly in time of need. "I wish that I had grandparents nearby I could run to, especially when my parents fight with each other," said Jonathon, twelve, whose grandparents live 1,000 miles away. "I wish I had grandparents to tell my parents to get along."

GROUP III: NO CONTACT

What happens when children who never met their grandparents and know nothing about them are asked to draw one? There are uncounted millions of such "grand-parentless" children in American society and some of those we visited refused to pick up a crayon. They had no grand-parent image within them to project onto the paper. All we found was a wound where, the children felt, a grandparent ought to be.

"What's a grandparent like?" Wanda asked us. She knew that some of her friends had grandparents but she had never seen hers. Wanda's mother is divorced and es-tranged from her own parents as well as from Wanda's pa-ternal grandparents. Wanda and her mother have moved many times since the divorce and the nearest experiences to grandparental love Wanda has known are temporary at-tachments to ever-changing teachers and aides in various day-care centers. Wanda drew the best grandparent she could imagine: a human form without human content. (Fig. 40)

> I guess I must have grandparents somewhere. Everyone has grandparents, I guess. I wonder what mine are like? What are they doing? Do I look like them? I asked my mother about my grandparents but she didn't say anything to me. I'd rather come home from school to a grandmother than come here (the day-care center), even though I like the people here. I guess that you could say that my teacher, Miss Jeffries, is like what a grandmother would be to me. Could I draw another grandparent? I'd draw one like the one I saw on TV.

For children without known grandparents, trying to draw one is like taking a test in a subject never studied—or worse, like admitting you were born with an important part of yourself missing. Thus, many children in this group tended to draw either small, profiled faces floating expres-sionlessly in a sea of empty paper (Figs. 41, 42), or else large puppet figures smirking like primordial beasts. (Fig. 43)

Tim, age ten, has grandparents who live across the country, 1,500 miles away. He has never seen them. But he has heard his parents talk about them, so he complied when we asked him for a picture of his grandfather. (Fig. 44) The image is ample, rising toward the upper portion of the page. The face is slightly grotesque, flushed and mottled with wrinkles. When he had finished Tim shrugged at the Frankenstein that he had created. "He's alive," Tim said of his grandfather, "but for me he's dead."

Lynn, eight, had lost all of her grandparents. Nonetheless, she was eager to draw one. But when she had finished, she jerked her head back, startled at what had come out of her. She had drawn a very good likeness of a butterfly. (Fig. 45)

> What did I do that for! I wasn't even thinking and that's what came out. I guess that I would like to have a butterfly for a grandparent because it's pretty and sweet. Besides, I don't have a grandparent to draw.

Paul, eleven, has no grandparents either. He was unable to draw anything more substantial than a phantom grandfather. But Paul had an inkling of what grandfathers are for and what he and his younger brother would do with him if they had one. (Fig. 46) "If I had a grandfather," Paul told us, "this is what we would be doing together, just what I see grandfathers doing with their grandchildren on TV." When we asked Terry, nine, a sad-eyed girl from the Midwest, to draw a picture of her grandparents doing something with her family, she grew even more withdrawn. She has no grandparents and no father. Reluctantly, Terry filled her paper with a backyard scene: patio, table, chair and a barbecue. (Fig. 47) But the stage she set was devoid of actors. Empty. "There's no one there," she said.

Since nature abhors a vacuum, many children search for

an elder to fill the void left by their grandparents. Robert, seven, drew his teacher for us. Patricia, also seven, started on a drawing but quickly crumpled it up and threw it on the floor. She has no grandparents and both of her parents work long hours to support the family. Patricia has no brothers or sisters either, and after school she spends long hours alone in the family apartment watching television.

> I guess my grandparent would be Fred Flintstone. He's always there when I come home from school. I even talk to him. I tell him what happened at school. Sometimes I even think that he looks out at me from the screen. It's almost like he can see me. I know that he can't but sometimes my mind thinks that he does. I love his family and his friends so much. I feel like I'm one of them, that they are like my own family. Do you know what I mean?

D. Commentary

The children have told us, better than experts can, what grandparents mean to them. In this case, they are the experts and all we need add by way of commentary is a summary of the major themes of their words and pictures. As part of our study, we compiled a list of comments of what children in each group said when we asked them what their grandparents were doing, saying, and feeling in the pictures they drew. This sample of comments was drawn for all 300 children we visited and is included for reference in Appendix B on page 227. Here, we will briefly underscore what we heard these child "oracles" tell us.

Group I. Children who were close to one or more grandparents described themselves as "lucky" to have such a warm relationship. They were indeed a fortunate few since only 5 percent, or about fifteen children in all, enjoyed such a close attachment. They felt accepted "as is" by their grandparents, even "adored," and some allowed that they did not "deserve" such unqualified affection. Grandparental love was not contingent upon performance; it came with "no strings attached." Only grandparents, we surmise, are free to bestow this kind of love, and the children returned it in almost equal measure.

These children portrayed their grandparents in a variety of roles. They functioned as mentors, caretakers, mediators between child and parents, same-sex role models and family historians. From them, grandchildren learned about how it was in "the old days," what mother or father was like as a child, their own roots, and an inkling of "how to be" in the future. These vital connections were real to them because they were transmitted through close personal experience and embodied in living "Great Parents."

When these children talked about their grandparents, they rarely mentioned things their grandparents had given them, other than heirlooms. Their conversations turned on what grandparents did with them, how they smelled, their personal quirks and foibles. Chief among the experiences of grandparents was the family dinner. Where this was a regular ritual, the scenes the children re-created strongly suggested that the grandparents were the "center" of the family universe.

Grandmother was, in most instances, the dominant figure: part madonna, part "Earth mother," very much the provider of good things to eat. Even though she might be employed, her grandchildren ignored this aspect of her life. It had no relevance for them. Grandfather entertained, told stories, taught crafts and in general introduced the children to a world beyond the immediate and familiar. Grandfather's work was an important part of his identity to them. There was no hint of a "generation gap" in the conversations of these children. On the contrary, these grandparents appeared to be compelling, reliable models for old age. Their very presence stimulated the children to anticipate without undue fear their own aging and, among older youngsters, death. These children were able to extend their feelings for their grandparents to older people in general. They were, on the whole, quite solicitous of "elders." Finally, these grandparents seemed to extract from these children deep and various emotions which greatly enriched their grandchildren's lives. Secure in the knowledge of their grandparents' love, these children freely expressed resentment, anger, concern, compassion and, especially, humor while drawing their pictures. In short, these "Great Parents" had added emotional subtlety and dimension to their grandchildren's young lives.

Group II. These children reflect the experiences of most American grandchildren. Grandparents have, to one degree or another, receded into the background of these youngsters' lives; yet, when they spoke with us, their grandparents turned out to be very much in the foreground of their emotional concerns. They felt attached to grandparents who were physically and/or emotionally separated from them. In their drawings and conversations, their grandparents emerged as intermittent presences in their lives. Leave-takings were frequently mentioned. And when these children attempted to describe their grandparents, they relied on a combination of first-hand knowledge—usually remembered rather than freshly experienced—and second-hand knowledge obtained largely through parents' stories and memories.

In their relationships with grandparents, children in this group spanned a wide spectrum from attachment to alienation. Correspondingly, their emotions reflected the range of protest-despair-disinterest typical of "separation." Those who had only recently "lost" a beloved grandparent spoke in elegiac tones. Many of them cried. All of these children were sad and puzzled by the separation in time and place from their grandparents. In their pictures, the children sometimes portrayed their grandparents as "happy" in the sun "playing all day." Paradoxically, however, when we asked them to describe what their grandparents were feeling inside, many of these same children imagined that they were "sad," "bored," or "lonely." In their despair of ever having their grandparents return, children whose grandparents had been absent for a long time tried to rationalize their behavior by devaluing their importance to them. Others completed the separation cycle by mirroring their grandparents' disinterest with their own. One child complained that her grandmother "doesn't want to be a grandma," and then added, "What good are grandparents anyhow?"

If we were to be privy to the inner thoughts of a Group II youngster, his thinking might sound like this:

> I am the center of my world. My grandparents are separated from me and I am helpless to retrieve them. If I were good (or worthy) enough, they wouldn't allow us to be separated. Therefore, I must be not good enough or else they don't care enough about me. Either way, I won't like them. I won't think about them because that makes me sad. I especially will not think about the nice things that they do for me because this confuses me. I will not become attached to them because they will leave me.

Younger children, in particular, cannot comprehend the meaning of abstractions, such as "retirement," which govern the lives of adults. They experience life organically in terms of connections with other people and are deeply disturbed if these connections, once established, are suddenly severed or attenuated. When divorce or death disrupted families of Group II children, the grandparents tended to withdraw, often in confusion, from their grandchildren, thus exacerbating the situation. Far from being the center of the family universe as in Group I, these grandparents actually added to the polarization brought about by divorce.

Overall, the children in this group saw their grandparents as preoccupied with their own friends, jobs, health or other problems of aging. This "one-sidedness" in their relationships was evident from the profiles they drew when the attachment was still more or less intact. In their conversations, children reported that such grandparents typically "bossed" them or were "grouchy." There was no "specialness" in the relationship. Gifts of "things" replaced gifts of self. Grandparents who chose to maintain connections via birthday cards and other occasional greetings were judged severely if those cards were carelessly selected or sent.

The most distressed children were those whose grandparents were physically near but emotionally distant. These children complained bitterly when forced under parental pressure or grandparental expectations to give "command performances" of affection toward grandparents who only pretended to return that affection. The resentment of these children was palpable and frequently lined with anger. The "charm bracelet" image captured their attitude precisely.

Because of their sporadic and not always happy connections to their grandparents, these children were keenly conscious of a gap between the generations. They derided elders as being "too old" and "out of touch," "the kinds of people they did not want to be like." They saw no reason to turn to older people for advice because their own grandparents were emotionally unreliable. Finally, these youngsters had little knowledge of how they would be and act when they were their grandparents' age. On the contrary, they found it difficult, even annoying, to discuss their own future as "old people."

Group III. These children, about 15 percent of those we visited, had never experienced any attachment to a grandparent. They were children of severely "nuclear" families, or less; some were being raised by single parents, many spent the bulk of their days in schools and day-care centers. Often, these children were hesitant to end our interviews because the complete and undivided attention of an older person was a treat for them.

During our interviews, these children appeared anxious to learn about grandparents. They wondered "what it would be like to have a grandparent." Since they had none of their own, they filled the vacuum with stereotypes borrowed from books and television programs. Some of their projective drawings were pure fantasy or figures of wish fulfillment. They drew butterflies, dolls, empty family settings. They felt that something was missing in their lives but they didn't know precisely what. Their emotions ranged from longing and melancholy through confusion to a barren lack of feeling. "I don't know what to think or feel," many confessed.

Understandably, these children possessed no knowledge of ancestry, no sense of bloodline. Similarly, they could muster no sense of future as older people; they had encountered few elders as role models in the institutions that sheltered them. In short, they were alienated from the aged by the fate of their family situation. They exhibited no love, bore no resentment, harbored no hatred. They lived in a state of detachment accompanied by a dangerous emotional apathy.

E. The Immortal Grandparent

A number of children we visited had lost their grandparents through death. Those who had never known their grandparents intimately did not mourn their loss. Those who had, conferred upon their grandparent a form of immortality that only grandchildren can provide. Within these children, their beloved grandparents lived on as constant objects, fixed forever as large and compelling, almost "heroic" figures in their minds.

The "reality" of the grandparent who lives on within the grandchild depends upon the child's age at the time of the grandparent's death and the degree of intimacy they shared. If the grandparent was a kind and beneficent person, so much the better for the grandchild. At the very least, recollection of such a grandparent evokes warm "feeling memories" within the grandchild, no matter how vague the child's recall of actual experiences shared with the grandparent might be. Lisa, nine, was four years old when her grandmother died. She recalled that her grandmother was "fun to see" and how she "made a fuss over me" whenever they were together.

> I can't tell you anything too much about her. It's just a warm and nice feeling when I think about her. I look at her pictures but I don't think about anything except that I just enjoy looking at the pictures. I don't know why, but I stare at them a long time.

Vinnie, six, had only recently lost his grandfather in an airplane crash when we visited him. The boy had been very close to his grandfather, which was evident from the large figure he drew, dominating the page (Fig. 48), and from the precise details that Vinnie recalled as he drew his picture.

> He hated spinach and broccoli, just like me. And he was funny just like me and when we would take a family picture he would always go in for his red suspenders and he would wear them for all the pictures. I have those suspenders and I will wear them just like him because we were so much alike and I will be like him when I grow up. He can't say anything now because he's dead and he can't talk. But the priest said to me that someday I may see him again in heaven.

For Vinnie, grandfather is still alive but in heaven. "He is looking at me," Vinnie explained as he completed his picture. "He's saying that he's sorry that he died but that he couldn't help it." Vinnie's grandfather is present to him in other ways as well. He is there in the suspenders the boy will wear, there too as an adult model whom Vinnie aspires to be like when he grows up. Finally, he is present as the grandfather he hopes to meet again, someday, in heaven. In sum, Vinnie's grandfather made such an emotional impression on the boy that he continues to exist for him in the present and the future as well as in the past. Vinnie's grandfather, we might say, is fortunate, at least in this respect. He died when Vinnie was young and their relationship was one of pure joy to the child. This will never change. The bond between them is immune from changes inflicted by time and is fixed forever as a totally positive attachment.

The longer a child enjoys the intimacy of a loving grandparent the more "alive" and idealized that grandparent will be after death in the mind of the grandchild. Evelyn had a close and loving grandmother for the first six years of her life and now, three years after her grandmother's death, Evelyn continues to experience her as a valuable inner companion. In her picture, Evelyn placed her grandmother on the left (past) side of the paper but she drew her full length, a tall person who is "wrinkled and old" in the face. (Fig. 49)

> She's still alive for me. I remember how she smells and how she held me in her lap. She was big and very soft. I used to melt in her. It's like I expect her to be there when I get home from school. I know she won't be there, of course, but she's not dead for me. I talk to her picture when I've got a problem. I've never told anyone this—it may sound crazy—but I think she is watching over me. I mean I really feel it. I can talk to her in my mind. She loved me so much.

It would be difficult to underestimate the durability of grandparental love within grandchildren, or to limit its perduring influence. One of the oldest grandchildren we visited was Charlie, sixteen, whose grandmother had died two years earlier. When we met him he was wearing the uniform of the contemporary teenager: worn jeans, jogging shoes and a T-shirt with the name of a rock band emblazoned across his chest. Charlie felt a bit awkward when we asked him to draw his grandmother, but he complied. He drew a large picture in the middle of the page, and as he did his eyes began to tear.

> She's saying "How are you, Charles? I hope that you are being a good boy." She's wondering if I still have the ten silver dollars. When I was born she bought ten silver dollars for me to keep and it was a special thing beween us. When I look at them I think about her, like a lot of lucky charms, and she said that we can count them in heaven some day. She said that she was sure to go to heaven because she ran her life so she would go there and I should do the same so that we can meet again and be together. Wouldn't that be something?

Charlie put the crayons down several times and finally stopped drawing altogether. "There she is, my grandmother," he told us. "It's not too good but I've done worse." Charlie was at an age when he preferred to talk about his grandmother rather than draw a picture of her and he had a lot to say. She had lived in the same house with him and had been his constant companion.

> She was always wondering how I was doing. Always concerned for me. She was so worried when I was on the school wrestling team. I talked to her most out of all the people in my family. She would always bake for us and help out without complaining. She'd make sure that we were obeying our parents. When she died, things were never the same . . . they aren't. I'd look at her old rocking chair and make believe that she was in it. I'd talk to it. She was always there, helping Mom. When I would come home from school—you know how kids like to see someone there when they get home from school—well, I'd tell her about the day, even things that I couldn't tell my parents. I never had a babysitter because she was always there, in the same house. She did so much for me when I was little.

Charlie couldn't tell us enough about his grandmother. Nor could he quite get to the bottom of all the things she still means to him.

> She is not dead for me, not in my mind. Do you know what I mean? She taught me a lot of church stuff. She would make sure that we all went to church, the whole family. My father didn't want to go but he listened to her. If he didn't listen to her, we wouldn't have to listen to him, right? We were proud when we all sat in church together, one big family. She was very strong on religion. Look to the church when you are in need, she would say, you will when you get older. Do the right things.

Grandmother's "message" to Charlie has stayed with him because of what she did for him and how it made him feel. That feeling was and remains different from the feelings generated by his own mother.

> If I was having a hard time with my parents, she would stick up for me, ease the way, you know. She would clean up

the kitchen for me so I could go to the movies, do my chores sometimes, and I wouldn't feel guilty. But when my mother says "go ahead" and I have a chore to do I feel so guilty that I don't enjoy going anywhere.

Charlie lived with his grandmother long enough to experience the inevitable changes in grandparent-grandchild relations that come when the child reaches adolescence. Charlie was very perceptive about those changes and was candid about the feelings they generated in him.

In one way, I'm glad she went when she did because when she got older she was more tired and I wanted to do more outside of the house. She irritated me a little because she didn't want to be alone. She'd want me to stay with her. I always did because I never would hurt her, never. After all she did for me. But I guess that even though I did it, sometimes I didn't like it. But I never told her that. I would think of how she came to the bus stop with me when I was little and would bring a raincoat for me if it was raining. Always thinking of me . . . no, I could never hurt her. Now I only have wonderful memories of her. She died quickly one day . . . a heart attack.

Shortly after his grandmother died, Charlie started to work as a volunteer at an old folks' home. The director of the home told us that he was so pleased with the residents' response to Charlie that he has offered the youngster a paying part-time position. In particular, the director praised Charlie's patience, kindness, and ability to make even the most cantankerous residents smile. This is an unusual gift in an adolescent, a degree of altruism not normally found in young people his age. On a subsequent visit, we asked Charlie why he had decided to work with old people.

Why? Maybe it's because I'm giving something back for my grandmother. I don't know. I just feel good around them and I feel that it is a worthwhile thing to do. I like being around these old people. They are funny and nice. It's hard to find people to care for them and it's too bad. They are people and they are lonely.

Charlie knows what is inside "old folks" because his grandmother is inside him. He is not simply doing something for her but responding to older people the way his grandmother responded to him. Through her, Charlie experienced the attachment of grandparental love and was able to return that love when his grandmother wanted him to stay at home with her. Her legacy to him is his extraordinary altruism, which is his for life. Because of his grandmother, Charlie has gained early in life a profound understanding of the humanity he shares with all people and a respect for elders that is rare in our society at any age.

> Yes, it's like she's a part of me, different from my parents. She's part of them, we're all part of each other, I guess. I feel different than many of my friends do about older people. When they make jokes or put down older people, I don't think that's funny and they laugh about it. I know I'm right because I make believe that the person that they are laughing at is my grandmother, and I wouldn't laugh at her, wouldn't let anyone else do it either. She is part of me and now that she is gone that will never change. "What good are older people?" my friends say. Too bad they never had a grandmother like mine.

F. The Substitute Grandparent

We observed earlier that if grandparents did not exist children would surely invent them. A few children we visited did precisely that: they ventured outside the family circle to find an elder to be their grandparent. One of these children is Kyle, eight, who is hardly a lonely child. She has five brothers and sisters—but no grandparents. Instead, she has a sixty-five-year-old widow living nearby whom Kyle visits every day after school. Sometimes the neighbor is startled to find Kyle in one of her bathrooms or to come upon the child cooking soup in the kitchen. But, the widow told us, she is pleased that Kyle feels sufficiently at home in her house to wander in and out at will. Kyle's mother doesn't mind; with six children she has enough to do. And Kyle is delighted with her substitute grandmother, as we could see for ourselves when we visited her at her neighbor's house:

> It's so peaceful here. No fighting, no kids running around. I'm the only child here and I can do almost anything I want to. Mrs. Nickel is lonely. She lives alone and I cheer her up. We just need each other, I guess. We're good for each other.

Kyle's neighbor fulfills a number of needs that only a grandparent can supply: another "place" to be, time alone together, and the undivided attention of an elder. Moreover, they have forged a special bond that can only exist, it seems, between the very young and the old: a bond of mutual need and support.

The need for a grandparent dawned on Connie when she was six. Four years earlier, a series of family tragedies left her without any grandparents. When the need became pressing she went out and literally recruited her mother's eldest sister.

> I noticed that my friend was talking about her grandparents and what she did with them and how much fun she had with them. I was really jealous. I wanted to have grandparents too. I really did. I used to dream about going somewhere with my grandparents, like Disneyland, or about cooking with them like my friend did. My parents always seemed to be busy. I told my parents that I wished I had a grandparent and they laughed at me. Well anyway, I had an Aunt Lucy who wasn't married and lived alone. I told Aunt Lucy that I wanted her to come and live with us and that I could

be special to her and she could be like a grandparent to me. My parents were surprised at this but Lucy did come to live with us. We had plenty of room in the house and we did all the things I had wanted to do with my make-believe grandparents. Aunt Lucy's like a fairy godmother to me . . . My mother got a little jealous but that was O.K.

At fifteen, Connie finds that she still needs and enjoys her substitute grandmother. What's more, she wanted us to know she has no intention of ever abandoning her:

Aunt Lucy is much older than my mother. She's the oldest and my mother is the youngest. When I'm married she'll be pretty old. She'll come to live with me after I'm married if she has nowhere to go. She'll always have a place with me. I'll give the love back to her when she needs it. It's like a circle. She was there when I needed her, I'll be there when she needs me.

2

What Grandchildren Mean to Grandparents

> When the news came that Sevanne Margaret was born, I suddenly realized that through no act of my own I had become biologically related to a new human being. This was one thing that had never come up in discussions of grandparenthood and had never before occurred to me.
>
> Margaret Mead, BLACKBERRY WINTER

A. *The Method*

The children told us that they feel a natural connection between themselves and their grandparents. They revealed, moreover, a strong emotional need for close attachment to at least one grandparent. When that bond was broken or never acknowledged by a grandparent, the children felt wounded, as if some vital part of themselves were missing.

What about grandparents? Do they feel a natural connection to their grandchildren? Do they crave a close attachment to at least one grandchild? Do they also feel wounded or incomplete if that attachment has been broken or never forged in the first place?

To find out, we visited 300 grandparents, including some whose grandchildren we had met during the course of our

first study. Once again, our "field trips" took us up and
down the East Coast of the United States, from Maine to
Florida, with a few forays to the Midwest and the West
Coast. Once again, our concern was with variety of life situations, not regional or ethnic diversity. Thus, we visited
people in nursing as well as in private homes, those who
had moved to "retirement" communities as well as those
who had "stayed put" in their home towns. In our "sample" you will meet couples, as well as singles who have lost
their spouses through death, divorce, or desertion.

During each visit, we asked grandparents to respond to a
formal questionnaire which had two very different purposes. First, the questionnaire allowed us to quantify and
compare the results of all our interviews: Those tabula-
tions, together with a copy of the questionnaire, can be
found in Appendix C on page 233. Our major finding—
which came as no surprise—is that the grandparents mirror
the continuum we found among grandchildren (page 7);
that is, in terms of shared time and emotional intimacy,
the vast majority of grandparents were only intermittently
involved with their grandchildren, including some of those
that lived nearby. About 5 percent were regularly and
deeply involved, while approximately the same number
were *totally* disconnected from their grandchildren.

Second, and more important, the process of answering
the questionnaire created a channel—much like the children's projective drawings—into the grandparents' innermost feelings and thoughts. Like many of the children
we visited, most of the grandparents were surprised that
someone actually cared about what was on their minds and
hearts concerning their roles as grandparents, and that we
were interested in learning what they had to say. Initially,
most of the grandparents sputtered out disconnected
thoughts and observations, as if clearing their minds. Grad-

ually, however, the questionnaire helped them focus on their relationships with their grandchildren. Once focused, these grandparents poured out a genuinely revelatory stream of reflections. Often a grandparent talked at such length and with so much intensity that there was not enough time in a single day to complete the interview. We sensed that we had tapped a deep well of emotion long repressed. The interview itself became an "event" in their lives because we had put them in touch with their own inner "oracles."

Our approach was simple. At the core of our interviews we asked our respondents to go back in time and recall where they were, what they did and, particularly, how they felt when they learned that they were to become grandparents for the first time. We wanted to know how they anticipated grandparenthood; what they felt when the child finally arrived; what thoughts arose in reaction to the event and what action they took to see the baby. Only later did we inquire about the evolution and character of their subsequent relationships with their grandchildren. In short, we wanted them to relive for us those moments when, as Margaret Mead put it, they suddenly realized that through no act of their own they had become biologically related to a new human being.

B. The Instinct to Nurture

A grandmother recalled the birth of her first grandchild:

> I was so glad I was there, just to be there and to share that wonderful moment with the children. And when I saw that baby, well the way I felt was unbelievable. When I first saw my grandchild I was bursting with joy and pride. I'd never

had a feeling quite like that before . . . to see your own child produce another child and to know that it came through you.

It was a wonder, a mystery, and there was something else, too—a wonder at nature. It was a spiritual or religious experience. You know, just as if you would sit there and look at a flower for a long time—that kind of feeling, a religious feeling.

A grandfather recounted a similar rush of thoughts and feelings:

I was so happy now that this little grandson would carry on my name, my father's name, this connection between all of us. It was a deep and mysterious feeling within me that I could never hope to put into words.

I had been waiting eagerly for a grandchild. I would be a good grandparent to this grandchild, as my grandparents had been to me. Besides, I had nothing better to do and now I had a new job.

Another grandfather described how his mind reeled off a succession of images of how life would be with his new granddaughter:

I daydreamed of the things my granddaughter and I would do together. How nice it would be, how I could do things for her that her mother didn't have the time to do . . . how we would enjoy each other in peace, now that I had so much time, especially in today's hectic world.

Now I'm immortal. Through my little grandchild I will continue, my blood will be mixed with the blood of other people. This will make us all a family.

These responses, typical of those we heard, provide privileged insights into the initial reactions of grandparents, and so into formative stages of the grandparent-grandchild bond. On becoming a grandparent, the impulse to nurture is reawakened and earlier experiences of motherhood and fatherhood are relived. Thus, a grandmother looks at her daughter's baby and feels her own maternity telescoped: "To see your own child produce another child and to know that the child comes through you." She has, in effect, given birth once more through the labor of her own daughter. Once again, she is absorbed in the recurrent "mystery" of new life unfolding like a flower within the womb. She becomes, by virtue of a biological process over which she has no control, a "Great Mother."

Although grandfathers cannot relive the physical sensations of giving birth, they do have a strong emotional reaction, accompanied by thoughts of extending their kin. They experience themselves as bearers of a bloodline, newly extended beyond fatherhood and certifying, through grandpaternity, their own sense of continuity. They anticipate how they would protect and provide for this new addition to their enlarged family. They become at one stroke "Great Fathers."

These common experiences indicate that *the connection between grandparents and grandchild is natural and second in emotional power only to the primordial bond between parent and child.* Moreover, the arrival of the first grandchild seems to quicken the attachment between parents and grandparents as well. This was confirmed by several mothers who, remembering the birth of their first child, talked to us about the sense of longing for their own parents at that time. Although the experiences of new mothers are part of a separate study, we have included two of them for the evidence they provide that these vital attachments are not felt by grandparents alone. In each case, the absence of the maternal grandmother (and to a much lesser extent, the maternal grandfather) was keenly felt and regretted.

A new mother described her mix of feelings when the nurse first presented her with her baby:

> When my baby came I was so happy, so happy. After all

that pain I wanted to see my husband's face when he saw the baby for the first time. We looked at the baby together and we had all that happiness. But in some way I felt empty. The baby was gone from my stomach, but that wasn't it. It was something else deep within me. Things didn't feel "complete."

And then I knew what it was. I wanted my father to be proud, but most important, I wanted my mother. She had to hold my baby too. In a way, it was a part of her, a little baby from her through me . . . and from her mother . . . a connection.

A second mother, who like so many younger women has left her parents and maintained little contact with them after marriage, felt a similar need when her first child was delivered.

I felt the absence of a mother most when my baby came. I needed a mother then, but not my mother. She drives me crazy and I can't stand her. But I needed a mother, an older woman. My husband wasn't enough. Not that he wasn't what he was supposed to be . . . he just isn't a mother and that's what I needed at that time. My husband tried, but he can't be all things to me. It just wasn't a natural situation—me, him and the baby. Just the three of us. It's not complete. My mother should have been there, too. Then it would have been right. And my father, too. I wanted to see his smile. But mostly my mother. That seems natural. It would have felt right.

The arrival of the first grandchild is a biological event that creates a new network of human connections and triggers in grandparents—especially grandmothers—their dormant instinct to nurture the young. *"To grandparent," in other words, is as natural as the instinct to parent.* The evidence for this instinct was especially pronounced among grandparents who were not present at the birth of their first grandchild. A grandmother explained the visceral re-

sponse she felt to the news of her first grandchild, born
1,000 miles away:

> I felt a pull in me when the baby was born. My daughter
> was in New York and here I was in Florida. I was very emo-
> tional when my son-in-law called. I "became" a grandmother.
> A strange, sinking feeling came over me. I felt empty. It was
> like there was something that I had to do and I just wasn't
> doing it. Something I never had to learn, that people just do,
> an instinct. I had something to do. I thought and thought
> about it. I felt like a migrating goose would feel if it couldn't
> go with the flock when it was time to go.
>
> It was time for me to do something and I just wasn't in the
> right situation to carry out my duties or to do what I felt that
> I was supposed to do . . . It was more than seeing the baby
> and helping my daughter. And it wasn't that I missed out on
> the excitement of the new baby. It was much deeper than that
> —it got to the point where I became very active and busy
> doing nothing. I was doing the wrong activities. It sounds
> crazy I know, but I felt that. I believed that I should have
> been with my daughter and that I should have been doing for
> her and my grandchild.
>
> I discussed all these feelings with my husband and he said
> that he couldn't explain it either, but he knew exactly what I
> was feeling. Neither of us could make any sense out of it.
> It's like birds that build nests by instinct. Something like
> that . . .

Indeed, women are not alone in being seized by a "hom-
ing" instinct when a grandchild is born. A father described
how he reacted to the phone call announcing that he had
become a grandfather:

> When my grandchild was born I suddenly became aware of
> the great distance that separated my family and me on such
> an important day. My own son had become a father, like me.
> A new bond had been established. His wife had given me a
> grandchild and I had not been there to share the experience.
> You see, it was *my* grandchild.
>
> After my son called to tell me that the baby had arrived

and that everything was okay, I hung up the phone and went out to take a walk on the beach. I had to think things over. I felt deep feelings that I had never felt before. I cried with joy because I was a grandfather and with sadness because I had missed the celebration.

I had a moment of great spiritual clarity. I saw things for what they were. I sort of got carried out of myself for a moment and realized the absurdity of my being where I was and not with the children when such an important event was taking place in my life. An event that I was connected to . . . and responsible for. How did I end up here, I wondered. I took the next plane out to see my family and my new grandchild.

The birth of the grandchild automatically confers grandparenthood, whether the grandparent is willing or not. Not every child arrives in the world at the most convenient time or under the most welcome circumstances. Perhaps the most difficult experience of first grandparenthood occurs to those parents who still have young children at home. In this situation, a woman, in particular, finds herself thrust into the role of grandmother (with all its connotations of aging) before she has had time to exhaust her role and responsibilities as mother. Yet even in these difficult circumstances, we found, the grandparental instinct cannot be entirely ignored. As one recent mother/grandmother told us:

> Would you believe it? Here I am with a child ten years old and my daughter goes ahead and has twins. I need a rest. I said to myself that I'll be bringing up kids until I'm ninety . . . But that's what I'll have to do—after I finish complaining, of course.

A mother still in her mid-forties recalled a similar emotional conflict when her oldest daughter gave birth to twins:

> I didn't want any kids around for a long time. But when my

daughter brought her babies home and my own kids looked at them, it was all over. I wouldn't give those grandchildren up for anything. So I guess that makes me a willing mother and grandmother at the same time.

A young grandfather recalled the anger he felt when his first grandchild was born—and how his anger was overcome:

> I had a fit when I became a grandfather. I still had two young ones at home whom I had to help through school. I was really mad. But after a week with the baby, well, she won my heart.

One grandfather we visited still hadn't seen his newborn grandson, but the attachment he felt beneath his anger was drawing him toward the child:

> I told my daughter that she shouldn't get pregnant so early and I'm still mad at her. They can't afford a kid. They are both still in college. I haven't seen the baby because I'm too angry. I feel bad about it and I'm trying to get over it. After all, it is my grandchild and everyone says how cute he is. I won't be staying away much longer, I suppose. I couldn't, no matter how hard I tried.

For grandparents, as well as for parents, the instinct to nurture creates a need within the individual to "do" something. It is an imperative for action. The primary act is to see the baby and thereby establish a "visual imprint" of the child. This initiates the process of object constancy. Visual imprinting is an explosive experience, well known to obstetricians and dramatically demonstrated in cases where an infant has been designated before birth for adoption. In such situations, the mother typically is not permitted to see the baby after birth because visual imprinting unleashes such strong biological forces of attachment that the mother often refuses to give up her child—or else suffers much greater emotional pain upon surrendering her baby to someone else.

Similarly, an infant who is seen and held by its grandparents imprints itself like a brand on the hearts and minds of those grandparents no less indelibly than on its parents. Such moments are not only precious, their emotional impact "fixes" them in the mind as lasting memories. A grandmother who nurtured some of her grandchildren, but not all of them, put it this way:

> I feel much closer to the grandchildren I helped with after they were born. Don't ask me why. It was like those early moments were the most important, sharing the joy with my children and being helpful and loving my grandchild at such a young age, I'll never forget those times. I feel warm all over when I think about them.

Another grandmother reflected on the continuing effects of her "being there" when her first grandchild was born:

> I was with my daughter from the beginning. We all were. Couldn't wait until we heard the news—"It's a girl!" We were all so happy. We all helped during the first months. That brought us so much closer as a family and I got to know the baby real well. Now, we are all very close. When I look at my granddaughter, I still see the baby she was. In fact, I still speak to her as I used to, and she gets annoyed about it.

For grandfathers, sight of their newborn grandchildren provides living confirmation of their own continuing paternity and, beyond that, of their family bloodline. "Now that my grandchild is born, I feel fulfilled," one newly minted grandfather told us. Another said, "My grandchild means that I count, that I'm someone. I just feel that way and I can't explain it." A third, more eloquent grandfather recalled the sense of "cosmic connectedness" that engulfed him when he gazed at his first grandchild:

> It's a strange feeling. A child of mine and a child of a per-

son whom I never knew unite and give us a grandchild, thereby connecting us through this child. In the old days, they did this to unite countries so they wouldn't war with each other. A child could stop a war—think of that. What came from Adam and Eve . . . their descendants . . . are reunited again through this child. Think of that!

In sum, the birth of a child unleashes in grandparents a natural sequence of reactions which are rooted in biology and are manifest by automatic psychological responses. First, grandparents anticipate the birth of the grandchild by recalling their own experiences of parenthood. Unconsciously they review their life as a grandchild and relive their experience with their own grandparents. From these factors they formulate an emotional and behavioral policy that they intend to implement with their own grandchildren—a script for their future grandpaternity. This *"mental rehearsal"* for becoming Great Parents is, we argue, universal. Second, the arrival of the child elicits *feelings of joy* in grandparents (even though the timing of the birth may otherwise be considered unsuitable for other "social" reasons), and these feelings of joy are universal. Third, a grandchild's birth triggers in grandparents a rush of *wondering thoughts* about continuing fecundity and immortality, such as images of their connections to posterity, to the cosmos, or to God's ongoing creation. These expansive thoughts, though they vary in details, are also universal. Fourth, the child's birth releases an *impulse to action*: to see the baby, most of all, but also to hear, hold, and care for it. This impulse to act, too, is universal. In other words, this sequence of responses is instinctive,* as was clearly evident in a long conversation with Mrs. Brimmer, a seventy-nine-year-old grandmother.

* How society affects this instinct will be discussed later.

Mental Rehearsal:

I knew I would love the child before it came because I was
so happy about my daughter's marriage to Charlie. They were
so well matched. I think that if people are uncertain about the
person their child marries it is bound to influence their feelings about their grandchildren. At least I feel that way. I also
hoped that they would have a girl for the first one—to break
them in, so to say. You know how boys drive one bats with all
the noise. Better to break in with a girl, I say. And I told myself that I would be a good grandparent like my father was to
my children.

Feelings:

Well, my son-in-law called us up to tell us about the baby
and I hugged him over the phone. What a happy feeling! I
was impossible, jumping for joy. And my husband—he was one
of those silent Swedes—he just stood there grinning from ear
to ear. "Pretty with curly hair," my son-in-law said, and I'll
never forget it. I was so excited.

Thoughts:

I was thankful that they were all right—healthy, I mean.
That was my first thought. Then I thought of my grandfather.
He was really a stepgrandfather, but even though he wasn't
the same bloodline I thought of him and believe it or not I
take after him a lot. I thought of all the Sundays he used to
take me to the park and buy me a red balloon. I thought I
would do something like that with my grandchild because it
was unforgettable for me. Even now, every time I see a red
balloon it sets me off.

Impulse to Action:

We packed up and within two days I was with my family
and I saw my new grandchild. What a thrill, seeing whom she
resembled. It was a little disappointing that she looked like
my son-in-law's side of the family . . . I'm a little ashamed of
that feeling. It wasn't my grandbaby's fault, now was it? I fell
in love with that baby as soon as I saw her and held her. But I
probably loved her before she was born.

C. Developing Vital Connections

Up to this point, the grandparents have taught us that the biological connection between generations elicits a natural instinct to "grandparent." We have learned that once a grandparent actually sees the grandchild, the biological bond between them is vitalized by a direct personal attachment. The baby is no longer "my child's child" but "my grandchild."

Yet like all relationships between two people, this nascent attachment, no matter how natural and wondrous its inception, must be developed through *shared time* and *intimate contact* if it is to mature into a vital connection. For example, numerous clinical studies have amply demonstrated what mothers instinctively understand: namely, that the early years of life are crucial to the physical and emotional development of children. The baby clings, sucks and follows its mother about with its eyes, thereby releasing nurturing responses in the mother. She, in turn, cuddles, feels, smiles at her baby. Through this intimate exchange—and on through early childhood—the child learns emotional dependency and trust. Thus the initial attachment between mother and child develops into a perduring human bond.

The early years are also crucial for cementing the bond between grandchild and grandparent, although this bonding process has not received the professional attention it deserves. As we learned from the children's projective drawings, those grandparents who are closely involved in their grandchildren's lives are pictured as large, lively figures. That's because the world of the child is wholly populated by very few people; therefore, emotionally significant members of that world occupy a very large place in the child's mind. Put another way, a child's relationship to a Great Parent is based on the same feelings of dependency and trust as its relationship to a parent. There is a difference, of course, but it is one that cuts two ways: on the one hand, the child's bond to a grandparent is normally not as indispensable for the child's physical survival and emotional health as the bond to a parent; on the other hand, *a child need never—and usually does not—abandon the feelings of dependency and trust generated by loving grandparents*. These aspects of their relationship remain stable. The relationship between parents and children, by contrast, is naturally tumultuous and unstable as the child grows into adulthood. In other words, a caring grandparent can be a Great Parent forever—so long as a vital connection is established early in a child's life.

Emotionally, the early years of a child are as crucial to grandparents as they are to parents. As we learned from our interviews, the birth of a grandchild arouses a compelling instinct to nurture. The mental rehearsal, the feelings, the expansive thoughts and the eventual visual imprinting are powerful experiences which grandparents never forget. But this nurturing instinct can be thwarted. Unless it is exercised in the child's early years, grandparents cease to *feel* like grandparents, however much they may continue to think of themselves in that role. This is typically what happens to grandparents who become separated from their grandchildren during the latter's early years, or who maintain only intermittent contact with them. In the grandparents' minds, a grandchild remains the child they once knew while the real grandchild grows, changes and becomes, in effect, a stranger—a charm on grandmother's bracelet. Thus, a vital connection is never established and grandparents who might have been Great Parents for life become, in the eyes of their grandchildren, merely "old folks."

In varying degrees, this was the state of grandparent-grandchild relationships among the majority of grandparents we visited. Initial attachments between them and their grandchildren had become attenuated or severed altogether. The reasons and rationales these grandparents offered varied enormously. "Bad blood," some said, had developed between themselves and their children. Others just didn't want to "interfere" in their children's lives and families. Many felt helpless when their grandchildren moved away; many others "retired" and moved away themselves. A few felt that they were simply "too young" to be grandparents and resented being regarded as such. Some were too busy working to have time for their families. None, however, was entirely pleased by the separation from their grandchildren. Not a few wept when they talked about it. It was "wrong" or "unfortunate" or "too bad," they told us. When we probed deeper we discovered that many grandparents simply did not know anymore what was expected of them. Some said that they never knew that grandparents were important to children.

Clearly, there was no single explanation of why so many grandparents had failed to develop or maintain vital connections with their grandchildren. So we turned for insight to those few who had. We went to them as apprentices might to master craftsmen, hoping to learn what it takes to be and function as grandparents. We also wanted to find out how their own lives—their sense of themselves and their place in the world—had been affected by their long and intimate relationships to their grandchildren.

Vitally connected grandparents, we discovered, are unusually talkative people. They are rich in experience and full of memories and observations. One of our most useful visits was to Mrs. Mason, whom we had already met "second hand" through our long conversation with her granddaughter, Deborah (page 17). Mrs. Mason is sixty-eight and lives alone in the center of the small town where she has spent most of her life. She has been a widow for seven years and supplements her Social Security benefits by working part-time—"helping out," she calls it—at a local women's-wear shop. She is an enthusiastic, bouncy person— has been all her life, her family says.

Mrs. Mason's apartment is clean and orderly but not fussily so. The first thing she shows visitors are the family photographs and children's art work which decorate the walls and tables of every room. A special section of her "gallery" is reserved for photographs of her own parents and grandparents, which she keeps close by her bed on top of a dresser.

> This (picture) is an oldie, an aunt from the old country. I just love to look at these, of course. I look at them often. When the family comes by we look at them together. The kids love to hear the stories about all these people. My grandparents told me the stories and I pass them on. The children all know which pictures they will have someday to tell about to their families. They'll get them when I die. They've picked theirs out already.

Mrs. Mason sees herself as the family "curator," but also as an individual with a full life of her own. We recalled Deborah's admiration of her grandmother as an "independent" person and asked Mrs. Mason how she felt about being on her own at a "mature" age. She pounced on our euphemisms immediately:

> I object to being classified as an "older" person. I'm a person—period. We're all just people, young, old, grandparents. I don't like to be with people who think of themselves as "old" people. I know I'm old, but I want to be as old as I feel, not

the way I'm supposed to be. Am I supposed to act old? I'll never retire, you know, so much to do. When I reached my last birthday and I said, "Well, that's it kiddo, you're over the hill now." But the heck with it. I really don't feel that way so I'm continuing life as usual.

We asked Mrs. Mason what makes her so active. Was it her personality? Her friendships? Her part-time job? Her community work?

Well, I'm a friendly person but it's really the contact with my family. Yes, that's it. I don't interfere—only when I'm asked. Well, most of the time. The grandchildren, that's where it is. I like the vitality and the interest of the young. I'm interested in what they do. The older ones can fend for themselves, more or less, but the little ones, they need me. I teach them cooking—even sewing to Deborah, and that takes patience.

Mrs. Mason's memory of her grandchildren as infants is still vivid. She has these permanent memories in her mind:

I still picture them in my mind when they were little ones. How precious they were . . . I just couldn't spend enough time with them. My husband went absolutely wild over Deborah, the first grandchild. He would say, "I'll be a little late for dinner because I've got to stop over and see the baby." He used to go over at lunch time. My daughter would run out and shop for an hour and he used to babysit.

Remembering the past, Mrs. Mason went on to talk about the effect her own upbringing had on her attitudes toward her children and their families.

You see, when I was young I had a large family. Most of our fun and pleasure came from the family. The world was just a place to get enough money to live from, so the family could eat. We lived for each other. We talked about each other all the time. When we were all together talking and gossiping—I love gossip—no one wanted to be the first to go home because they knew that they would get it after they left. But it was all in fun. We never knew what "bored" meant.

No one wanted to move, either. What for? Once you move you loose contact. Then you forget what's really important. Even the problems are important. Fight, kiss and make up. What's life about? Work, work—life is the family.

Moving away is foolish . . . for what? My family has resisted moving. My daughter wants me to live with her but I told her that I want to live alone. I would probably interfere too much. My daughter says "no" but I'll think about that when the time comes.

We asked Mrs. Mason to describe the sorts of things she does with her grandchildren and the part they, in particular, play in her life:

I guess my grandchildren are a big part of my life right now. They come over very often, spend the night. I show them the old movies if they are in the mood to see them and we laugh together. I make them their favorite foods. Many of my friends are envious. Their grandchildren have moved away or else my friends are too lazy to put themselves out for the kids. The little ones do break things. I don't care but I guess that bothers my friends, breaking things.

In some way it is my job to spoil the kids a bit when they are young, listen to them when they are older and do things for them that their parents do not have the time to do. It's different from being a parent. Special for me and for the kids. I truly feel sorry for those people who don't have grandchildren or who have them and don't pay attention to them, leave them.

Mrs. Mason became quite animated when we asked her why she felt that her grandchildren need her:

Let's get it straight—I need them. Well, I take care of them and I participate in their activities, like going to school night and other things. I teach them things and I tell them stories. I help them with their parents and I help their parents with them. And I'm around to nurse them when they are sick.

Mostly, I give them an awful lot of love. They really feel it—
they tell me that.

Also, it may sound conceited to say this, but some of the
kids have told me that they are a little like me and it's kind of
nice that they have that . . . and for me to know that they
are a part of me and that my great-grandchildren will see pictures of me. I guess it's immortality, a little bit of me going
on. And the children know that they will live on also because
they see me do it. Besides, this is my job now, to see that the
grandchildren come along well. Everything has its place and
they now have a place in my life.

If we look again at Deborah's drawing of her grandmother (Fig. 20), at her picture of Sunday dinner with her
grandparents (Fig. 18) and at what she said about her
grandmother, we can see that Mrs. Mason's feelings and
thoughts are mirror images of her granddaughter's. They
have enjoyed a reverberating relationship which has developed as each has changed over the years. Mrs. Mason has
reproduced herself twice over through her children and her
grandchildren. Today, Deborah not only looks like Mrs.
Mason—a result of biological connection—she also looks at
herself and the world through a sensibility shaped in fundamental ways by the on-going vital connection with her
grandmother.

From what Mrs. Mason told us, we can isolate four factors necessary to achieving and maintaining vital connections between grandparents and grandchildren. The first
two factors are the critical dimensions of *time* and *place*,
without which there can be no intimacy. "I couldn't spend
enough time with them," Mrs. Mason said of her grandchildren, and Deborah could remember no time when she
was without her grandmother. But time means staying
close by, always being there. "Once you move, you lose
contact." The third factor is *commitment to family*. This
commitment includes a sense of family history and heri-

tage and is rooted in the conviction that ties to family take emotional precedence over ties to society. In Mrs. Mason we glimpse the origin and development of this commitment to family. She grew up within a family network where no one was ever "bored," where outside work was for the sake of the family, not the reverse. Her commitment to her grandchildren follows upon this early experience and her later experience as a parent. Thus Mrs. Mason has managed to fuse her natural instinct to grandparent with a rich gestalt of family attachments that supports her role as a Great Parent.

The fourth factor is personal. It is Mrs. Mason's evident sense of *altruism*. She readily understands the needs of her children and grandchildren and responds with love, insisting that "I need them." Unlike many widows and widowers, Mrs. Mason has not withdrawn into narcissism or become an aging "dependent." Instead, she has intensified her connections to many people and thereby achieved the "independence" which Deborah, at sixteen, admires so much in her grandmother. Readers who are familiar with Erik H. Erikson's theory of the human life cycle, with its eight stages of psychosocial development, will recognize in Mrs. Mason the virtues Erikson associates with "Maturity," the seventh of his "eight stages of man." She has achieved—indeed, she resonates—the kind of concern for others which Erikson calls "generativity"[1]; that is, "concern for establishing and guiding the next generation." Erikson opposes generativity to the "stagnation," or excessive self-concern, that often besets adults of grandparental age. From the grandparents' standpoint, therefore, it appears that vital connections are crucial for achieving the psychosocial well-being consonate with adult maturity.

But, as Erikson also observes, adults in their later years need not have natural grandchildren in order to behave in a generative manner toward the upcoming generation.[2] The same altruism that Mrs. Mason focused on her extended family can also be directed toward others who have no biological claim upon us. In other words, one can be a grandparent to many children as long as this role can be institutionalized in society. This is the role that elders play in some so-called "primitive" societies. But it also is possible, within a society such as ours which has no place for elders, for caring adults to create an elder role for themselves.

This is what the O'Flahertys did by extending their sense of vital connections to the children of an entire urban neighborhood in New Jersey. Mrs. O'Flaherty is seventy-nine, her husband is eighty-two. Between them they have raised six children and now have seventeen grandchildren. Beyond that, however, the O'Flahertys have "grandparented" almost every child within walking distance of their modest home. Their doors are never locked. Children wander in at will, pick food out of a full refrigerator or sit in the O'Flahertys' overstuffed chairs and play. The house is anything but childproof. Sticky fingerprints dot the door frames and the kitchen is covered, from stove to table top, with steaming pots and dishes waiting to be washed. Saturday morning is clean-up time and the morning we visited the O'Flahertys quickly drew us into their own bubbling by-play.

"If only you'd clean up after you finish what you're doing the place wouldn't be such a disaster area," Mr. O'Flaherty complains good-naturedly. "He's been saying that for fifty-five years, he has," Mrs. O'Flaherty says to us, rolling her eyes up in her head. They both laugh. "My wife is in charge of the children," Mr. O'Flaherty adds by way of explanation. "That's right," his wife responds. "I don't listen to him because he's such a sourpuss. I just go ahead and do what I want. He always comes around."

What Mrs. O'Flaherty does, among other things, is move about the neighborhood constantly talking, forever meeting people, magnetizing children as if she were the community's official fairy godmother. She readily acknowledges that she's different from her contemporaries:

> I'm not your general run of grandmother, as far as being fond of children goes. My friends think I'm daft to go to all this trouble, like making turkey and mashed potatoes for the kids in the neighborhood. The kids stay in the kitchen with me when I cook the stuff and we spend the afternoon cooking and tasting as we go along. We have a good time. My friends don't understand. They say it's too much work, couldn't be bothered with strangers.
>
> One of my friends is sick and her family never comes near her. Can you imagine? But let me tell you, my friend never put herself out, never. I always said, in this world you only get what you give. Give nothing, get nothing. I just think that too many grandparents are selfish and that the grandmother's trying to please the husband too much, because their husbands get annoyed with the grandchildren. I wouldn't care if my husband was annoyed or not, he wouldn't stand between me and my children, I say.

Several of the neighborhood youngsters whom Mrs. O'Flaherty has "adopted" dropped in while we talked. Even older teenagers who no longer have the same need for her still come by to visit. From Mrs. O'Flaherty's conversation it was sometimes hard to distinguish when she was talking about these children from when she was talking about her own grandchildren. But she was particularly prescient about the need all children have for a Great Parent:

> Nothing gives me more pleasure than to be needed. If my children or grandchildren call, I'm there. I love to stay with the kids when my children want to go away on vacation. It's not like it used to be. It's hard for young people nowadays . . . too much work for the young mothers, too busy, not relaxed. Parents need time together and that's one of my jobs,

to see that they have the best opportunity to get along, to be happy. I can help without interfering.

We talk openly and they know how I feel about things. All they have to do is ask me. What makes me sad is that I have to defend myself with my friends. I mean, sometimes I doubt myself. Maybe I should dry up and grow old, but I feel good with the kids and then I feel I'm doing the right thing.

Although Mrs. O'Flaherty did most of the talking, she frequently glanced at her husband for reassurance and support. She is gabby and outgoing; he is a listener, but equally assured when he speaks. We had the impression that Mr. O'Flaherty is a stable maypole around which his wife felt free to scurry, busy and secure. Words are not important to them; their evident affection for each other is built on deeds. They share the same altruistic outlook, as Mr. O'Flaherty made clear:

> You don't have to be a grandparent to love the young and to enjoy them. There are a lot of kids who need love from older people. Look around. I think there are too many selfish people around. Lousy parent, lousy grandparent, if you ask me. Selfish—some people don't put themselves out at all.

The O'Flahertys have reached a stage in life when a person is what a person does. They have no time for fancy theories. Still, Mrs. O'Flaherty wonders whether something hasn't gone wrong in society:

> There are some people who do and others who don't give a damn. They'll walk over a body lying in the street. Selfish is selfish, and that's it. Look at what is going on today, everyone's interested in themselves. The good people ain't in the right places anymore, because if you're a good person you won't do what is necessary to get there. It's the selfish people who are running things nowadays, yessir.

The O'Flahertys call it "selfishness." Behavioral scientists call it "narcissism." The scientists' word doesn't mean much to the O'Flahertys but they know the effects. Mr. O'Flaherty summed them up in his own terse manner:

> There are people who don't like people and there are people who are sensitive to others and that's that. There's a lady down the street who was a lousy mother and doesn't give a damn about her family. What's anyone going to do for her, tell me that?
>
> I just don't know how anyone can resist those faces on the little ones. It's beyond me. Lately, the faces that come to the door are colored. My neighbors don't like it, but to me they are kids. I'll never move from here like some other people want to. This is my house and all children are welcome. The more the merrier—even though they drive me crazy sometimes.

Grandparents like the O'Flahertys are probably rare. But what they told us about themselves helps us to understand the benefits to grandparents when they combine the instinct to nurture with a spirit of altruism to act compassionately and responsibly toward young people beyond the circle of their own kin. At an age when most of their friends have "retired" and disengaged from life, the O'Flahertys have found a full-time "job" as Great Parents within their community. Their time belongs to others and so does their home. Their legacy of vital family connections now extends to the entire neighborhood. They are earthy, direct, and confident as only "old folks" who have shed the last vestiges of narcissism can be. They are unaffected by the alienation of their peers. By drawing on their own emotional resources—and without asking anyone's permission or advice—they have become true elders of society. When we asked Mrs. O'Flaherty how she was able to act in a way that was so opposed to the drift of the surrounding culture, she responded without hesitation: "I'm just the spitting image of my grandmother. She did the same thing."

D. Disconnected Grandparents

The vast majority of grandparents we visited are not at all like Mrs. Mason or the O'Flahertys. Although many had successfully "retired," most felt wounded, emotionally, by their disconnection from the grandchildren. For the most part, they found it difficult at first to put their feelings into words. Not a few were defensive, many were confused. Our questions, together with their own reminiscences, often ignited feelings of regret—for lost opportunities, for rash decisions to move South, for the failure to pass on more of the family heritage to their grandchildren. They spoke movingly of dashed dreams, of unfulfilled promises, of bleak futures bereft of close family attachments, of grandchildren they no longer knew, or never did.

If it is difficult for grandparents to describe the pain of disconnection, it is more difficult yet for us to parse its particular grammar of emotion. Nonetheless, based on what we learned from active grandparents we were at least able to discern certain common denominators in the stories disconnected grandparents told us. Simply put, in each instance one or more of the factors crucial to maintaining vital connections—*time, place, commitment to family,* and *personal altruism*—were either weak or missing altogether from the grandparent-grandchild relationship.

Unfortunately, altruistic grandparents are the ones who suffer most from lack of intimate contact with their grandchildren. Theirs is the language of loss, bordering on despair, as was evident from listening to the Fosters. A couple in their late sixties, the Fosters live in Chicago, less than an hour's drive from their son's home in the suburbs. The

Fosters also have a childless married daughter whom they
see quite regularly, but this relationship cannot compen-
sate for the rupture with their son and his two children.
The son's break with his parents came shortly after his
marriage; his wife is of a different religion and so, now, are
their children. This is one barrier the Fosters feel between
themselves and their grandchildren, but it is not the only
one. Another is their son's affluence; he has done well in
business and is now much more prosperous than his own
father. The son's consequent change in lifestyle, the Fosters believe, adds to the alienation they feel. Mr. and Mrs.
Foster have a strong sense of family and commitment to it.
They cannot understand why their son and daughter-in-law
seem anxious to keep them at a distance from their own
grandchildren. During our visit, the Fosters were reluctant
at first to acknowledge what had happened or the feelings
that disconnection had caused. Mr. Foster was glum and
only gradually did Mrs. Foster summon the strength to dis-
close her feelings:

> My daughter listens to me but I can't get to first base with
> this son. I don't know why . . . and his wife, I think, just
> doesn't care for me. They have respect for me but no personal
> relationship. We get along well, I think. No animosity or re-
> sentment . . . well, maybe on my part because I have been
> deprived of my grandchildren. I don't know why and I don't
> want to ask.

Mrs. Foster stared down at her lap for long moments as
if it held some explanation of her son's behavior. Slowly,
she recalled the knifing frustration she endured because her
natural instinct to nurture her own grandchildren had been
thwarted from the birth of her son's very first child.

> I met resistance as soon as they had the first baby. I wanted
> to help, but I was refused. I was left out. I don't think that's
> right. I mean, I think young people should be independent

and all, but this . . . Then the other was born and I wasn't allowed to be included. They always got a nurse. I wasn't even welcomed when I came to see the babies in the hospital. I guess it's their lives and they can do whatever they please.

Mrs. Foster's sense of loss was all the more painful in light of her warm memories of her own grandparents. She had been endowed with a legacy of love and care by her grandparents but was unable to act on that inheritance.

I would have loved for my grandchildren to grow up the way I grew up. A close family, lots of people around all the time. I loved my grandparents. I would go over to their house all the time. It was wonderful. I would so love to have that feeling of closeness to the children. But there's a wall, a barrier.

I've even taken the initiative. I've called and said, "Come." They say, "Sure." But they never do. They never call me, even the grandchildren. The love is all one way. It's fine when we visit, but it's a sham. I've lost my grandchildren and they've lost me.

Mrs. Foster is at an age when the instinct to grandparent flowers. She is an altruistic person. She feels this, and in her frustration she talked perceptively about the effects of disconnection on herself and, by extension, on all mothers:

I should mean more to my grandchildren than I do. I truly want to do more with them. It hurts me and my husband. Men can handle it better than women—than mothers. My husband said the hell with it several years ago and quit trying to get closer. But me, it's what I've always done all my life—raise children. My children have always been the center of my life and now it's going to end here.

My friend has such a wonderful relationship with her grandchildren. Most of the others don't, come to think of it, but the one who does talks about how wonderful it is . . . I want to have that. They are a part of my blood, after all. They belong a little to me, don't they?

Eventually, Mrs. Foster's reflections turned, ever so lightly, into self-recrimination, almost bitterness:

> Maybe I should have asserted myself more, fought more for them. My son is so successful that maybe I've been a little afraid of him. He's done well in business. I brag about him to other people but I really feel like a fake. My grandchildren were never taught to love their grandparents, to be taken to their homes, to know them, to go places with them. What bothers me the most is that they do not feel a part of us or connected to us at all.

The Fosters are typical of adults who have everything it takes to be active grandparents except one: they have been denied the time needed to develop vital connections with their only grandchildren. For such grandparents, the emotional experience of disconnection is similar to the process of protest-despair-detachment that occurs in infants who suffer from "hospitalism" (page 5). At first, grandparents feel uneasy about the lack of intimate contact with their grandchild. Gradually, this uneasiness becomes a sense of hurt which eventually turns into anger. The grandparents may protest against the separation but if it persists, they experience despair—a gnawing sense of remorse that a vital relationship will never be established or re-established. As they become resolved to the separation, the grandparents become intellectually and finally emotionally detached from the grandchild. This is the point Mr. Foster has reached in his efforts to be a grandfather: he is intellectually detached but emotionally he has yet to withdraw from the painful separation. "We've been put out of a job and there is nothing we can do about it," Mr. Foster said at the close of our conversation. "I try not to think about it anymore, but when I do . . . shit!"

Grandparents who had chosen to move away from their grandchildren responded differently to the ensuing disconnection. They did not protest the severing of vital connections with their grandchildren because they themselves were responsible for fracturing the critical dimensions of time and place. In most cases, the husband had worked hard and felt entitled to the rewards of retirement. Grandmothers, on the other hand, tended to be less reconciled to disconnection. Few of them protested, however. Some talked in tones of quiet despair of ever reknitting family connections but most—grandfathers and grandmothers alike—had already become emotionally detached from their grandchildren by the time we spoke with them. Emotionally as well as geographically, they had become "displaced persons," eager to talk about the "old days," rather befuddled by their present state in life and passive, almost fatalistic, about the future:

> I don't know what happened. We retired to this lovely place in Florida. I have eight grandchildren and I do see them a couple times a year. I guess I don't do very much of anything. I mean, I enjoy myself, but sometimes I think, "Is this what I want, to be a grandparent who is not involved with her grandchildren?" I don't know, I don't know how I got here, truly, I think my husband wanted to retire here, but we talk about it and he tells me the same thing—that he thought I wanted to do it.

The speaker is Mrs. Mincher, seventy-six, who has moved away from her children in Forest Hills, New York. She doesn't feel that she knows them anymore—a fact that causes her considerable pain when she remembers her own maternal grandmother. During our conversation, Mrs. Mincher revealed a profound sense of her family heritage. She recalled how she felt long ago when her grandmother came from Germany to visit while Mrs. Mincher was still an adolescent:

> I would talk about my grandmother to my parents before

she came to visit and, when she did come, it was amazing—it was as if I'd always known her. Grandmother said it was harder for her because we were growing faster than the kids in her pictures.

We had a continual party while she was here. It was hilarious. She dyed her hair but didn't want anyone to know about it. She used to sneak around at night and touch her hair up in the bathroom and make up the funniest reasons about why she was prowling around. We'd all be giggling about it, my sister and I. Everyone wanted to come and visit her and we'd sing. It was a wonderful time.

I went back to the old country for a visit and I swear I felt that I had lived there, that I belonged there. I saw my grandmother and it was like home, not strange. My grandmother wanted to visit us for my wedding—she told me that. I was the number one granddaughter. I was named after her. But she died on the day that my husband and I became engaged. I felt terrible. I looked like her, you know. There was something incomplete about her not coming to my wedding, just a feeling.

I realized when I was very young how important a grandparent can be to a child, and I promised myself that I'd be a really good grandmother. But all of the time, not just for a short visit.

Now, Mrs. Mincher confided, she feels that she has broken her promise. She regrets having moved South away from her grandchildren but "at my age," she says she feels powerless to change her way of life:

I guess we had thought that this (retiring to Florida) was the thing to do a long time ago and we just did it. And now we're in a rut and too lazy or something to get back to our families. I just don't know . . . No, I don't think that we will ever leave here. I would very much like to move back home but I don't think we will. I don't know why, but we probably won't. I miss the children terribly . . . but, well, my sister's down here and I see her.

When divorce occurs the sense of family is cracked at its very foundations. We have already heard what the grand-

children think and feel when they lose a beloved grandparent because of their parents' divorce. Now we hear from
grandparents who have lost their grandchildren for the
same reason. We spoke to Mr. Congdon, a grandfather
from Maine, who was deeply attached to his three grandchildren before their parents' divorce. His ex-daughter-in-
law has taken the children with her to Cleveland, leaving
Mr. Congdon angry and confused:

> To tell the truth, I resent my son. He could have tried
> harder. Now, I've lost my grandchildren. My wife can't even
> talk about it. We used to see them every day. We've been
> deprived of our grandchildren—the joy we felt with them.
>
> Should I call them more often? Write them? Forget about
> them? I don't know what to do. Maybe they want to forget
> us, although they do write often. Should I go visit them? I
> don't want to interfere. Maybe their mother doesn't want to
> see us. They have a new life now. Different. I don't want to
> disrupt it. If I call they might be happy—or sad, even. If I
> don't . . . I don't know what to do.
>
> We used to spend a lot of time together, working, fishing,
> hunting. I took all of them, the boys and the girl together. I
> was looking forward to seeing them grow. I was looking for-
> ward to spending time with them—my old age. What do I do
> now? This is not natural.

Mrs. Crimmins, a grandmother from Massachusetts,
faces a similar dilemma. Her son and daughter-in-law have
been drawing apart for years and will soon divorce. The
strain in the marital relations has produced considerable
friction between mother and grandmother, and the children have become pawns in the family battle. Mrs. Crimmins already feels their loss:

> Maria, one of my daughter's children, is just a dream. She
> says, "Hi Nanna" and wants to hug and kiss me. My daughter-
> in-law's children never do that. Sometimes they laugh at me
> behind my back. It's awful.

> I truly feel uncomfortable with those children, my own grandchildren. I have them down, I try to buy them presents. They are polite, they are nice. But they are not lovable. If I give the oldest boy a kiss he'll just wipe it off. And he looks just like my son, too. She always comes here with them—I am never allowed to see them alone. I just don't know what to do about this.

Those grandparents who had become both physically and emotionally detached from their grandchildren were not for that reason devoid of all grandparental feelings. On the contrary, as these displaced grandparents opened up to us, they discovered that their deepest emotions were in conflict with their thoughts. This conflict created a revealing dialectic between buried feelings of attachment and the rationales they had constructed—if only for themselves—to justify their decision to disconnect from their grandchildren.

Here, for example, is a portion of a long conversation with the Donaldsons, a sun-tanned couple in their early seventies who moved to Florida in 1967, leaving eight grandchildren behind in New York. Mr. Donaldson was eager to explain his views on a grandparent's responsibilities. How he views his role as a grandparent:

> I did my job. That's it. My children should get by without me now. I owe them encouragement, perhaps, maybe a little financial support or help if they need it. But that's it. I can't be bothered to supervise things up there. They can run their own lives.

Mr. Donaldson fell silent for a moment, then continued:

> I do miss the grandchildren, but they've no time for me and I'm not too fond of children. My wife is pretty high strung anyhow and the kids cause a commotion when they come.

> They break things and she has some nice vases and stuff. They make her nervous.

After another pause, Mr. Donaldson shifted the focus of his thoughts:

> Personally, I love the climate but I don't care for the age factor in Florida. I feel that the people down here are all tired. They talk about their illnesses. I never hear any children laughing, that's what I miss. I guess I sound confused, saying that kids annoy me but I miss hearing them laugh. Wonder why I feel that way.

Mrs. Donaldson took advantage of another pause to clear the record, as she saw it. She was palpably annoyed by her husband's version:

> I wouldn't have come down here if you didn't want to in the first place. All my friends say the same thing. It's the men who want to come down here. Most of the women want to stay with their families. A lot of the women are mad but they don't say anything. After all, the man has usually worked hard most of his life and deserves a rest.

Mr. Donaldson made no effort to defend his earlier remarks, or his wife's account of why they had moved to Florida:

> You're right. I wouldn't do it over again, sitting here looking at these old people looking at me. Why, when a kid walks into the apartment house you'd think it was Jesus Christ the way everyone carries on, kootchy-cooing and all that.

Mrs. Donaldson agreed:

> It's not a natural way to live . . . and no one ever told us. I mean, retiring was what we were supposed to do. We just never thought about it.

Mr. Donaldson amplified his wife's remarks:

> The sense of family is gone. The kids don't need us and we don't need them. Older people nowadays are more healthy

and financially better off. No one gets the benefit and background of a family because we move so much . . . and we
never really thought about the things we're talking about.

After a moment of mutual silence, Mrs. Donaldson
sighed and said:

> I really miss the grandchildren. I really do think about them
> often. I think about what I will do when I see them, but it
> doesn't happen when we are together.

Her husband interjected:

> Let's face it, we don't know them.

Mrs. Donaldson nodded in agreement. Things hadn't
gone right, now that she thought about retirement:

> You know, when I was young I always wanted to leave
> something behind—to show that I was here. Like my uncle, an
> architect. He left a beautiful building behind. I feel like a peb-
> ble on a beach . . . small . . . and I look at my youngest
> granddaughter. She looks like me. She has musical talent like
> me and I look at her and think to myself: that's what I'm
> going to leave behind, and I'm sad because I truly wish that I
> had put more into it.

The Donaldsons' dialogue touches on a number of important themes—notably "retirement"—that we will explore in the next chapter. At this point, we are concerned
with the emotional consequences of disconnection. As we
observed at the outset of our grandparent study, the process of answering our questionnaire created a channel to
their innermost thoughts and feelings. In this way, the
Donaldsons discovered the regret they felt over the loss of
vital connections to their grandchildren. They had removed themselves from their grandchildren's lives during
the latter's crucial early years and now they are hopelessly
out of phase with their grandchildren's development. In
her isolation, Mrs. Donaldson imagines what she will do

with her grandchildren next time they visit, but her plans do not work out. One reason is that Mrs. Donaldson, unlike Mrs. Mason, lacks the experience—the craft, really—of grandparenting. But the major reason is that the grandchildren have grown and changed. Mr. Donaldson is on target when he says, "Let's face it, we really don't know them."

This is a statement of emotional truth. Mr. Donaldson can say nothing about his grandchildren because he cannot feel them. What he does talk about are his own conflicted feelings. Children are disruptive and he both misses and is happy to avoid such disruptions. His thoughts focus on ideas rather than persons: "I did my job" or, more abstract yet, "The sense of family is gone." Mrs. Donaldson, perhaps because she is a woman and mother, feels the lack of vital connections in a more concrete way. But her feelings are focused on images of her own creation. Her dormant nurturing instinct, when aroused through conversation, attaches to figures of fantasy, not to memories relived in her mind through regular and intimate contact with her own "flesh and blood." Her plans do not work out because her grandchildren do not match the fantasy figures in her head.

Ultimately, the Donaldsons are not mourning the loss of their grandchildren, however much they may regret their disconnection. They are mourning the loss of themselves as grandparents—and as human beings. Thus Mrs. Donaldson imagines her youngest granddaughter as a kind of building, based on herself as (biological) blueprint, which she hoped to "leave behind" as a monument certifying her own existence. But, to continue her own metaphor, Grandmother Donaldson left the construction site long before the job was complete. She wishes that she had "put more into it" because now little of her self remains. The entire image reveals the real consequences of disconnection: emotional isolation, stagnation, and narcissism.

If disconnection breeds narcissism in grandparents, the reverse is also true. Most grandparents who move away from their families without considering the emotional impact of their decision on their grandchildren have already grown emotionally detached from them. We might well conclude from this that only grandparents with narcissistic "personalities" are capable of disconnecting from the grandchildren. This may be true. But what is more to the point is that even grandparents who are deeply attached to their grandchildren and have a commitment to family find it surprisingly easy to move away and thus relinquish their vital connections.

Recall Norma, the twelve-year-old who used to bake "tons and tons of brownies" with her grandmother before her grandparents moved to Florida. Norma told us how distraught she felt when she realized that her grandparents' move was permanent and how reluctant she is now to act as if nothing has changed when her grandmother, since widowed, comes back to visit. During one of those visits, we talked with Norma's grandmother, Mrs. Andrews, to find out how she feels about being disconnected from her grandchildren. Mrs. Andrews is an altruistic person with a strong sense of family. She is also emotionally acute and quite upset by the consequences of her decision to move away from her family. She told us why she and her husband had retired to Florida:

> My husband was a proud man. He did not want his children to see him die. He said that he had had enough of cold weather, so he decided that we would move to a place that was warmer. I told him that it wasn't bad for the children to see him die, that we all had to face that. But he had his way and I went.

I was heartbroken to leave my life behind—friends, my business, and most of all my children. I'm over seventy-five and I feel fine, you know. I was so close to my grandchildren. So many of my friends have nothing to do with their grandchildren, I'm not like that . . . Maybe there's something wrong with me, but I loved to be with young people.

There are no young people where Mrs. Andrews lives in Florida and this has made her feel different about herself:

I used to feel important with my grandchildren, teaching them things, playing with them, proud of them, going to school with them. You know, I was a grandmother in my community. It meant something there. The grandchildren were proud of me. They would show me off to their friends. I would cook for them. It was a way of life that I miss now.

When we retired I was so bored. I didn't have that job anymore of being a grandparent. When I went away, the kids grew up without me. They don't need me the same way. I missed the boat . . . It's hard to say, but I resent my husband a bit for that. But then, he didn't make me go. I should have listened to my heart.

In Florida, Mrs. Andrews found an outlet for her altruism by caring for others. But it wasn't the same as caring for her own grandchildren:

While I was away I worked in a retirement home. I cheered up the residents there. I would bring them flowers and their faces would light up. I used to get sad sometimes and think that this was fine, but I've got family somewhere else and what am I doing here?

I feel kind of exiled now. My business doesn't need me anymore, my family doesn't need me now and I wasn't there when they did. I feel that I've gypped myself. My husband died and now I'm alone. If I had it to do over again, I would never do it. And if anyone ever asks you about it, tell them that moving away and retirement are bunk.

Mrs. Andrews can hardly be described as a narcissistic person. Wife, mother, and businesswoman, she was by all accounts a devoted and enthusiastic grandmother, a lode-star of her family and of her community. Yet when her husband asked her, she agreed to break all those bonds. And even now, much as she regrets her decision, she feels she must remain "exiled" in her Florida apartment. Why? The only adequate answer, we believe, transcends notions of "personality" altogether. Rather, the question goes to the texture of American society and what Christopher Lasch has labeled "the culture of narcissism." If this phrase means anything at all with respect to Americans of grand-parental age, it means that the pressure of such a culture is in the direction of encouraging otherwise strong and al-truistic people to sever their vital family connections. Put another way, it means that regardless of how grandparents may feel, the culture can inhibit them from acting on those feelings by interposing attitudes which dictate different be-havior.

Precisely *how* this has happened is the subject of the next chapter. That it has happened is evidenced by the fact that the overwhelming majority of grandparents we visited elected not to become closely involved with their grand-children. Most had *not* moved away from their grand-children; indeed, the best estimate to date is that only about twenty percent of Americans sixty-five and over move out of their communities upon retirement. Nor is their emotional detachment from their grandchildren sufficiently explained by the increased mobility of their children. America has been a conspicuously mobile society since the colonial period, and with modern modes of trans-portation and communication, today's grandparents can re-main in close if not intimate contact with their grand-children if they so choose. The salient fact is that the majority choose to keep their distance without altogether severing their family connections. In other words, they acknowledge their biological connections but they do not, for the most part, vitalize those connections. Why?

E. The "New Social Contract"

Pieces of the answer surfaced like flotsam in the course of virtually all our conversations. The pieces began to take shape only in interviews with grandparents like the Bennetts, a Rhode Island couple who deliberately limit their contact with their grandchildren to two holiday visits a year. They are, by choice, "part-time" grandparents, even though Mr. Bennett knows what it's like for a child to have a "full-time" grandparent. Mr. Bennett's recollection of his grandfather framed his conversation:

> I'm not the man my grandfather was. He was a tremendous fellow. Big and strong, ran the whole family farm. When he spoke we all listened. He was a hard man but he was on our side. That gave us a good feeling. It was a sad day when he died. Never said a bad word about anybody. I still have the watch he gave me. I haven't decided who to give it to yet when it's my turn to go. No, I'm not like my grandfather and I think it's a damn shame.

Mrs. Bennett interjected on her husband's behalf:

> It's not your fault. After all, things are different today. No farms. The family's not in one place anymore.

Mr. Bennett continued, almost as if he hadn't heard what his wife had said:

> Well, I tried. In the time that I have with the children I try to teach them industry—that's what made our nation great. I like to advise them, too, without being dictatorial. I fix their bicycles for them when I visit them. But now that they are older I don't have much in common with them. I've tried to show them a good example. You know, if one is in a business

where they are cheating someone, the kids see that and they will be scallywags too. I try to set an example.

Mrs. Bennett modified her husband's remarks, casting their shared attitude toward grandparenting in a more personal light:

> The grandchildren are close in our hearts, even though they don't know us that well. I guess we remember them when they were little babies but they don't remember us from that time, naturally. I love to talk to my friends about them and show them their pictures.

Mr. Bennett explained that their attitude toward their grandchildren is shaped by their relationship with their children:

> We don't want to be overbearing. They are free to come and go as they please. We don't want to demand and say, "Come Sunday." I must say, though, that I do get a kick out of stirring them (the grandchildren) up.

Mrs. Bennett interrupted:

> Well, you bring them up and that's it.

Her husband didn't quite agree:

> Well, not exactly now. I'd like to see the family name go on, so it's not exactly over after all.

Mrs. Bennett corrected herself:

> I mean it's up to them. Our job is over.

Mr. Bennett wasn't so sure:

> That's it with our children. But I guess we bunched it together—our children with our grandchildren—and threw the babies out with the bathwater. I guess we still got those grandchildren. Can't get rid of them.

The Bennetts told us a great deal about themselves in a very short time. Mention of grandchildren stirred in Mr.

Bennett memories of his own grandfather, a "tremendous fellow" who made Mr. Bennett in his youth feel very secure. But what Mr. Bennett remembers most about his grandfather is the high standard of behavior he exacted from his children and grandchildren. This, in fact, is the grandfather's legacy to his grandson. Thus, when Mr. Bennett reflects on his own behavior as a grandparent, he prides himself on setting an "example." He has a thinking ("I try to teach them industry") and a doing ("I fix their bicycles") relationship to his grandchildren—but no emotional attachment. He does not want to be "overbearing," as his grandfather surely was, because this would be intolerable to his children and grandchildren without the simultaneous investment of personal feelings, which he feels powerless to make.

Mrs. Bennett understands all this very well. She justifies her husband's disconnection by blaming it on changes in the family structure. Yet she is as detached as her husband is. The grandchildren, she says, are "close in our hearts," where they are lovingly remembered as babies. But the truth is that their grandchildren are no longer babies. In short, they are strangers to the Bennetts—little more than faces on the photographs which Mrs. Bennett likes to show her friends.

Except for pro forma gestures, the Bennetts have written themselves out of their grandchildren's lives by holding themselves at a discreet emotional distance from them. They realize that they are emotionally detached grandparents yet, for that very reason, they say that they are powerless to change their relationship with their grandchildren. They feel sapped of the emotional strength necessary to assert themselves as Great Parents. But why?

The answer, it seems clear, lies in the Bennetts' attitude toward their children. "You bring them up and that's it," says Mrs. Bennett. Her remark has the force of a dictum, a statement of fact which commands ready assent. The Bennetts are disconnected from the grandchildren because they are disconnected from their children. *More important, they have ceded to their children the power to determine their own relationship to their grandchildren.* Thus, much as Mr. Bennett enjoys stirring his grandchildren up, he does not want to violate his children's "freedom" by insisting on seeing his grandchildren more often. *In sum, the Bennetts do not recognize, much less assert, a connection to their grandchildren which is independent of their connection with the children.* Little wonder, then, that they feel powerless.

The Bennetts—and all grandparents like them—seem to belie our earlier assertion that the instinct to grandparent is universal. In fact, however, the evidence provided by such grandparents leads us to assert the existence of a powerful counterveiling force which vitiates the instinct to grandparent and, with that instinct, the primordial bond between grandparents and grandchildren. This force is rooted in history, not biology, and is manifest by thoughts rather than feelings. We call it *"the new social contract."* It is social because it is based on attitudes which have been learned and digested from family experience in a changing society. It is contractual because it assumes that parents can and should decide whether—and to what extent—grandparents will nurture their grandchildren. And it is new because it has developed within the lifespan of the current generation of grandparents.

The provisions of the new social contract have never been explicitly stated. But they are all the more powerful for that. They exist as a climate of opinion which insinuates rather than commands. Nonetheless, they were readily discernible in the conversations we had with many grandparents who had elected to remain emotionally detached from their grandchildren. We first met these grandparents second hand in the shrunken figures and sad, often angry commentaries of the grandchildren we visited. They were, it will be recalled, the majority of grandparents (Group II of the children's study). Later, we met some of them first hand through their own comments and reflections. Here we present a few who differ from the rest only in the explicitness with which they articulate the provisions and principles of the new social contract.

We visited Mr. and Mrs. Wilson in their spacious country home in Danbury, Connecticut. Mr. Wilson is seventy-one, his wife sixty-five. They have eight grandchildren, four living two hours away by train in New York City, and four in New Mexico. The subject of grandchildren at first made the Wilsons slightly defensive, but they quickly captured their composure. Mr. Wilson, a tall, vigorous and handsome man, commented sardonically on the trials of being a grandparent:

> I've lived a Godly, upright and sober life, as they say, and I vote regularly . . . I don't get too involved with children and grandchildren, really, because no one listens to anybody anyway. Of course, I'm free to express my wisdom, but who's going to listen to it? Anyway, you can't really teach anyone anything. They have to learn for themselves, don't you think so? Young people don't believe anything you tell them anyway. Take drugs, for example. They'll go out and try it.

Mr. Wilson made it clear that this attitude was not the result of frustrated efforts to influence his grandchildren but a rationale for not getting involved in the first place.

> When the grandbabies were born, my wife and I said that we weren't going to get involved, let them (their own children) lead their own lives. We didn't babysit. We were too busy with our friends, I guess . . . We did spend time with

the grandchildren when they were young. In fact, we still have some of the toys here that they played with when they were young. They come for a visit now and then. But they have their lives and we have ours. We keep to ourselves now. We don't want to meddle in the children's lives. I let the youngsters run their own lives, make their own mistakes.

I don't see them too often now. We go out to New Mexico once a year to visit my son and his family. I don't know the grandchildren too well. We send birthday cards but I don't really know them . . . It's too bad because there's not much time left.

Mr. Wilson insisted that he is an important figure in his grandchildren's lives but he was hard put to say just why.

I guess the best example of that would be the card I got from one of the grandchildren in New Mexico. It said that I make him happy. Making him happy—that's important. No, I don't have much influence with them. Haven't been around them that much. I guess I'm sad about that.

Mrs. Wilson analyzed her relationship to the grandchildren:

If I think about it, I might have some influence. The fact that I exist means I have influence, but I don't know how or what. Anyway, it's not too good to get too close. I don't want my grandchildren or my children to feel that they owe me anything, that they are responsible for me, that I would interfere with their family or their financial status, or be a burden.

I think I have a good relationship with my grandchildren. I mean, I don't see them too much and it's not bad. We get along when we see each other. We're not pals but . . . let me put it this way. I wouldn't want to be too close to my children. I wouldn't like to live on the same street.

I don't think it is right for any family to know what is going on in the other family. I think there should be a period of time—weeks—when I haven't the faintest idea what anyone is doing. I wouldn't like it if they knew my business. If we were too close I might become critical of them. It's better for

me not to be a busybody. I don't know how the grandchildren
feel about that.

Mrs. Wilson was quite candid and detailed in explaining
her relationship to her grandchildren during their infre-
quent family visits:

> I don't like to go out alone with the grandchildren because
> I don't want the responsibility of driving in case something
> happens. The grandchildren come to visit but I ask them to
> bring a friend. I find it tiresome to play with my grand-
> daughter and talk to her. It tires me. I get a little bored, I
> guess, so she can amuse herself with her friend. It takes too
> much out of me. I guess I can't be with my grandchildren too
> long. I don't like to eat dinner with them. It was always like
> that.
>
> I feel though that they are an important part of my life in
> the abstract. I love them when they are not here. Do you un-
> derstand? It's hard to say . . . I do not build my life around
> my grandchildren. I know people who are crazy about their
> grandchildren and others who never acknowledge them. I
> don't want to leech onto them.

Mrs. Wilson paused for a moment, struggling to find the
precise words to formulate her attitude toward her grandchildren:

> I don't know why, but I don't want to depend on my
> grandchildren for emotions. That's it. I would feel bad if I
> couldn't see them once in a while. But maybe that's selfish.
> We're very lucky to have normal grandchildren.
>
> I think that we have a normal relationship with our grand-
> children when I look around at other people. I would think
> that almost anybody could have a good relationship with their
> grandchildren. I would think it's natural. I mean, you couldn't
> woo them. I don't give them anything. I don't bring them
> toys and presents and try to buy their affection. And we don't
> take them places. We appear on the scene and we're there
> and that's about it. I don't know how to make them like me
> and I wouldn't know what to do if they didn't like me.

Mr. Wilson was not entirely comfortable with his wife's assessment of their relationship to their grandchildren.

> I wish I spent a bit more time with the grandchildren because I enjoy them more as they grow up. I really don't know them too well, when it gets right down to it, even though we don't live too far from one of the families . . . There's no doubt that there's something missing now. It's an emptiness inside, perhaps where the grandchildren were supposed to be.

The Wilsons are among the most disconnected grandparents we met. Yet they regard their relationship with their grandchildren as "normal." They are not emotionally or physically close to their grandchildren, nor are they totally detached. They have worked out a relationship of sporadic contact which they feel is "natural." They visit the grandchildren twice a year and exchange postcards from time to time. Mrs. Wilson candidly admits that she enjoys the children more "in the abstract" than when they are near her. Little wonder, then, that on this basis she believes that "almost anyone could have a good relationship with their grandchildren."

The Wilsons' grandchildren, however, do not "feel good" about their relationship with their grandparents. When we visited the grandchildren in New York City, they drew the Wilsons as small, emotionally expressionless figures frozen on an otherwise empty page. "They're just standing there," a granddaughter explained to us. Her brother said he feels that his grandparents "don't like me" because they never come to see him. "If they liked me," he reasoned, "they would spend time with me."

Mrs. Wilson is correct when she says that she doesn't know how the grandchildren feel about the relationship the Wilsons have established with them. That's because the grandchildren's feelings were never considered in the first place. The Wilsons' relationship to their grandchildren is derived from the implicit social contract which they have established between themselves and their children. The basis of that contract is not mutual support but mutual independence: "They have their lives and we have ours," Mr. Wilson told us. This was not said harshly but as a matter of principle. Under the terms of the social contract, no one is obliged to anyone else. Put in a more positive way, each party to the contract is to refrain from any activity which would put the other party under emotional "obligation." Thus, according to the contract, financial or emotional support equals "meddling." Advice or opinion equals "controlling." Interest in lives of the other party equals "interference." More broadly, the contract rests on the assumptions that intimacy equals emotional dependence and that emotions equal weakness. Thus the new social contract exists to prevent emotional bonding from taking place. Mrs. Wilson underscores this fact with devastating clarity: "I don't want to depend upon my grandchildren for emotion."

The grandchildren, however, are not parties to the new social contract. Nonetheless, they are its primary victims. The Wilsons' children may, as young parents, cherish the distance between themselves and their parents as evidence of their own independence. But grandchildren, as we have seen, crave intimacy with their grandparents. They do not recognize contractual relationships, only emotional bonds. *Bonding, however, implies emotional "bondage" to others.* This is what grandparents like the Wilsons want to avoid. And that is what the new social contract is designed to prevent.

Thus far we have looked at the new social contract solely in terms of its negative effects on grandchildren and grandparents. Obviously, the new social contract must hold a positive attraction for at least some grandparents or else they would not choose to fashion their behavior in later years according to its provisions. In other words, if disconnection is so painful why do some grandparents actually welcome separation from their grandchildren? The answer, we believe, is that the new social contract provides an alternative by which grandparents can develop an identity, roles and a sense of self-fulfillment which are determined by their relationships—as *individuals*—to society rather than to family.

This "positive," perhaps even "liberating" aspect of the new social contract was evident in our conversations with those few grandparents who professed no interest at all in their grandchildren. Such a grandparent is Mrs. Jaynes, sixty-two, who holds a responsible position in the business office of a hospital in New Hampshire. Her husband is a prominent businessman in their small town and together they very much enjoy the freedom they have from grandparenting their six grandchildren. Mrs. Jaynes is a businesslike, self-possessed woman. Nonetheless, she became quite agitated during our interview. She spoke rapidly, as if her verbal output were necessary to block questions that might otherwise kindle feelings she would prefer to ignore:

> Me grandparent? Heck no. I don't want to get involved in that. If my grandchildren stay away, on the other side of the country, I can escape that grandparent category. I don't want it. I hate labels. If I don't have grandchildren around, that's fine with me. People have some nerve making up those categories. I don't want to be a grandparent.

When we asked Mrs. Jaynes why she objected to being a grandmother, she responded at first with the usual justifications of the new social contract.

> I don't want them to become dependent on me. Then I'll owe them something because they'll need something from me.

Of my six grandchildren I've seen only two of them and that was just once. Just as well.

Mrs. Jaynes recalled her own experience as a mother by way of reinforcing her attitude toward her grandchildren:

When my babies were born—I had three in a row—no one helped me. My family wasn't around. I didn't get the help from them that I needed then. I had a big family and I felt close to my own grandparents but I lived too far from them. If my daughter is in that situation now I would rather send her money to hire someone to help her than do it myself. I had enough. I did it, so can she.

Mrs. Jaynes was quick to assure us that her grandchildren are not neglected:

I'm sure that the grandchildren are well taken care of. They live in the woods and have dogs and a horse. They have mothers who stay home and take care of them. If I lived closer to them I might feel differently. But I don't, so I feel the way I do. I don't know, maybe I'd still feel the way I do. I don't want to interfere in anyone's life. I do not want to get into childcare and babysitting as a grandparent because it would tie me down. They have their life and I have mine.

By way of contrast, Mrs. Jaynes described her present life in terms of being free of close emotional attachments.

When I am finished at my job at the end of the day, I am finished. I am not responsible for people I work with and I'm not emotionally involved with them.

Grandparenting means taking care of little kids. I did that and never cared for it. I won't do it again if I don't have to. So the grandchildren won't know me. As long as I keep busy, I don't have to think about that, now do I? I don't know them either . . . I'd rather not think about that. In fact, I don't want to talk about it anymore. The whole subject bothers me.

It is possible that Mrs. Jaynes feels the way she does about her grandchildren because she has "had it" with chil-

dren. It is also possible that she feels that she must devalue
their emotional importance to her because they all live
nearly a continent away. Whatever the reasons, she is quite
content, she says, in a world of adults where vital family
connections are not necessary for happiness. In that world,
being a grandparent is not important. In fact, it is a "label"
imposed by others which Mrs. Jaynes refuses to accept. At
age sixty-two she has developed an identity and sense of
self-worth which are defined by her job, her husband, and
their place in the society of their small town. This social
milieu does not crowd them; they do not have to get "emotionally involved" with anyone other than themselves and
friends of their own choosing. Not even Mrs. Jaynes' colleagues at the hospital can make emotional claims upon
her. She is an "individual," independent of all connections
save those that bind her to the "adults only" society she
moves in. In a phrase—one that is dear to psychoana-
lytically oriented social critics who would liberate everyone from family-connected roles—Mrs. Jaynes has become
"separated-individuated." To her grandchildren, however,
she is just another old woman, living far away, who was
their mother's mother.

F. Summary of the Grandparent Study

In visiting some 300 American grandparents we found
that only fifteen of them were intimately involved with
their grandchildren. Another fifteen or so were totally detached from their grandchildren's lives. The majority, therefore, were intermittently involved with their grandchildren
and this, we conclude is the dominant pattern in American
families.

All but the most disconnected, however, attested to the

fact that the attachment between grandparent and grandchild is natural and second in emotional power only to the
primordial bond between parent and child. The arrival of
the first grandchild, we learned, creates a new network of
human connections between three generations; more important, it triggers in grandparents—and especially in
grandmothers—a dormant instinct to nurture.

This nurturing instinct, we discovered, unleashes in
grandparents a natural sequence of reactions which are
rooted in biology and are manifest by universal and automatic psychological responses: (1) A mental rehearsal for
becoming "Great Parents," during which grandparents anticipate the birth of the grandchild by recalling their own
experiences of parenthood; their own experience as a grandchild, and prepare a mental script for grandparenting; (2)
feelings of joy elicited by the arrival of the child; (3) expansive thoughts about continuing fecundity (especially in
women) and continuity (especially in men); (4) an impulse to act, the primary act being to see (and hold) the
child, which has the effect of visually imprinting the child
on the grandparent's mind.

These sequential events, grandparents told us, are powerful, unforgettable experiences. But they are not enough to
ensure vital connections with grandchildren. By listening
to active grandparents such as Mrs. Mason and the O'Flahertys, we were able to isolate four factors necessary for
developing and maintaining vital connections: the critical
dimensions of time and place, a commitment to family and
a sense of altruism, which we linked to Erikson's understanding of "generativity" as the virtue proper to adult maturity. In the O'Flahertys, we found an example of how
grandparents can extend the sense of vital connections to
an entire neighborhood and through their generativity be-

come true "elders" in a society which reserves no place or honor for elders.

We then turned our attention to the majority of grandparents, who were to varying degrees disconnected from their grandchildren. We saw that disconnection occurs when any one or combination of the four factors necessary to vital connections are weak or missing. From listening to altruistic grandparents whose grandchildren have been separated from them by circumstances beyond the grandparents' control, we learned that the painful experience of disconnection is similar to the process of protest-despair-detachment experienced by little children who are separated from their parents. More narcissistic grandparents, who were often responsible for the disconnection, mourned the loss of themselves more than the actual separation from their grandchildren.

At this point we moved to consideration of why most grandparents, including some otherwise altruistic persons, accept and even prefer a less than intimate relationship with their grandchildren. We rejected as insufficient the usual answers, such as mobility and changes in family structure. Instead, we located within the rationales offered by the grandparents themselves the existence of a "new social contract" which controls—and in most cases greatly limits—the degree of intimacy between today's grandparents and their grandchildren. We observed that this contract is implicit rather than explicit, the rule rather than the exception and all the more powerful for being unstated. Thus, grandparents who see their grandchildren no more than two or three times a year told us that their relationship with them is "good" or "normal" and like that of most other grandparents they know. Further, we argued that this new social contract is part of a climate of opinion which has emerged within the lifespan of this generation of grandparents. We said the contract is rooted in history, rather than biology, and has had the ultimate effect of thwarting the grandparents' instinct to nurture, thereby severing—or at least severely attenuating—the vital connections between today's grandparents and grandchildren.

We also found that the more disconnected grandparents are, the more they describe their relationships with their grandchildren in terms of a contract. According to those terms, intimate involvement with grandchildren equals "meddling." Interest in their grandchildren's lives equals "interference" in their children's families. Intimacy is interpreted as emotional "dependence," advice is viewed as "controlling" and emotions themselves imply "weakness." The new social contract, we concluded, also functions as a "positive" alternative for those adults who do not want to acknowledge their grandparenthood, much less establish emotional bonds with their grandchildren. As one highly disconnected grandmother summed matters up: "I don't want to depend upon my grandchildren for emotion."

3

Today's Grandparents:
An Emotional History

> For man is that creature without any fixed age, who has the
> faculty of becoming, in a few seconds, many years younger,
> and who, surrounded by the walls of the time through which
> he has lived, floats within them but as though in a basin, the
> surface level of which is constantly changing, so as to bring
> him into range now of one epoch, now of another.
>
> Marcel Proust, REMEMBRANCE OF THINGS PAST

Today's grandparents are very different from their own
grandparents. Many of these differences are obvious. Today's grandparents are, as a group, healthier, longer lived,
and financially more secure than their forebears. The re-
markable thing is that these very welcome differences did
not interest the grandparents we spoke to. The point most
made, over and over again, is that they wanted to be more
like the grandparents they had known as children but, with
few exceptions, they said they couldn't. "The times have
changed," they told us, "things are different." They felt
somehow cheated by history, robbed of roles as grandparents and elders which they thought would be theirs.
They wanted to know what had happened.

We have already suggested an answer. In the previous
chapter we argued that the degree of intimacy between

most grandparents and grandchildren was controlled by a new social contract which has the ultimate effect of thwarting the grandparents' nurturing instinct and vitiating the vital connections between them and their grandchildren. By itself, however, the new social contract does not tell us all that we want to know. It is an idea that needs unpacking if we are to discover why most of today's grandparents are unable to respond to their own emotional needs and those of their grandchildren. Recall, for example, that while the contract erodes the bond between grandparents and grandchildren, it is actually a relationship between grandparents and their own children. This fact alone suggests that the new social contract came into being as the result of a much longer process involving the emotional relationships of today's grandparents with their own parents and grandparents.

In this chapter we will look behind the new social contract to see how and why it evolved within the lifespan of today's grandparents. To do so we have constructed a common "emotional history" out of the life stories told by the grandparents we visited. Such a history has never been attempted before, so far as we know, and what follows can be no more than a cursory sketch.

Emotional history, as we understand it, is not simply a history of emotional experiences. It is a history of vital connections. Biologically, on the one hand it is a history of the "telescopic" connections between today's grandparents and those out of whom they have emerged (their parents and grandparents); and on the other of those who have emerged out of them (their children and grandchildren). Psychologically, it is a history of these grandparents' experience of receiving and giving nurture, a history which touches five generations of Americans and so spans the entire twentieth century. It is a form of social history because the nurturing

process is an inherently social process and is affected by social change. We have chosen to describe this history as
"emotional," however, because our focus is on the ways in
which certain changes in the process of nurture have
affected the emotional well-being, outlook and behavior of
today's grandparents.

A. *The Method*

The emotional history we have constructed cannot be
separated from the process by which that history was elicited. Initially, most grandparents we visited responded to
our questions in the emotionally detached way that people
typically reply to public opinion pollsters. They reported
that they were, on the whole, quite satisfied with the material conditions of their lives. They felt healthy and, in most
cases, were financially better off than they had expected to
be at their age. In general, they were content with their
relations to their children and grandchildren, which they
felt were "like everyone else's we know." In short, their responses reflected satisfaction with the way their lives had
been arranged according to the provisions of the new social
contract.

It was only when we began to probe their vital connections that our respondents were able to get beneath these
surface attitudes and into the stuff of emotional history.
To help them do this we employed a method whereby our
subjects could become aware of their vital connections—
despite the effects of the new social contract—and thus
view their individual life histories through the prism of
emotional attachments and detachments. Our method was
simple: we asked them to recall their own grandparents. In

order to do this, they had to summon forth the child within each of them; it is impossible to recall one's grandparents without, at the same time, calling forth the child who experienced those grandparents. In this way, our respondents were able to re-enter a world of emotional relationships which existed before they became parties to the new social contract. Gradually, this process put them in touch with all their vital connections and, eventually, they were able to articulate the pain and disorientation they now felt as a result of their separation from their own children and grandchildren.

Of necessity, emotional history is deliberately "nonobjective" in method but not, we judge, in results. Our primary "evidence" might best be described as "emotion recollected in tranquility" and so resembles the matter of poetry, as Wordsworth defined it, more than the matter of "fact." Yet the way things feel is the way things are, especially to children. And for the old, the way things felt is the most important dimension of what they have to tell us about the way things were.[1]

To discover "the way things felt," we asked grandparents to tell us their life stories, focusing on their experiences of receiving and giving nurture. One can, of course, tell the story of one's life by focusing on other experiences. But no matter how one chooses to tell the story, or at what age, at least two things are necessary: a sense of the beginning and a sense of the ending. Since we cannot remember our birth and can only anticipate (if that) the circumstances of our death, our sense of beginnings and of endings must extend beyond both events. In other words, our sense of beginning is necessarily rooted in the lives of those people out of whom we emerged and our sense of ending necessarily incorporates the on-going lives of those who have emerged from us. Whatever else they might be about, therefore, all life stories are inherently stories of vital connections.

Finally, we want to anticipate an objection regarding our method. How is it possible, one might ask, to construct an emotional history from life stories told by many different people from diverse backgrounds, each with different kinds of forebears and progeny? The objection is further compounded by the fact that every life story is a mix of memory (the past) and anticipation (the future) and is always told from a particular subjective standpoint: the present. Thus the same person will tell his or her story differently at different ages and stages of life. In addition to these quantitative factors relating to time, life stories also vary qualitatively according to those events which each person regards as "turning points" in his or her life; the outcomes of these events affect how the past is remembered and how the future is anticipated.

In answer to these objections we observe, first, that in constructing a life story the teller selects and edits the materials for his own story. What interests us, therefore, are the choices and emphases the story teller makes. Secondly, the similarities that unite the story tellers are, for our purposes, more important than their differences. All the life stories we heard were told by people in the grandparental stage of life. They had all experienced the turning points central to a history of vital connections: that is, most of them had been nurtured by grandparents and parents and, in turn, had nurtured their own children. Thus their present relationship to their own grandchildren is the common standpoint from which each of them told us their life stories. This shared standpoint makes it possible for us to isolate the central themes, at least, of the stories we heard and out of these to construct the outlines of a common emotional history.

B. "The Way Things Were"

In listening to the life stories told by some 300 grandparents, the first thing we discovered is that most of them
had amazing recall of at least one grandparent. This was
not unexpected since children who were born in the early
years of the twentieth century, we surmised, were more
likely than children today to live close to their grandparents. Moreover their image of older people was not
compromised as it is today, by images of the aged derived
from television, the movies, and other mass media. As a result, today's grandparents started out in life with a generally realistic anticipation of old age. This finding corrobo-
rates what we learned earlier, namely that a child's image
of old age—and therefore of his own "ending"—is shaped
to a large degree by the presence or absence of at least one
close grandparent. A child who has a close grandparent, it
will be recalled, is less likely to fear old age or to revile the
aged than a child who is bereft of such a grandparent.

But—and this is crucial to understanding any history of
vital connections—these elders out of the nineteenth century are not merely well-remembered ancestors. Psychologically, they are also powerful "constant objects" or emotional reference points in the minds of their grandchildren,
who have become the putative elders of the twentieth century. Thus, they not only provide today's grandparents
with a strong sense of their own beginnings, but also color
their anticipation of their own ending. The result, we
found, is that most of the grandparents we visited regretted
that they had not measured up to the image of vital old age
which they had inherited from their own grandparents.

Mr. Johnson, who was born in the early months of this

century, typified the majority of the grandparents we visited. He had no trouble at all recalling his grandfather for
us:

> I think of him so often. No matter where I was, he used to
> come and visit me. When I went away to school, he would
> come regularly, unexpected, just to see how I was doing. He'd
> pick me up in the car and bring me home for a weekend or we
> would just spend the weekend together.
>
> He would bring down fishing gear with him and we would
> go fishing. He would do that most every weekend when I was
> a small kid. He would seek me out. Most of all he was full of
> stories, funny stories, sad stories. I loved his war stories best of
> all. He did very well in business and he used to tell me what
> was going on, how he was doing, what deals were coming off.
> It was like a serial. I learned about business that way.
>
> He never bought me things, you know, except maybe some-
> thing that we would use together, like a new fishing reel. Now
> that I think of it, we used to make each other's gifts, rarely
> bought anything. He would always ask me to bring a friend if
> I wanted to but I liked to be alone with him, so I rarely did.
> My friends knew him, though, and would ask me if they could
> come along when he was around.

Mr. Johnson lives alone in a nursing home, a childless
world for physically dependent "senior citizens." Except
for the fact that he needs a nurse's attention from time to
time, he sees no reason why he is there. He never expected
to end up in a nursing home, yet he wouldn't think of "im-
posing" on his children. As for his grandchildren, Mr.
Johnson hardly knows them. All he knows is that "things"
aren't at all like they were in his grandfather's day.

> Funny how things change. My grandchildren come and see
> me here a couple of times a year. I don't even feel that I miss
> them. I kind of put it out of my mind, I guess. If I think
> about it I get angry . . . or maybe it hurts. Yeah, I guess
> that's it. I can't give what I've got. I don't have the opportu-
> nity to pass it on, the funny stories. I don't know these people

who, after all, are my flesh and blood. Can you believe that it has come to this? My flesh and blood and I—there's nothing there.

I'm not giving these youngsters what I should be passing on, what my grandfather passed on to me. I've still got it inside of me. What do I do with it when I'm gone? What will happen to the stories that he told me?

Biologically, Mr. Johnson sees himself as a link in a human chain. Emotionally, he feels like the end of the line. The stories his grandfather told him will die with him because he has no one to tell them to. "There's no one there," he laments, no vital connection between himself and his own grandchildren. He has been a father, but not a grandfather. To make matters worse, he cannot account for the break in this final vital connection. "Funny how things change," he muses.

What he means, among other things, is that he did not turn out to be at all like his own grandfather. His grandfather was important to him in childhood and now, at the close of his life, he himself is important to no one. Old age did not turn out the way he had been led to anticipate it through his image of his own grandfather. Therefore, his life story reveals no symmetry, no narrative line ("Funny how things change"), reaches no conclusion. It will only stop. This sense of their own insignificance compared to that of their own grandparents is the first major theme common to the life stories we heard.

The second major theme is the memory of childhood as an emotional Eden. To be sure, any adult whose basic needs for food, emotional dependency, and trust were satisfied in childhood will recall that period of life as a paradise of good feelings. Indeed, the image of childhood as paradise is ancient—perhaps archetypal—as is the cognate image of Paradise Lost. What is significant about the emotional history of today's grandparents is that the good feelings they remember are not the result of their family's economic status. On the contrary, nearly all the grandparents we spoke with either came from humble origins or else remembered childhood as a time of relative economic hardship. By their own accounts, their early emotional paradise was solely the result of close family connections.

Mrs. Kane, who grew up in a working-class family in the Bronx, recalled her early years:

> Childhood was a wonderful time for me, although I heard the adults complaining that the "times" were hard. I felt that I counted. I could make them smile. I could "ungrouch" them. "Sunshine" they called me. I always had a good time what with so many people around.
>
> Only when I grew older did I realize the poverty, what my parents had gone through. And I got sadder too. I felt happy until I started to work. Life was less fun. But before that I had all I needed, all the people I needed, and I was happy.

The story Mrs. Kane told us was of childhood "before the fall" into work and adult responsibility. Outside, the world was rapidly changing under the impact of industrialization; soon, the effects of this process would be felt within the family as well. For the time being, however, the family clung together for emotional as well as economic security (as many so-called "ethnic" families today still do). Children thrived in this family environment because there were so many adults who lavished attention on them. The hardships these adults faced were plain enough for the children to see. But they did not *feel* hard put themselves so long as there were people around to provide emotional support and trust; people to be "with," people to be "like," even people to be "unlike." In short, within the family circle of parents and grandparents, of aunts and uncles and cousins, people counted, not things. It was, as long as it lasted, a paradise of vital connections which stretched out in all directions, like spokes from the hub of a wheel. And for grandparents like Mrs. Kane, it remains a touchstone in their emotional history:

> I never felt I was poor until I knew what poor meant. It was hard, but we were alive. It was us against the world. Not all of my friends' families were as close as we were, but we were pretty typical. We all lived in one house—including, on and off, my grandparents and four uncles. One by one they eventually left, but while we were living together they would come home and on Friday they would put most of their wages into a big pot on the table and my grandmother and my mother would use it to keep the family going. There were always people around to help, or just to be with. There would be people at the kitchen table, having tea and cake. I didn't see much alcohol around in those days and only an occasional relative with a "drinking problem." Selfishness was out of style then. One for all and all for one was the way. Family closeness was taken for granted. It's so different now. Nowadays, people have what they want but, well, they've lost the closeness.

The Great Depression of the thirties was particularly hard on families. Yet, to Mr. Ignatius, his childhood and early adolescence on the family farm in rural New Jersey were golden.

> The grown-ups were always talking about hard times but it didn't bother us kids none. Mother was of a cheerful nature and although my father was away working most of the time there were plenty of relatives around to give me all the attention I craved and to teach me all I wanted to know. "Curious George," they called me. I got used to being with a lot of people and now, if I'm alone too long, I just don't feel right. Lonely. Even though people can drive me batty at times, I'd rather be with them than not. Know what I mean?

Like Mrs. Kane, Mr. Ignatius remembers his family as a close network of kinfolk whose collective opinion outweighed all outside influence. As long as the family had enough food and other basic necessities, "Curious George" was perfectly happy within its bosom.

> I never really had to leave the farm. I had plenty of people to play with—and to fight with. Sunday, we went to church, of course. We were known in town and I felt good knowing that I had my family behind me. You know, my-brother-can-beat-up-your-brother, that sort of thing. And we did it. Not many kids can say that nowadays. Our family was important in the town because we lived there for such a long time. We all worked, every one of us, but work was not important. It was important that a person had a job, of course, but the type of work wasn't much the mark of the man. It was the family that judged you. My uncle, for example, was the oldest son of my grandparents. Well, he worked as a blacksmith and you would've thought the sun rose and set at his command the way my grandparents and everyone else treated him. He was just a plain person, like you and me, and if he lived today he would be stricken with an inferiority complex, being a blacksmith and all. But money didn't matter much, except of course for the things you need to survive. We had the other, the real necessities. Sounds corny but it's called love and togetherness.

Paradise did not last long for today's grandparents—the third major theme of their emotional history. The same close family ties which generated the good feelings of childhood also required children—certainly by the time they reached adolescence—to assume a large part of the family's support. Everyone who could, worked. Along with these responsibilities came an abrupt change in the relationship between today's grandparents and their parents. The nurtured became youthful coproviders for the family and, often enough, conurturers of younger siblings. Emotionally, they were put in the position of helping to support their parents while continuing to obey them. Unlike their own children, today's grandparents told us that they had little opportunity—or even the desire—to rebel. To be

sure, a privileged few were sent off to college and so gained
both a measure of independence and a delay in their entry
into the world of work. But even these lucky young people
did not escape the sense of family responsibility. They had
to succeed for Mother and Father, but especially for
Mother. They knew that eventually a portion of their success would be added, like their uncles' wages, to Mother's
family pot. Mrs. Gilbert, a retired grandmother we visited
in Florida, recalled how she felt when this transformation
in paradise occurred.

> I know what "Paradise Lost" means. I had it when I was
> young, when it really counted. Then, one day, it was all over.
> From that day on I don't think I even did anything for my-
> self. It was all for my parents. From the day I could help, my
> life was devoted to them. My friends were just the same. Life
> at that point became a drudge. Work. Help out the family.
> Nothing for me. And I never even questioned it or thought
> about it. That's just the way it was. We all did it. I did it
> with my parents and then I did it with my children. It was
> duty.
> I was my family's insurance policy. My brothers and I
> worked, gave Mom the money, took what was needed, which
> was little. I made good marks in school—for her. She was a
> good person. I loved her very much. I wanted to make her
> happy, and I did. I never thought of rebelling against her.
> Sure, we'd sneak around a little, perhaps, but we wouldn't
> openly antagonize her. She was too nice . . . and I would feel
> guilty. Who disobeyed their parents in those years, not me or
> my friends. What Mom said I did, and never wondered why.
> The mistake I made is that I thought my own kids would
> treat me the same way. Was I wrong!

According to this emotional history, doing for others was
a duty. It is what their parents did, and, consciously at
least, they accepted it. But their childhood was too short.
Thinking back on it during their conversations with us,
grandparents re-experienced buried feelings of resentment

—the fourth major theme of their emotional history. Some of these feelings were directed against their parents for binding them so closely that they could do nothing other than accept and act upon the sense of duty bred into them. Unconsciously, however, they resented this bondage. They would raise their children differently, they told themselves. They would teach them independence, send them to school longer, and allow them the "freedom" and extended childhood that had been denied them in their own youth. With one ear they listened to their parents, wanting very much to bind their own children to themselves as they had been bound to their parents. With the other ear, they listened to the burgeoning corps of child-rearing experts who stressed—often rightly enough—the child's need for emotional independence from parents. Emotionally, they were in a bind: they still wanted to please their parents and, at the same time, please their children by freeing them of the parental control they themselves had experienced in youth. Mrs. Pillsbury, sixty-four, put the matter succinctly:

> I did what the experts said. I read Dr. Spock. I let them have their way. I gave them all the love I could and now they are all living in different places in the country. All three of them. They spoke their minds to me, all right. Now they have no contact with me at all.

Most grandparents we talked with became quite bitter at this point in their conversations. They felt cheated twice over—first by their own parents, for failing to give them the freedom they wanted in youth, and now by their own children, for failing to give them the dedication they had come to expect. This is the fifth major theme in their emotional history. Grandmothers, it seems, feel the resentment more than grandfathers because of the greater emotional investment mothers typically make in their children. Mrs.

O'Connor, who grew up in a large family in Boston more than a half-century ago and raised four children of her own, summed up for many grandmothers the sense of disillusion she now feels with the way her life turned out:

> I lived for my parents most of my life and then I lived for my children. My husband worked his fingers to the bone for all of us and he deserves to retire, to rest. But the children have taken the horse and run. After the Depression, my husband and I saw the opportunities that were open to kids and we worked to send them through school, all the way. I took care of the family and worked part-time. My husband worked full-time, and then some. All five of them are something today. But they are all different. Married into different religions. I feel self-conscious around them. So I ask myself, "What did I do this for?" My son said I don't own him when I asked him to stay in Boston to settle down. I felt that way about my parents but I could never say it out loud . . . and here my own sons say it to me. Do you believe it? I've had it.
>
> I'm living my own life now, with my friends. And with my sister. She lives nearby. We fight a lot but we are still sisters and this is all that is important. When the time comes, I can count on her. I hope that it would come to that if I needed my kids . . . but I wonder. I know that they wouldn't take me in when I get older. Now, retired, I'm just going to look out for Number One, and that's not the way I would like it to be. If I had to do it over again, I wouldn't have sent them to school. But who knows? Maybe the same thing would have happened anyway. Maybe it's just the times . . . What do I look forward to? What else is there? You obey your parents and you raise a family and that's it. *Fini!*

The men were victimized in another way. Told to go to work, they obeyed. Now, most told us, they regret the emotional price they paid for their dutiful commitment to work. Work, they had learned early in youth, is what men did for their families. In time, however, work became something they did *despite* their families. Mr. Markhem, a grandfather we visited in Utah, looked back over his life and tried to chart for us the erosive impact of work on his vital family connections:

> When I was young, work wasn't that important. Family first, work down the list. It's changed so much now. Work has consumed my life. The older I got, the more it chewed me up. The bigger it became, the less time I had for my family . . . and I knew it when it began to happen. The kids begged me to stay home. My wife began to complain. But I worked.
>
> At the beginning, it was for my family, but after a while it was for me. Life at work, out of the home, was easier to cope with, fewer demands. I found myself finding it hard to come home at night, to face the hassle in the family. It snuck up on me. I thought a lot about retirement, the day when I could be relaxed with my children. But when I was ready, they weren't there anymore.
>
> My wife, she was the one who knew the children. She is the one they turned to. I'm so out of it. And I did it myself. When I got guilty, I would buy my way out of it. I'd get toys for the kids. I made a good living. I became a playmate, not a father. When I disciplined them I would overreact. My wife ran things and I guess I was trying to be the man of the house, to establish my father image. But we all knew it was a fake. I was frustrated and took a lot of it out on the kids. They in turn avoided me. I was pushy at times because I wanted to make up for when I wasn't there.
>
> I hope I can make up for it with my grandchildren, now that I've got the time. I hope that my kids will settle near me. I try to talk to the kids about this work thing, about how it made me miss out on all of the birthday parties and important events in the family and I don't think I'm getting through. It seems that the young people are more workaholic than I was. I could teach them something important, but they don't listen.

For Mr. Markhem and countless grandparents like him, the vital connections he might have had with his grand-children were vitiated long before his grandchildren were born. Having disengaged himself from his own children's lives, he now feels powerless to develop close emotional bonds with his grandchildren. What's worse, he is unable to persuade his grown children not to make the same mistake he did in neglecting vital family connections for the sake of his work. He senses, rightly, that his children will do as he did, not as he says, and so continue the process of emotional detachment with their own children and, eventually, with their grandchildren as well. Such is the way in which patterns in emotional history evolve.

We are now in a position to locate the origins of the new social contract and to isolate the forces which allowed it to supplant vital connections. Based on what today's grandparents have told us, we can summarize their emotional history as if it were the story of a single couple stretching the length of the twentieth century. It is a story, as we shall see, of a gradual transformation in the nurturing process.

Childhood: Looking back over their lives, grandparents recalled early childhood as an emotional Eden. They were born into close-knit families with blood relatives living nearby or even in the same household, at least for a time. Materially, these families were not well off and depended on mutual support for economic survival. Emotionally, however, the children prospered under the closeness, commitment and undemanding love they experienced from many available adults, particularly from grandparents. For as long as it lasted, this emotionally bountiful environment was indeed a "haven in a heartless world" in which vital connections between the generations were firmly established and flourished for children.

Adolescence: This emotional paradise did not last long because it depended upon the availability of many adults who, collectively, could devote a great deal of time and attention to the children. As economic opportunities gradually improved, however, aunts and uncles dispersed. Father worked longer hours, often taking employment at a great distance from home in order to put the family on a firmer financial footing. As soon as they were able, the children themselves were recruited to help support the family. Mother alone remained at home and so became the center of family life and the nodal point of the children's emotional attachments. Behind her was at least one grandparent (usually her mother) who continued to remind the children of the Eden they once knew. As the children matured, the emotional bonds between them and their mother became unusually strong (for some, even strangulating) and, unconsciously at least, the youngsters began to experience emotional conflict. On the one hand, they loved their mother and willingly complied with her wishes. On the other, they came to resent her control over their lives and their truncated childhood. And as they moved into late adolescence, they came to resent the lack of freedom to pursue their own interests, and began to see the emotional bounty of their youth change into emotional bondage. They could not leave their mother to venture out into the world because of the guilt they felt. Thus many of them did not wander too far from home when the time came to establish families of their own.

Parenthood: These conflicting emotions carried over into adulthood and eventually transformed the way in which they nurtured their own children. On the one hand, they sought to give their children the kind of happiness they had themselves enjoyed in early childhood. On the other, they vowed to give their children greater independence than they had known as children and so avoid the emotional bondage that paralyzed them. Above all, they set out to rid themselves of the fear of poverty, which they had inherited from their parents. Thus as young parents they

continued to work hard—not only for their mother, who
continued to exert a powerful influence as a "constant object" in their minds, but also for their own children, who
would one day act out their own hidden fantasies of freedom and self-fulfillment.

As today's grandparents discovered too late in life, the
goals they set for themselves and their children were con-
tradictory. In order to provide his family with a "higher
standard of living," Father had to invest his deepest ener-
gies and interests in his job. He became an absentee father,
like his father before him had eventually become. He gave
his children things instead of his time and attention.
Meanwhile, Mother stayed home just as her own mother
had done, but she too was imbued with a drive to "produce." Her "product" was to be a generation of independent children who would be free to seek happiness on their
own terms. These children would not have to work for
Mother in the same way that she had worked for her
mother. But they did have to fulfill her desires for them.
Emotionally, Mother and Father agreed to endure the present and looked forward to a future "retirement" when they
could do things for themselves.

Although Grandmother was close by in most cases, she
was not much help to Mom in rearing the children. She
was old-fashioned in her ways and the times had changed.
Moreover, it was Grandmother who had prevented Mother
from achieving her own emotional independence. So
Mother, with Father's approval, turned for guidance to
"parent educators," experts who taught her the latest
methods in feeding, training, and disciplining children. She
even learned when to give and when to withhold praise and
affection. In short, she learned to subjugate her own emotional responses to an alleged higher authority in order that

her children might some day enjoy a "higher standard of living."

When the children reached school age, Mother gave them to experts who took a more direct hand in her children's lives. At school they were tested and graded, taught to compete against other children for admission into the liberating realms of higher education. Parents, in turn, responded to their children's success or failure as if it were their own. Without realizing what they were doing, parents allowed thinking to replace feeling as the gauge of vital connections and performance emerged as a measure of the quality of the emotional ties between parents and children. Children felt more and more that they were loved for what they could "do" not for what they "are."

Here, then, are the emotional origins of the new social contract. Today's grandparents could not foresee the long-term results of the changes they had made in the nurturing process, but they soon felt its implications. When their own parents died, their emotional bondage to the previous generation was terminated. They had only their children left as a source of vital connections. But when they looked their children were no longer there. Having been raised emotionally to "stand on their own two feet," the children literally walked away from their parents. They moved from farms to cities, from cities to suburbs, from one state to another as part of the largest internal migration in American history. Between 1940 and 1960, for example, the farm population declined by half. In the same period, college enrollments more than doubled. The children became more "learned" than their parents and what they learned determined to an unprecedented degree where they would live and work, and thus the kind of vital connections they would establish. Instead of returning home, this "new class"[2] of college-educated young adults married classmates who were equally detached from parents and established independent households wherever the job market took them. By 1978, they would, on an average, move fourteen times in the course of their lives.

To be sure, many of today's grandparents protested against this disconnection. In some cases, the pull of ethnic, religious and other family-centered traditions drew children back to their places of origin. But the majority of grandparents were helpless to recover what they had already given away. By the very terms of the new social contract they were not to "interfere" in their children's lives, unless asked to, nor in the lives of their grandchildren. Thus, they became titular grandparents with no real or vital connections to their "children's children."

Obviously, the loss of vital connections is not the only experience which makes today's grandparents feel the way they do. Mention must also be made of four other "events" in their lives which set them apart from their forebears and which have heightened the emotional impact of the new social contract.

Longevity: As a group, today's grandparents have lived longer than any previous generation. Within their own lifetime, or roughly since the turn of the century, they have seen the average life expectancy in the United States (and other Western industrialized nations) jump from around forty-seven years to seventy-three. "Nothing like this has been known in human history," observes British essayist V. S. Pritchett, himself a hardy septuagenarian. "We are almost a new species."[3] The experience of so many people living out a full span of life is so new, yet so ordinary, that it is hard for younger people to appreciate their elders' unease at the prospect before them. Little wonder, then, that in their quest for elders to imitate, today's grandparents look behind the devitalized images of old age they see reflected in contemporary society to those hardy figures out of their childhood.

Economic Independence: Unlike their own grandparents, who looked to their families when they could no longer look after themselves, virtually all of today's grandparents can now count on pension programs, Social Security and other old-age subsidies provided by nonfamily sources. Indeed, with the advent of Medicare and Medicaid, "the substantial proportion of the federal budget going to the elderly now represents the largest income-redistribution scheme in the nation's history."[4] To be sure, many of the aged on fixed incomes are victimized by rampant inflation. Yet the fact remains that most of today's grandparents are financially independent of their children. More important, they are *expected* to be, in terms of the new social contract. Thus, one recent study indicates that "parent-caring"—a decided breach of the contract—has replaced the climacteric and the empty nest as the major problem of family life among middle-aged American couples.[5]

Mandatory Retirement: When the forebears of today's grandparents entered the work force, they expected that only illness or death would terminate their employment. Within their own lifetime, today's grandparents have experienced "forced retirement" as a process of segregation-by-age in which the elderly are regarded less as individual workers than as a "problem" class to be dealt with by employers and ultimately by the state. Despite the undoubted merits of retirement itself, most of the grandfathers we spoke with rued the loss of authority, prestige, power, identity, and purpose conferred by steady employment. For many men and women retirement also means the loss of friendships built up through years of being together on the job. Even those who welcome retirement, or escape it, experience their sixty-fifth birthday as a traumatic event. In the absence of other criteria, the "age of retirement" has become the accepted, if arbitrary signal that one is officially "old." Thus, as family historian Tamara K. Hareven has observed, retirement at a standard age "represents the most drastic development in the emergence of old age as a separate stage of life."[6]

"Acceleration of history": The phrase is Margaret Mead's, one which the late and distinguished anthropologist used to explain why, in her view, each generation now has the feeling of living in a world markedly different from that of its forebears. In *Culture and Commitment*, Mead described her own generation, which is that of today's grandparents, as strangely isolated: "No generation has ever known, experienced, and incorporated such rapid changes, watched the sources of power, the means of communication, the definition of humanity, the limits of the explorable universe, the certainties of a known and limited world, the fundamental imperatives of life and death—all change before our eyes. We know more about change than any generation has ever known, but we also stand over against and vastly alienated from the young who, by the very nature of their position, have had to reject their elders' past . . . We have to realize that no other generation will ever experience what we have experienced. In this sense, we must recognize that we have no descendants, as our children have no forebears."[7]

More than most grandparents, Margaret Mead was aware of and able to elucidate the cultural disjunctions between the generations. In retrospect, it may turn out that she exaggerated those disjunctions in reaction to the youth movements of the sixties, which were so much on her mind. Indeed, in her own life and work Dr. Mead belied her own arguments that the generations are hopelessly out of touch with each other. Nonetheless, the disjunctions are real enough and the emergence of the new social contract is the major reason, we believe, why most grandparents we visited feel in their bones that they truly have no descendants.

The effect of the new social contract was felt differently by Grandfather and Grandmother. Eventually, Grandfather retired. He had been working, it seemed, for as long as he could remember—for his boss, for his mother, his own family and, as mandatory retirement became institutionalized, for his future retired self. Now he could afford to rest, to just "be" without doing someone else's bidding. But retirement, he soon discovered, means that he no longer has a role in society. He is no longer the somebody he used to be. Without work he is just another retired man —and an "old" man at that. Yet he doesn't feel old, only disconnected. This sense of disconnection was sharply evoked by Mr. Ortiz, a retired policeman we visited in Westchester County, New York:

> What the hell do I do now? I thought I would feel differently now that I'm retired. I still want to work but they won't let me. My friends feel the same way. I always thought that I wanted to rest and fish at this age. I never dreamed that I would be in such good physical health. I thought I would be all dilapidated. But I'm not—and believe me I'm amazed about that. I'm rarin' to go, but there is no place to go. Rest is O.K. for a couple of months. In fact, I've looked forward to this all my life, lying around, doing what I want to do. But now I know this is crazy. A person's got to be wanted and needed. A person's got to do something, be with people. This retirement stuff is a myth, a rip-off as the kids say. I need a new kind of job.

At the age of sixty-eight, Mr. Ortiz is vigorous and alert but he has nothing—and no one—to expend his considerable energy on. He is looking for "a new kind of job" because work and the workplace supplanted his family as the source of his vital connections. His job diverted the critical dimensions of time and place to work instead of to his family. His sense of commitment was deflected from members of his family to colleagues on the job. Even his sense of altruism found an outlet through his work, in so far as he helped guide the young men who eventually became the replacements for his generation of workers.

Like most grandfathers we spoke to, Mr. Ortiz is just beginning to realize the price he has paid for ignoring his family connections. As a father, he never learned the value of simply "being with" his children. He had to produce for them and now it does not occur to him that the people he might most enjoy "being with," the people who might need and want him most are his own grandchildren. Indeed, it is too late for Mr. Ortiz to establish vital connections with his grandchildren. They are already approaching puberty and do not regard him as a significant person in their lives. Whatever he may decide to "do" for them cannot make up for the fact that he never invested his time just being with them. Thus, as he enters the last stage of a long life, Mr. Ortiz is doubly disconnected: from the world of work, which consumed most of his life, and from the world of his progeny, which consumed too little of it.

There is a rather different ending to the story of today's grandmother. Like her own mother, she was the prime, usually the sole, nurturer of the young, unlike today's grandfather, therefore, she usually lived her life through and for others in her family. Although she herself was anchored emotionally in her own mother, she raised her children to be more autonomous. She did this partly to fulfill her own suppressed yearning for greater autonomy and partly in response to the demands of a rapidly changing society. That society required that children measure up, get educated, and be emotionally independent as well as intellectually prepared to meet the demands of a national job market. It was today's grandmother who accepted her husband's absence from the home, justified it to her children, and prepared them to disconnect from the family.

But now that the children have left, she feels the lack of vital connections more deeply than her husband, just as she felt more keenly than he the instinct to nurture when her grandchildren were born. More than the grandfathers we spoke to, the grandmothers were able to articulate the separation and loss that most grandparents feel. Among them is Mrs. Rutledge, whose words and images expressed the pain of disconnection with almost oracular power:

> Never did I think that I would live this long and have nothing to do—never! I didn't retire, I've been replaced. Television entertains the kids better than me. My grandson would rather imitate the Six-Million-Dollar Man than copy his grandfather. French fries and hamburgers are hard to compete with. Even my home-baked cookies come out second best to ones that are store bought. And what can I tell my grandchildren that they don't already know? My grandparents knew everything. There is no place for me.

Mrs. Rutledge thought for long moments, searching her mind for apt images of her feelings. Then she said:

> I'm not a philosopher but I'll try to explain my feelings. I feel like I'm in a nowhere, one of those black holes in space. You see, all of my life I knew what to do, more or less. Now, I don't know. I'm at the end of my life and I'm more unsure of myself than ever before. More confused about a future I never thought I would have.
>
> It's like you are sitting in a theater and the movie is over and you are supposed to leave and it's night outside the theater and you don't know where to go. It's like waking up from a dream and being disoriented. I don't know what to do with the rest of my life. No one ever told me.

In these few words and images, Mrs. Rutledge spoke not only for herself but, in our judgment, for most of the grandparents we visited. In summary, she said that today's grandparents feel:

1. Powerless. Compared to her own grandparents, who "knew everything" and did much, she feels unable to tell her grandchildren anything that they do not already know or to "do" anything with them.

2. Role-less. When she and her husband retired from work they found that there was nothing for them to do and no one to do anything for. They are merely titular grandparents with no real role or function.

3. Disconnected. Now that her own parents are dead and her children no longer need her, she feels like she is living in a "nowhere." She feels an emptiness inside where her children once were. She feels like a "black hole" of spent energy and light . . . and life.

4. Superannuated. She never expected to live so long or be so healthy at her age. But these benefits are of no use to her. She is physically alive but in terms of vital connections she no longer exists. The "movie" of her life is over but she is still sitting in the audience. It is dark outside the theater and there is no one out there waiting for her. She has no "place" to go.

5. Disoriented. All her life she knew what to do. She had a job to do and she did it. She did what her mother told her to do, what the "experts" told her to do, what her children wanted her to do. She was so busy for so long, so immersed in her "work" at home and on the job that she never gave thought to what life would be like once her work was over. She feels like she has just awakened from a dream to unfamiliar reality.

6. Replaced. Not only have Mrs. Rutledge and her husband been retired from the world of work, they have been

replaced as grandparents. Not by parents, which is emotionally impossible, but by a phalanx of impersonal institutions, services, and "personnel" which have emerged in the
wake of the new social contract to fill the vacuum left by
grandparents. Mrs. Rutledge cited a few of these replacements; here we will add briefly to her list:

The Functions of Grandparents	*Institutionalized Replacements*
(Based on the children's study)	
FEEDERS (Sunday dinner at Grand-mother's house)	Restaurants; fast-food outlets; junk food
CARETAKERS	Baby sitters; day-care centers; schools; medical professionals; jail; television
NEGOTIATORS BETWEEN CHILD AND PARENTS	Child's peer group; family and per-sonal therapists; experts on child-rearing
MENTORS	School teachers; television; peers; rock stars and other celebrities merchandized by the entrepre-neurs of the youth culture; cults
ROLE MODELS	Media stereotypes of elders; nobody
CONNECTIONS WITH THE PAST	Television; movies; family albums; parental memories
CONNECTIONS WITH THE FUTURE	Television; movies; science fiction; other sources of fantasy
REALISTIC EXAMPLES OF OLD PEO-PLE AS INDIVIDUALS	Media stereotypes

No doubt the reader can extend the number of entries
on both lists. Our point is that the functions of grandparents have not disappeared. In the absence of grandparents, these functions have been taken over by surrogates
which have no personal, lasting, or emotional commitment
to children. These surrogates are either "dead" (media im-

ages), temporary (teachers, peers, therapists), or exploi-
tative (rock stars, merchandized celebrities)—and often all
three at once. No doubt many of these surrogates would
exist even if grandparents had not abdicated their roles.
But their intrusion into the lives of children—and their
families—would not be as powerful or as pervasive if grandparents were physically and functionally present for their
grandchildren. But the grandparents are not there. And
their absence has served to hasten the trend, already well
established, in which, as one psychologist approvingly puts
it, "the relationships of each individual to the larger society
are more important than his or her relationship to the
family."[8]

C. Places Where Grandparents Used to Be

To say that today's grandparents have been replaced
does not mean simply that their functions have been
usurped. It also means that they are no longer "in place" in
the ways that grandparents used to be. We owe this insight
to Mrs. Rutledge, whom we interviewed when our field
work was already more than half completed. Our conversation with her was one of those serendipitous encounters
that can occur when the source of historical data is, as in
emotional history, stories people tell. Mrs. Rutledge's profound sense of being out of place, of being in a "nowhere"
with no place to go, moved us to ask subsequent grandparents where they remembered being with their own
grandmothers and grandfathers, how time passed in those
places and what they learned and felt. We had already seen
in the projective drawings how children who are close to
their grandparents typically locate them in a particular
place doing something of emotional significance to the

children. (By contrast, children who are not close to their grandparents, it will be recalled, tend to draw figures floating on an empty page.) In much the same fashion, we found, grandparents easily recall particular places where emotional attachments between them and their own grandparents were cemented.

For today's grandmothers, the most prominent of these "feeling places" was the kitchen. From there, their grandmother ruled over her domain as Great Nurturer, preparing meals, "setting table" and summoning the "gathering of the clan." Often, all these activities took place in the same room and grandmother's presence filled every corner. A grandmother in her sixties recalled how her own grandmother's kitchen felt to her as a child:

> There was a big wood stove against the wall and a big round table in the middle of the room. That was the center of the house. We did everything on that table. Grandma would always have something cooking or baking in the kitchen and the odors were wonderful. I can smell them even now as I talk of her.

In feeling places, we discovered, grandparents and grandchildren shared unmeasured time together. From the stories we heard, grandparents did not always focus their attention on their grandchildren. It wasn't necessary. Instead, they incorporated the child into their world, a world which was similar to yet very different from a mother's world. In this way, grandchildren learned new ways to "be" as well as new things to "do" through emotional attachment—and without being graded for effort or results. A grandmother, eighty-two, conjured up those timeless moments with her grandmother, more than three-quarters of a century ago:

> In the kitchen, being next to my grandmother and just quietly watching her, I learned how to cook and sew, table

manners and how to serve a dinner and so much more . . .
Most of all, how to be gracious and patient. At least I try to
be. It's a shame that kids nowadays have to go to a home economics course to learn all that, and to take tests. I learned all
that and I wasn't even aware that I was learning. And I never
forgot what I learned.

Another grandmother, Mrs. Eppley, described how it
felt to be a "student" in her grandmother's kitchen even
when she was allowed no more involvement than that of
admiring observer:

> I remember just sitting in the corner on a tall wooden stool,
> like the ones naughty kids used to have to sit on when they
> were being punished. I would just sit there and watch my
> grandmother in that kitchen. I don't know how much I
> learned like that. But when I grew up, I found that I could do
> the same things without thinking about them. I never really
> learned them—things like cooking, mixing spices, serving table.
> I finally realized that all the while I was sitting there, watch-
> ing her, I was tucking away all that learning. Just watching.
> And how time would fly. Nary a word would pass . . . Some-
> times she would ask me to taste something, or smile at me, or
> shoo me away if I got a little rambunctious. Grandma was a
> very quiet person, but whenever she finished something she
> would stand back, let out a big sigh and look over at me. I al-
> ways felt that we did it together.

If the kitchen was the emotional "learning center" in
grandmother's house, larders were sensuous sanctuaries
where children could dawdle indefinitely, as in a library,
amid the multiscented treasures of jams and jellies, herbs
and spices, smoked meats and other foodstuffs "put up" by
grandmother. For Mrs. Grenier, seventy-three, her grandmother's larder remains a place unmatched in its magic by
any other place she has visited as an adult:

> The room was small but as a child it was like a big depart-
> ment store to me. The smells were unbelievable. My sense of

smell became alive in there. Most of all I remember the smell of the oilcloth she used to line the shelves in her larder. I used to cover my school books with it. I would touch the different spices—there were so many of them. I would sit in the middle of the larder on a small stool and Grandma would come in when she wasn't busy and show me what was there. We would taste things together and she would tell me what each spice was used for and we would cook or bake something with it. Time stood still there.

From the stories we heard, it appears that grandfather's main impact on his grandchildren occurred outside the home as a guide on fishing expeditions, walks through the woods or visits to the store. When he was home, which was seldom, his special "feeling place" was usually a basement workroom or tinker's shop, well away from the center of the house where grandmother held sway. Within his own environment, grandfather was the presiding magician, making broken things whole, crafting toys, or sharing his way with tools. Partly because he knew things that others in his grandchildren's world did not, and partly because grandmother was usually the rule-maker in his own home, grandfather functioned as a kind of elderly co-conspirator, legitimating the grandchildren's urge to rebel by involving them in his own. Mr. Gaffney recalled his grandfather's workshop:

I always knew where my grandfather would be if he was at home. He would be down in the basement of our two-family house making something in his workshop. In fact, he had a bottle stashed away in his toolbox—my grandmother used to get furious at him if he drank. Anyway, he would let me taste his whiskey. I hated it, of course, but I can remember the smell of freshly sawn wood, the harsh smell of alcohol, even the smell of his large wooden toolbox. I can smell those same smells. All I have to do is close my eyes. I can see him in his overalls, a big, fat carpenter's red pencil in the top pocket. He's cautioning me: "Shhh . . . don't tell Grandma," as he reaches for another nip.

For very different reasons, porches were also major feeling places—"inside-outsides"—one person we interviewed called them. They were places grandparents went to be neighborly, to see and be seen, places where the paper could be read in the evening with one eye on what the children were doing in the street, and the other viewing the comings and goings of the neighbors. During one of our visits to a typically porchless modern home, a mother tried to evoke for her children what life was like on her grandparents' porch:

> It's too bad they don't make them anymore. When I was a young girl I lived right down the street from my grandmother who had a porch all around the house. It was glassed-in on the sides and open in the back and front, where it faced the street. Grandma had a box of toys for me on the porch. Since I lived so close I could wander over to Grandma's whenever I wanted. I would look in the box right away; my grandfather would often put a new toy in the box for me or leave a note for me. And I would answer him, all very secret of course.
>
> Many of the neighborhood children would play on her porch and many's the fight I had to keep them out of my toy box. Her porch was a kind of day-care center for the neighborhood. While I was there my grandparents would sit on the porch and chat or visit with the neighbors, or just sit quietly watching the people coming and going. After dinner, most of the people on the street would sit outside and talk back and forth to each other across the street.
>
> My grandparents were the watchdogs of the neighborhood. Nothing escaped their scrutiny. My sister used to complain about it all the time, especially when she wanted to be alone with her boyfriend. She said that she was living in a fishbowl. That didn't bother me because it was O.K. to live in a fishbowl for a youngster and besides, I enjoyed the attention. I had nothing I wanted to get away with.

Porches were also places where elders who had nothing else to "do" could go and simply "be." It was, nonetheless, their base of operations within a larger neighborhood or town community. A middle-aged father told his children what the porch meant to his elderly grandfather with whom he lived as a boy:

> Grandfather was ageless. We all used to bet how old he really was but we never found out. He was the wise man of the neighborhood. "King of the Front Porch" we used to call him. In the morning my father put him out on the front porch before he left for work and put him back to bed at night. That was Grandpa's life except for a break now and then to do the necessaries.
>
> But Grandpa knew everyone and everything that was going on. He held court from nine to five every day. He made a living betting on the horses. People used to come from all over to ask him about horses and he used to bet on them and take bets. The sheriff tried to catch him. He knew what Grandpa was doing, of course, but what could the sheriff do if he did catch him? Grandpa would have been too much trouble for the sheriff to take care of.

Another father, who had been raised on a farm in Idaho, recalled how his grandfather served the community without ever leaving the family porch:

> He was about ninety years old and had eight children, six of whom survived. Well, all of my life I remember Grandfather sitting on the front porch in an old rocker with a brass bell on the floor in front of him so he could get some help if he needed it. He would sit there and rock back and forth and talk about the weather and the crops. He could predict the kinds of winters we would have. People would ask him and then the folks in town would say "Well, Grandpa Jim said it will be a bad winter"—and that was it.
>
> Grandpa Jim was sort of the town meteorologist. He used to scrape little lines in the battleship-gray paint on the porch. A long line for a good day and a short line for a bad day. Peo-

ple would know how he was feeling by looking at the lines in the paint. But aside from scratching the porch floor, spitting into the spittoon when he was chawin' tobacco and peeing off the porch once in a while when someone didn't respond fast enough to his bell, Grandpa Jim was no trouble to anyone.

Today, most elders of Grandpa Jim's age are either in institutions for the "Aged" or living in "efficiency" apartments by themselves. Modern homes do not have places like porches where Grandpa Jim can still be part of the world and the family too. Porches, if they are built at all, have become mere appendages on the backs of houses, out of sight of the street. Workrooms can still be found, sometimes expensively equipped, but basements are giving way to "crawlspaces." Larders have already disappeared; supermarkets and home freezers have made them superfluous and even grandmothers have ceased "putting up" preserves. Kitchens are all efficiency: they are not places to spend unmeasured moments in unless one is "into" cooking; home economics is now taught as a form of business management, not as a craft.

Attics are among the last places where grandchildren can still encounter their grandparents, if only through their effects. To children, attics are mysterious places, time warps, where they can encounter their family predecessors through the clothes they wore, the toys they played with, the books they read, the furniture they used. "An attic is a place where memories are stored," is the way one boy we visited put it. Marguerite, twelve, told us proudly that she is the only one among her friends whose grandmother still has an attic:

> My grandmother lives in a big old house in Boston. Whenever I visit her I make a beeline for her attic. What a place! It's so weird, like being in ancient Egypt. Old paintings and pictures hanging there and old toys from long ago. Grandma

used to be a flapper and she has funny clothes that she used to wear, like an old satin coat that hangs down over my rear end and behind my knees when I put it on. I always put it on when I go into the attic—it's my "adventure coat." When I was younger I thought the attic was so scary and mysterious and I thought that spirits were there. That was when I was younger, of course.

Marguerite's grandmother told us that she keeps the attic messy on purpose:

> The children love my attic. My grandchildren who live near me came home from school the other day and told me that they were the only kids left in their class who had a grandma with an attic. Isn't that a shame? I let the neighbor kids go up there, too—an adventure, they call it. An attic is a wonderful place for children. I loved my grandmother's attic so. I spent a lot of time there playing with the same toys that my grandchildren play with, some of the toys my grandmother played with. True, they're a bit tired but the children are fascinated by them. I did just like my grandchildren do now, come down from the attic all grimy, and my mother would get annoyed at my being dirty just like their mother does now. And I take the Fifth Amendment just like my grandmother used to do. I'm giving the children some of my stuff, bit by bit, so when they grow older they can have an attic for their children—that is, if they ever make attics again. My children tell me to get rid of all the "junk." That's what they call it. To me it is not junk. It's all part of my family and the grandchildren have a right to it. It's part of them, too.

The contents of grandmother's attic hold great meaning for her because her parents and grandparents were emotionally important people in her life. Similarly, these heirlooms have meaning to her grandchildren—if not her children—because she is an emotionally significant part of their lives. Without such vital connections, however, heirlooms are merely junk, dumb artifacts that cannot evoke the

memories by which possessions are transformed into heirlooms.

From the perspective of the new social contract, heirlooms are always junk—valuable, perhaps, as antiques but
emotionally of no significance. This is the lesson we
learned from Mrs. Carson, a seventy-two-year-old grandmother descended from an old New England family. Until
she retired and moved to the Southwest, Mrs. Carson
maintained a large country home where she had ample
room to store heirlooms that had been in her family for
several generations. When we interviewed Mrs. Carson
during a rare visit back East, she was deeply upset. She had
just discovered that her son had sold a framed portrait of
herself which she had given him as part of her legacy. This
event triggered in Mrs. Carson a series of emotional reflections not unlike those of Mrs. Rutledge:

> It's like I'm there but I'm not really there. Like being dead
> but still alive. I can't express what I felt exactly, but I feel
> that I'm in the way. In the way of what, I haven't the faintest
> idea. Antiques gain more in value with age. They become
> more unique . . . not me. I grow older and get more and
> more worthless. When I decided to retire and move away I
> gave my kids most of the stuff that I've accumulated over the
> years, even some of the furniture that my mother had given
> me. Do you know what they did with it? Sold it! Can you be-
> lieve it? They sold the good stuff to antique dealers and then
> sold the rest of it at tag sales they held whenever they moved,
> which was very often. I feel like I've been sold at a tag sale.
> My son says he has to travel light because of his job. Can
> you imagine? My things, given to my kids, sitting on someone
> else's shelf somewhere, my memories sold down the drain for a
> little bit of money! The young people today don't seem to
> have any feeling for these things. Only my granddaughters
> seemed happy to have trinkets I gave them. They say that
> they were Grandma's but if they imitate their parents, they'll
> probably sell them as soon as they need the money. I guess

sentimental is a word that is out of style now, but it is a beautiful word to me. When I was a child I used to love to say it over and over—sen-ti-men-tal. On the other hand, if I were a real antique the kids would probably sell *me*.

Like Mr. Johnson, the institutionalized grandfather who had no one to tell his stories to, Mrs. Carson has no one who will cherish her heirlooms. Her son, a rootless corporate nomad, has no place for them in his own life so they end up on someone's shelf. With each tag sale, her children erase another memory of her and her forebears. Not only has Mrs. Carson been retired and replaced, she has been removed, piece-meal, from home and hearts of her own flesh and blood. She differs from most grandparents we visited only in the fact that she is witnessing her own emotional internment. She feels "dead but still alive," a ghost returned from retirement to find that her presence is only "in the way" of the process of extinguishing her memory.

Mrs. Carson has seen the future and there is nothing of her in it. The reason is that she has severed her vital connections. As far as her grandchildren are concerned, she is already a ghost out of the past who will again disappear from their own time, their own place. Had Mrs. Carson maintained her old home, her grandchildren would at least know where to find her. They would have a place to be with her and perhaps, in the end, come to cherish the things she has saved for them. But Mrs. Carson, like most grandparents, is a victim of the new social contract, just as her grandchildren are. And just as her own children are likely to be when they become grandparents themselves.

D. Grandparents as Oracles: Emotional Effects of
Social Changes

We predicated our children's study on the assumption that every child is an oracle who, because he lives in an emotional "Now," can reveal what is really "going on" in his world if we consult him properly. In an analogous way, grandparents can be oracles, too. By recovering the child within them, as we have just seen, grandparents are able to enter an emotional continuum and reveal the emotional effects of the changes that have occurred in their lives. From what they told us we derived the outlines of an emotional history, focusing on changes in the process of receiving and giving nurture. These changes, as we saw, led to the loss of vital connections and the concomitant emergence of the new social contract. But these two "events" did not occur in a vacuum. Like everything else in human experience, emotional attachments require social supports. Thus today's grandparents are in a unique position to reveal the emotional effects of social and cultural changes affecting the family that occurred within their own lifetime. *What they have to say may serve as a warning, perhaps even as a corrective to those who will someday be grandparents too.*

In the first place, many of today's grandparents have experienced a reversal in the material and emotional dimensions of their lives. In childhood, they told us, their families were either poor or living in fear of poverty. But the children themselves were emotionally affluent because of the attention and concern they received from a variety of adults within an intragenerational family network. All had at least one grandparent, whom they especially cherished. Today, most of them told us, they are materially more secure than they had expected to be at their age and some were obviously very comfortable indeed. All but a handful, however, were ignorant of their importance as grandparents. They were also emotionally detached from their children and grandchildren. As a consequence of this detachment they felt emotionally unfulfilled. It appears, therefore, that what they gained in material security they lost in emotional satisfaction.

Secondly, the grandparents we visited revealed how they themselves had cooperated in diminishing or losing their own vital connections. In their efforts to put their own families on a more secure financial footing, the men invested most of their time and energy at work, often at great distances from home. Frequently, what vital connections they did develop were with colleagues on the job. The women complied with this division of labor; they became the essential, often the sole, nurturer of their children. But they did so with specific, socially sanctioned goals in view. Their children were to be as emotionally independent of them as they were dependent upon their own mothers. With the help of outside experts and institutions, their children were fashioned to be fit competitors for a national job market. Although emotional independence is not necessary for economic independence the two were indistinguishable in the minds of today's grandparents because of their childhood experiences. Their children responded to the way they were nurtured by leaving home and establishing families that were, as expected, both emotionally and economically autonomous to a degree that American families had never been before. Once established on their own, the children sealed the new social contract.

Most grandparents we visited were not aware of what

they had done. "Times have changed," they said, and even those who now regret what happened do not think that they could have done otherwise. They were bewildered rather than sorry about the way their lives had turned out. As a group, we found them proud of the self-sufficiency they enjoy in old age and concerned lest some financial or physical adversity force them to become dependent upon their children. At the same time, however, many of them lament the loss in later life of a family circle to be in.

This emotional paradox, which is well known to gerontologists, has deep roots in American family experience. Most modern historians of the family insist that the American family has been "nuclear" in structure for at least two centuries and that the aged have always preferred to maintain households separate from their children. According to this analysis, industrialization and urbanization only intensified a cultural preference for self-sufficiency which is as old as the Republic itself. But the maintenance of independent households does not—and for most of American history did not—preclude vital connections between grandparents and grandchildren. The loss of those connections, therefore, is related to changes in familial patterns and intergenerational relationships which occurred within the lifetime of today's grandparents and to which they are uniquely qualified witnesses.[9]

From what today's grandparents told us of their early years, the economic survival of the family depended upon mutual support between the generations. It did not matter whether three generations lived under the same roof—usually, they did not—or that there was acrimony between grandparents and parents, which certainly existed. What mattered is that some members of the same family (grandparents, aunts, uncles, cousins) lived near each other, were available to each other, and could depend upon each other's support in the face of economic insecurity. These "instrumental relationships" required, among other things, that children go to work early to help support the family and that grandparents take an active role in the rearing of children. In other words, these adverse economic conditions were ideal for the development of vital connections between grandparents and grandchildren. Their lives converged in the critical dimensions of time and place; survival alone demanded commitment to the intrafamily network as a community of kin. The insecurities of the job market encouraged altruistic behavior among young and old alike. Thus the emotional paradox manifested by today's grandparents rests upon a sociological paradox: in order to maintain their self-sufficiency as a family, members had to expand the family circle to include supportive kin.[10]

In their efforts to demonstrate the nuclear character of the family over the past two hundred years, social historians have tended to overlook the pervasiveness of intrafamily networks and to underestimate their emotional significance. Or so it seems to us. Even when historians do take note of grandparent-grandchild relationships, they tend to stress their economic purposes. In this respect, what today's grandparents have to tell us about the emotional benefits of growing up in a three-generational family milieu serves as a corrective to contemporary views of family history. Even as children, today's grandparents were not unaware of the "instrumental relationships" that existed between the adults around them. They knew the meaning of mother's "family pot" upon which everyone's survival depended. But what they remember—and what remains inside them to this day—is the way they felt simply because those grandparents were *there*.

In sum, the emotional history of today's grandparents follows a line from convergence to divergence of vital connections. Today's grandparents are the last generation of American children to grow up in the intimate company of grandmothers and grandfathers. They are also the generation which effected the withdrawal of grandparents from the intrafamily network, via the new social contract. In retrospect, we can see what these grandparents could not: namely, that their withdrawal coalesced with long-term changes in family functions. The direction of these changes has been toward shifting many of the responsibilities formerly under the control of the family—among them caretaking, education, medical care, food production, emotional counselling, recreation and even, of late, reproduction itself—onto outside institutions, agencies, and experts. As a result, each generation is now segregated in its own dimensions of time and place. More and more, the commitment of each generation is focused narcissistically on the needs of its own age group, thus giving the peer group increasingly greater authority. And more and more, each generation looks outside the family for support. These are the rippling effects of the new social contract.

The lesson one might draw from all this is that once elders cease to fulfill an economic function—in society or in the family—they cease to have any value at all. Much as this conclusion chafes at humanistic sensibilities, it is, in fact, the practical conclusion of all those social scientists, policy-makers and prophets who assign no role to grandparents in the future. Our own conclusion is precisely the opposite. In the past, children derived enormous emotional benefits from the presence of grandparents who were compelled by economic circumstances to be intimately involved with the grandchildren. As our children's study demonstrates, grandchildren continue to attach great emotional significance to grandparents, even though the vital connections between them no longer receive support from the family or from society. Emotionally, grandparents are important to grandchildren simply because they exist. Many grandparents came to feel this, too, once they were able to get in touch with the child within them. Yet the majority were unable to act on those feelings. The reason, we believe, is due less to the disappearance of economic functions than to the lack of an ethos which values emotions and emotional attachments.

E. Making Room for Emotions: The Ethos of Work vs. the Ethos of Being

In the process of telling their life stories, the grandparents we visited literally moved from one world to another, a passage which Mrs. Rutledge aptly compared to the experience of "waking up from a dream." That dream world is familiar to all of us. It is a world governed by an "ethos of work" in which the main purpose of life is production. As we have already learned, today's grandparents went to work very early in life and even when they became parents they approached child-rearing as if it were a "job." In a world where the ethos of work is all-pervasive, the worker "knows what to do and does it." It is a world in which reality itself is determined by work. The power that work possesses to determine one's sense of reality was well described by Freud in *Civilization and Its Discontents:* "No other technique for the conduct of life attaches the individual so firmly to reality as laying emphasis on work; for his work at least gives him a secure place in a portion of reality, in the human condition."[11]

But long before we even develop the capacity for work, we are already attached "to the human condition" by our vital connections. As we observed earlier (page 63), the initial human attachment is the primordial bond between mother and child. From the very beginning of life, the baby's experience of "reality" is, at the same time, an experience of its mother. Not only is the child nurtured and protected by the mother's body, even the emotional climate of the baby's world is conditioned by the mother's own emotional states. After birth, this bonding process expands and is replicated, in analogous fashion, in the child's emotional relationships with its father and other family intimates. At this time, life is lived according to an emotional priority. In this way, the child develops emotional dependency and trust, the attachments to reality which are fundamental to its subsequent social-psychological development.

The point, however, is that vital connections are formed not only *prior* to attachments developed through work, they also belong to a totally different order of reality. By work, we mean any activity which can be measured by standards of purpose, productivity, and achievement. This includes not only labor done on a job but also a child's effort to walk or to control its bowel movements. In the latter case, for example, a child who tries to eliminate body waste according to a schedule of toilet-training established by child-rearing experts and demanded by parents, is literally at work. The emotional satisfaction the child derives from producing on schedule has nothing to do with the pleasure of elimination, but it has everything to do with the emotional approbation he receives from the superintending parent. In other words, the child's achievement can be measured according to a performance schedule, but his pleasure is derived from emotions generated by his vital connections. "I can't measure feelings," said Jean Piaget, the eminent Swiss psychologist who spent a lifetime studying how young children think. "I can only experience them."[12] Just so. The irony is that the cognitive development of children cannot "progress" without emotional attachments, which are beyond measurement.

Whatever escapes measurement escapes the world of work. Concepts such as purpose, performance, production, and progress which make sense in a work ethos make no sense when applied to emotional attachments. Spouses, for example, can "work" at their marriage because marriage is a contractual relationship which imposes reciprocal obligations on the marriage partners. But it makes no sense to say that spouses must work at love, which is the substance of their emotional attachment. On the contrary, once spouses condition their love upon performance, they limit the emotional attachment between them. Hence the inappropriateness of phrases like "to make love," which is unintelligible other than as an euphemism for sexual "performance."

Emotional attachments, therefore, transcend the ethos of work. They are intelligible only within an "ethos of being," which governs a different range of human experiences. Chief among these are affective experiences such as love and caring; intellectual experiences such as creative intuition and philosophic insight; esthetic experiences and religious experiences such as contemplative prayer and mystical rapture. However much these experiences may differ one from the other they all share at least one common characteristic: they are gifts. They can only be given or received, not achieved. Moreover, each depends upon attachments to reality which transcend the purposeful world of work.[13]

Of all the people in a child's world, it is the grandparent who is best able to offer a pure and simple, unselfish emotional attachment. The same pressures which edge the elderly out of the work force serve to emancipate them from the tyrannies of measurement, production, and achievement which burden parents. Grandparents and grandchildren are natural allies, not only against the middle generation but against a world dominated by an ethos of work. The young child has yet to experience that world; the grandparent has already experienced its limits and survived. Both, therefore, can transcend its boundaries of time and place. To grandchildren, grandparents are familiar figures from an unfamiliar world. To grandparents, grandchildren are unfamiliar figures in an all too familiar world. Their natural mode of discourse is stories. Reciprocally, they suggest that the way the world really is is other than the way it seems according to the ethos of work. Disconnected, their voices are discordant. Connected, they are in tune with the world.

F. Parents: Bearing the Burdens of the New Social Contract

In a divergent society every generation suffers. When we began our field work, we sought out only grandchildren and grandparents. We did this because we sensed that this was the missing vital connection. But on most visits with children our interviews took us into homes where parents were the only adults present. Occasionally a mother or father, or sometimes both, were drawn into our conversations. Although what we learned from them goes beyond the formal scope of our present study, their involvement cannot be ignored. They too must be considered in any extended examination of vital family connections.

Look again at Billy's triangular drawing (frontispiece). Not only do the child and his parents rest on a foundation of four grandparents, the grandparents also serve as a buffer between the conjugal family and the society outside. At the same time, the grandparents provide a cushion for the conjugal family. Without the support of grandparents, parents must bear the brunt of child-rearing responsibilities as well as a disproportionate burden of society's workload. Unlike their own grandparents, they cannot rely on a community of kin to absorb family pressures, provide multiple adult role-models and diffuse social stress. They are on their own. They must nurture their children through periods of childhood and adolescence that are now more protracted than ever before. As the price of their children's admission to the higher reaches of social achievement, parents must finance an expanded and increasingly expensive period of formal education. Just to make ends meet, in the ways a consumer society insist that they must, more and more wives are joining their husbands in the workplace. As a result, millions of American children have little intimate contact with *any* adult. Moreover, as work claims more of the hours of both parents, spouses find less and less time just to "be"—together or by themselves. Love cannot thrive in an ethos of work. Little wonder, then, that so many marriages crack under the strain. Little wonder, too, that a new form of intrafamily network has arisen, based on divorce and remarriage, which mirrors and mimics the old community of kin.

Toward the end of our field work, a nine-year-old boy came to us. Roger is the eldest of six children and he was seeking treatment for abdominal pains that, as it happened, were psychosomatic in origin and quickly responded to treatment. On a deeper level, Roger, by nature a very sensitive youngster, was sounding the emotional alarm for his family, as children sometimes do. He "felt" something was wrong. He didn't know what it was. We asked Roger to draw a picture of his grandparents. The figures were small and expressionless. Roger explained that he did not know them very well and has difficulty understanding them when they talk. He said he didn't like their food, although his father is "crazy for it." Roger doesn't see his (paternal) grandparents very often. "Mostly, my father flies down alone to Miami to see them a couple times a year," Roger told us. "We're very different from them, my father says. He seems worried about that."

Roger's father, it turns out, is a successful neurosurgeon, the son of immigrant Cuban parents. While he was still a college student in the Midwest, he changed his surname from Casallo to Casey because, he said, other students taunted him about his accent and he wanted a name that sounded more "American." Now, at the age of forty, Dr. Casey regrets this impetuous decision but respects the fact that he went through a period in his life when he wanted to break away from his parents and submerge his ethnic identity. Nonetheless, he has a "Latin's" outgoing and emotional temperament. Mrs. Casey, by contrast, is a reserved New Englander. In many ways, they complement each other nicely. They both realize that they represent something to each other beyond personal compatibility. She is an "American" wife to him; to her, he is a man who can display warmth and affection—something she never received from her emotionally low-key family.

After a few visits with Roger it was apparent that the problems he felt encompassed three generations within the family. Dr. Casey became restless, then visibly upset when asked to talk about his own parents, and Roger's concern that he was "worried" about them. At our suggestion, Dr. Casey invited his parents to spend Christmas with the family up North, thus enabling us to visit with them as well. At first the Casallos balked. Both had emigrated to the United States as children and their lives remain enmeshed with the families who emigrated with them. The Casallos still speak Spanish to each other, are proud of their "ethnicity" and of their son's success. But they feel out of place in his world, upset that he has foresaken his name and heritage, hurt that his children—their grandchildren—are totally divorced from their own life and ways.

Mr. Casallo, an expansive, emotional man, told us how he spends many hours with his daughter's children, who live close to their home in Miami. His son's children, however, are uneasy in his presence. They are ashamed to have friends in when their Cuban grandparents visit, which isn't often. To Mr. Casallo, his son's children are sullen strangers:

> They are different from me. I don't know them. They don't understand Spanish, they don't enjoy the same things that I do. I have no chance to get pleasure from them. They have grown up without me. They are lost to me—it's like they are someone else's children.

Mrs. Casallo's eyes welled with tears when we asked her about her grandchildren. But her tears were for her son as well:

> We're so far apart, so different. Never would I have allowed my son to go away to school if I knew that I would lose him. My grandchildren now, too. I would never have his wife as my daughter . . . The old ways may be no good now, too old-fashioned for some. But what good is life now without half of my family near me? Thank God for my daughter and my other grandchildren. If I didn't have them, I . . . there would be no point to living now. Their children—that's what it is all for. Am I wrong? No, I don't care what anyone says, I know I'm not wrong.

The Casallos know how it feels to lose a son via the new social contract, though the phrase is foreign to their thinking. As children, they were taught that the United States is a land of opportunity and they raised their intellectually gifted son to take advantage of those opportunities. They worked hard to pay for his education. But they never dreamed that when he left them for college at the age of seventeen that he would return with a different surname. They expected him to practice medicine in Miami, within the Cuban community, and crown their efforts with his glory. They did not envision a daughter-in-law so utterly unlike themselves; in her presence they feel self-conscious about their language, their religion, and their food. Worse, they feel like "foreigners" to their own grandchildren. Their pain of disconnection is particularly acute because the Casallos' deepest values are rooted in a culture that prizes close family bonds. Had she to do it over again, Mrs. Casallo would not have sent her son away to school. His personal success, she feels, has been purchased by the loss of half her family.

Because their son's disconnection occurred so early and was so dramatic, the Casallos do not know how he and his wife feel about their isolation from a larger family circle. They recognize how much their son feels "at home" when he comes alone to visit them. But they do not realize the conflict he experiences migrating between his family of origin and his own family. Nor do they suspect that his "American" wife also feels burdened by detachment, not only from her own parents, but from her busy husband as well. After some hesitation, Mrs. Casey described her own feelings as an isolated dutiful mother:

> No one on God's green earth was made to care for six kids alone. Now I know why young mothers are leaving home . . . I even went back to school for one semester but that was ridiculous. The kids went crazy without me. Roger almost got an ulcer. The housekeeper was useless and the kids wouldn't listen to her. And besides, I don't like other people raising my

children . . . My husband resented me going to school. He said his mother never did that. I asked him why he is so far from his mother, if she is so wonderful and such a good cook. Things just get worse . . . the situation is ridiculous. My husband is never around. With work and meetings, the kids never see him.

Although Mrs. Casey lives less than a day's drive from her own parents, she has never called on them to help her out. Her parents have never encouraged intrafamily intimacy, she said, nor has she tried to maintain more than formal connections with them. In her own way, she too has tried to repudiate her family roots:

> I wanted to get away from them when I was married. Now, I don't know if that was such a good idea. The kids are all stuck here together. There's no one else to look to when there is an emergency, no one else to help. I can't even get sick. My husband has to take a day off of work and he resents that . . . I even resent him when he is sick—another baby to care for.

Mrs. Casey was surprised by her own rush of feelings, almost embarrassed to complain. She has been well educated, her husband is a professional of high status, and their family is affluent. But she also feels emotionally isolated and overburdened:

> It can't be as bad as all this. I'm amazed at what I am saying. I know that friends can't fill the gap, it's not the same as family. But I feel I can't go back to my family. I know that we need each other but . . . we're too separated now, too involved in our own lives, too disconnected.

The pressures Dr. Casey feels in his own family have made him rethink the value of his independence and the emotional price that he, his wife, and their children are paying for his own youthful decision to sever his vital connections:

> Two parents aren't enough family to raise six kids. My wife

and I are running away from this awesome responsibility—and the kids are suffering for it. I never thought about this when I was younger. I wish I had it to do all over again. I'm ashamed to say it now, but when I was younger I was so different from my classmates and I wanted so much to assimilate into the American way of life that I threw away many important things. I feel it now, even when my kids came along I didn't want to live near my parents. I wanted my kids to be *Americans*, to speak English. Now the eight of us are isolated. Alone. Too close, too interdependent. It's not a natural situation.

At the age of forty, Dr. Casey sees himself at the fulcrum of his family's disconnection. He acknowledges the suffering his separation has caused his parents and would like to weld the generations together. But he also recognizes that his children do not care for his parents and their "un-American" ways. He is at an emotional impasse:

As I get older, I feel a deep need for my parents and for the people I knew when I was younger. Maybe we all go through this. Thomas Wolfe said, "You can't go home again," but I'm beginning to have other thoughts about that. Even if I wanted to move to Miami to be with my family it wouldn't be right. My kids' world is *here*. They are so different from the people I was raised with . . . Education, language, food, religion, different people.

Dr. Casey wonders if his present emotional dilemma might have been averted:

I only wish that my parents had fought me more when I was younger. But then, I was so much better educated, so much more "with it," so much more American—and so young. What could they do? They didn't know either. They were helpless . . . It's as if we were all swept along by some force. We couldn't help doing what we did.

Dr. Casey feels the same force operating within his own family. His youthful disconnection, he senses, is being repeated by his children, even while they are still at home.

Now I feel myself separated from my kids, like they are also being swept along a course from which there is no deviation. I feel it most when they are watching television. I see them sitting there, enjoying it, and I want to be close to them, to talk and kid with them. But they aren't too interested in me now and that is what hurts. I still have fun with the little ones, but the older they grow the farther they get from me. Something is wrong, something over which I have no control. It's almost that I don't want to be independent anymore, that I want to get back the connections to my family and my children that I cut one time in my life. But there is no way back.

Like his parents, Dr. Casey is an emigré in a new land. Until age seventeen, he existed only in his parents' world, sharing their language, food, religion, friends, community. He was what he received by virtue of being his parents' child. He shed that world, symbolically, when he changed his name, but he did not become psychologically or financially independent until he became *Dr.* Casey. His life is now determined by an ethos of work; he is what he *does*, and what he does defines his connections—or lack of them —to his own family as well as to the Casallos. He has established an independent household that is equally disconnected from both his parents' family circle and that of his wife's parents. The Casallos are not "American" enough to accept the loss of "half a family." They grieve for their departed son and despair of ever becoming intimate with his children, their grandchildren.

Mrs. Casey was raised in New England by parents who expected that she would someday move away from them, though they did not imagine that she would marry into a family that is so "different." Mrs. Casey accepts the new social contract as given. Nonetheless, she feels terribly isolated within her family. She is sensitive enough to recognize that housekeepers and day-care centers are no substitute for a mother. And she is wife enough to want to "be" with her husband more often. But he is seldom home and as sole nurturer of six children she feels overwhelmed by the emotional as well as physical demands put upon her.

Dr. Casey senses that there is something "not natural" about his family's autonomous existence. At the age of forty he finds that he no longer values the independence he has achieved, yet he sees no way to re-establish close connections with his parents. As a compromise, he migrates several times a year from his new world with its emphasis on work, to his parents' home, where the emphasis is on feeling and emotional attachments. He eats his mother's food, which he misses, speaks his father's language, which he has not forgotten, and otherwise revels in an identity anchored in the ethos of being, where his life assumes an emotional priority.

Dr. Casey fears that the same "force" which swept him away from his parents is separating his children from him. When he fails to draw their attention away from the television set he gets a premonition that he is unimportant in the eyes of his children and is already being replaced. "The older they grow," he observes sadly, "the farther they get from me." Indeed, the same "force" which made his own parents titular grandparents is transforming Dr. Casey into a titular parent.

In conclusion, let us imagine that we are listening to the life stories told fifty years hence by the Casey children as grandparents. What emotional history will their lives inscribe? What grandparental figures will they summon forth as constant objects? Perhaps they'll remember a childhood paradise based on material rather than emotional abundance. Will they recall their mother as a solitary source of vital connections? What stories out of the past will they want to pass on? What treasured heirlooms? What places, apart from the television room, will they recall as time-warps where moments went unmeasured? Who was *there* when their parents weren't? With whom did they share their secrets? What image of old age will they have to guide them? Where will they spend their later years? With whom? Who will care?

4

An Agenda for Grandparents

A. Grandparents and the Aged

As part of a documentary on the decade ahead, a crew from a television station recently interviewed a friend of ours, still in her forties, who has raised six children, written or contributed to many books, has been a syndicated newspaper columnist, and now teaches social psychology to graduate students. She was asked to assess the future of the family in the decade ahead and to describe her personal aspirations. "I hope to become a grandmother," she said. That was the only one of her observations that did *not* appear in the subsequent television program.

There seems to be a conspiracy of silence concerning grandparenthood, one that is all the more noticeable in light of the widespread public concern about "being old" in America. Despite the much discussed "youth revolt" of the sixties and the subsequent discovery of midlife and its "predictable crises" in the seventies, the real revolution in American society has occurred among the old. The population as a whole is aging dramatically. When the first U.S. census was taken, in 1790, half of the population was under seventeen. Since 1970, the median age of Americans has risen from just under twenty-eight to just over thirty, and will reach thirty-five by the end of the century. The fastest growing segment of the population are those Americans seventy years of age and older. But the most powerful new age group in the United States may well be those men and women between the ages of fifty-five and seventy—the "Young-Old," as sociologist Bernice Neugarten has labeled them.[1] Healthier, more affluent, and better educated than any group of elders before them, the young-old "can be expected to develop a wide variety of new needs and will want a wide range of opportunities both for self-enhancement and for community participation."

The aged are also better organized than any other age segment of American society, although they have yet to coalesce into a single political bloc. In his comprehensive survey of the aged in America, "Why Survive?" Dr. Robert Butler lists 240 private and government agencies that have programs for the aged.[2] Significantly, perhaps, the nation's political leadership was unable to deliver on President Carter's pledge to hold a White House Conference on Children in 1980, but a similar conference on aging will be held this year—the third in as many decades. What do the aged want? Their social and economic goals are easily summarized: elimination of "Ageism" or discrimination against the old because of their age; expanded services and reduced costs for health care, nutrition, insurance, transportation, housing, and better police protection; and above all, an end to mandatory retirement and greater opportunities for part- as well as full-time work. Indeed, if there is a growth industry in the United States, it lies in those fields that cater to the aged. Already, a new corps of experts has emerged—physicians, psychologists, psychiatrists, nutritionists, physical therapists, sexologists, management consultants, economists, sociologists, historians, retirement planners, housing developers—who have made the problem of aging and the problems of the aged their specialty.

But the real experts on the aged are children. Only children understand what elders are *for*, and only they can meet the real need of the aged: the need to be needed. Children need grandparents and grandparents need children, whether they are their own flesh and blood kin or surrogate grandchildren. And until these mutual needs are acknowledged and supported, the aged will never achieve more than begrudging respect, much less outright affection, as elders in American society.

Throughout this study, we have referred to the oracular nature of the message children have for grandparents. Essentially, they have reminded us of the organic relationships that bind the young and the old to each other—and of the suffering that occurs when those bonds are severed or ignored. They have taught us the primacy of emotional attachments over instrumental relationships between human beings, especially among members of the same family. These attachments are as old as the human species and therefore more natural than the titular ties which now exist between most grandparents and grandchildren. In other words, the complete emotional well-being of children requires that they have a direct, not merely a derived link with their grandparents. That link is what we have called vital connections.

The willful and institutionalized segregation of grand-parents from grandchildren is a recent phenomenon within industrialized societies. It is manifest by the new social contract which, in turn, is supported by the values and mechanisms of an increasingly divergent society. In such a society, we have argued, each generation is progressively segregated from the other. Nor are we the first to make this observation. The late Margaret Mead repeatedly drew attention to the emotional superiority of age-inclusive primitive societies and tirelessly championed the development of age-inclusive communities in the United States. In *Two Worlds of Children*, a masterful study of child-rearing practices in the United States and the Soviet Union, Cornell University sociologist Urie Bronfenbrenner warned:

> . . . the phenomenon of segregation by age and its consequences for human behavior and development pose problems of the greatest magnitude for the Western world in general and for American society in particular. . . . we cannot escape the conclusion that if the current trend persists, if the institutions in our society continue to remove parents, other adults, and older children from the active participation in the lives of the children, and if the resulting vacuum is filled by the age-segregated peer group, *we can anticipate increased alienation, indifference, antagonism, and violence on the part of the younger generation in all segments of our society—middle-class children as well as the disadvantaged.*[3]

The trend persists, the vacuum expands, and as Bronfenbrenner has subsequently observed, "in terms of broken homes, working mothers, and child abuse, the middle-class family of today is approaching the level of social disorganization that characterized the low-income family of the early 1960's."[4] Indeed, while poverty continues to assault low-income families, forces of a more complex kind are eroding middle-class family life, forces which emphasize self-fulfillment at the expense of vital family connections. As sociologist Alice Rossi has noted:

> A remarkable shift has occurred during the past decade in society's opinion of the family, from a general endorsement of it as a worthwhile and stable institution, to a general censure of it as an oppressive and bankrupt one whose demise is both imminent and welcome. What was once defined a decade ago as "deviant" is today labeled "variant," in order to suggest that there is a healthy, experimental quality to current social explorations into the future "beyond monogamy," or "beyond the nuclear family." Today one is more apt to read that the nuclear family will oppress its members unless couples swap spouses and swing, and young adults are urged to rear their children communally, or to reject marriage and parenthood altogether.[5]

Behind this shift toward derision of the family, Rossi discerns an "egalitarian ideology that denies any innate sex differences and . . . urges several progammatic changes in family organization: a reduction of maternal investment in children to permit greater psychic investment in work outside the family, an increased investment by men in their fathering roles, and the supplementation of parental care by institutional care."[6] In sum, what Bronfenbrenner, Rossi and other scholars see is the development of a divergent family that replicates the division of a divergent society.

Is it too much to suppose that today's grandparents have a stake in what is happening to the family? From a reading of several agenda for the aged, it appears that it is. Nowhere among the goals outlined by various organizations representing the aged is the role of grandparents given importance. It's as if the bond between grandparents and grandchildren no longer existed. On the contrary, it appears that today's grandparents—in their collective identity as the "Aged"—threaten to intensify age segregation by "raising" the consciousness of one age group instead of expanding the consciousness of all generations toward greater mutuality. What some representatives of America's aged are demanding is simply more of what they once had in middle age: more jobs, more consumer products, more services. Such a limited range of goals, based as it is on competition, is merely an extension of materialistic values inculcated by an ethos of work. In themselves they cannot engender respect, love, and intimacy—values which are governed by an ethos of being. To address the problems of the aged according to an ethos of being, however, presupposes that the aged are not isolated individuals but men and women who are vitally connected to the young.

In the course of our field work we met a handful of extraordinary grandparents who placed an emotional priority on their lives, ignored the new social contract, and refused to be segregated from their children or grandchildren. Mrs. Mason, a widow, maintains her own apartment, keeps busy in the community, and holds a part-time job. Yet her primary role is grandmother to Deborah and her other grandchildren and emotional support to their families. As a result, she has a rich and full life. She is fully engaged in the present rather than living in the past, as many of the aged do. She has wisdom born of emotional insight which no amount of technological change, no "knowledge explosion" can replace. Her self-esteem is based on her mastery of the maintenance of vital connections. The later stages of her life have turned out to be as full and rewarding as those which preceded them—just as she expected them to be from experiencing her own grandmother nearly three-quarters of a century before. The O'Flahertys went a step further by becoming elders to an entire neighborhood. Without social sanction or a franchise from experts, they turned their own home into a community resource where any child could come and simply "be" with them.

Elders like Mrs. Mason and the O'Flahertys are truly heroic figures. By asserting themselves as Great Parents they challenge a system of age relations which patronizes the aged and conspicuously denies any real value to the grandparent-grandchild relationship. This system, in effect, issues name tags to men and women when they become grandparents, affirming their titular roles in the lives of their grandchildren. Most grandparents accept this token recognition because they are either unwilling or unable to establish vital connections. They feel powerless vis à vis their children and redundant in the face of institutions which have replaced them as grandparents.

Society, however, cannot change what a grandparent means to a grandchild. Our interviews with children lead to this unassailable conclusion. Any grandparent who cares can subvert the institutions which have replaced them in their grandchildren's lives. They can become conscientious objectors to a pattern of family relations which invites manipulation by outside authority and encourages the dependence of children upon strangers. They can resume their place as the foundation of the conjugal family and thereby diminish—perhaps even halt—the quickening pace of family disruption. To do so, however, they must understand the import grandparents can have on the lives of children.

B. Roles of Grandparents

In their conversations with us, children touched on numerous roles close grandparents play. These roles have survived the effects of the new social contract because they are based on biological and psychological realities which transcend particular social arrangements. From what the chil-

dren told us, the following roles of grandparents seem especially significant:

Historian: Children accept the world as they find it.
They know no other time or place. Grandparents, however,
are living ancestors who can liberate children from the
tyrannies of the present. A child with a close grandparent
as a guide has immediate access to "other voices, other
rooms." The child who comes to experience the world
through attachment to a loving grandparent sees reality in
a third dimension. In passing over to the perspective of a
grandparent, a child dilates time, transcends space, and
dwells in the wonder between the way things are and the
way things once were. Children love to hear stories of "the
olden days," demanding to hear them over and over again.
In this way, a grandparent's stories become part of the
child's own life story.

Grandparents are oral historians, a role that places them
in an ancient tradition that includes medieval troubadors,
Greek poets, and the tribal elders of more "primitive" societies. Today's grandparents, however, have experienced
more changes than any of these celebrated precursors; they
are living authorities on how life was before television,
superhighways, and packaged food existed; before the airplane, telephone, and the "horseless carriage" were in-
vented. To little children, especially, grandparents appear
to have existed at the very founding of the world.

The grandparent is also a family historian, bringing to
life relatives long dead or so distant that they exist for the
child only through the grandparent's words and images.
Above all, grandparents are the official biographers of the
children's parents. They confirm that parents once were
children too, that they were fully capable of inflicting joy
and anguish on their own parents. As family archivists,
grandparents are guardians of the family heritage. The con-

tents of attics, photo albums, and heirlooms are all part of the family archivists' "equipment." In the hands of children, these artifacts become tangible evidence of their unique family connections, their roots. To have roots is to know where you came from and therefore who you are. It is to know that you can be "at home" in other places, that scattered about—sometimes even in other countries—are family you have never met but who care about you, rather like grandparents do, just because you are you.

Family historians needn't be chauvinistic but they do need to be colorful. Most children would rather hear about an uncle who robbed banks than one who owned one. Children love to tell other children about their ancestors. In this way, family history provides children with a "we" to talk about as well as an "I." In this respect, the need for a family history and an authoritative family historian increases to the degree that children have fewer siblings. Family history, therefore, solidifies a child's sense of belonging.

In their capacity as living historians, grandparents transmit ethnic heritage. Culturally, all Americans are hyphenated—American in a particular ethnic way that makes them different from other Americans. This rich cultural diversity could not survive without families (and neighborhoods) in which the old tell stories to the young and manifest in their own lives just how differently people of diverse ethnic backgrounds feel, nurture, respond to pleasure and pain, cook, "get things done" and celebrate holidays. Thus grandparents not only preserve family history, they re-enact it in rituals which thrust the past into the present and reaffirm the particularity of those who are responsible for the family's future. That most of those rituals end up around a table, with the grandparents presiding, is not accidental. Such rituals of family communion have been going on ever since mankind can remember.

Grandparents also transmit religious faith and values. Grandchildren tend to see grandparents as "closer to God" because of their age. In many of the families we visited, the grandparents were the ones who took the children to church or temple. Although research indicates that the religious behavior of children is affected most by their parents' beliefs and behavior, grandparents who take religious commitment seriously put a break on parental indifference to questions of ultimate concern. Finally, grandparents provide a direct link to those ancestors who are dead. At the core of the city of man, Lewis Mumford has suggested, is the city of the dead—burial grounds.[7] And what is true of cities is true of families as well. Cemeteries are not only final "resting places" for ancestors, they are also important "feeling places" where bonds between the generations can still be honored with appropriate emotion. Indeed, we would argue that the gradual disappearance of family plots —and, what is worse, of any burial place at all, as when bodies are cremated and the ashes scattered—is yet another sign that divergent societies do not respect vital human connections.

Mentor: Children spend most of their lives in schools, doing school "work," taking tests given by experts, and being promoted from one "grade" (segregated age level) to the next. Among the array of teachers who pass in and out of their lives, however, children occasionally find a mentor who takes them under his wing, imbues them with his own love for his subject, shares advanced forms of his knowledge with them and, tacitly at least, fires his pupil with the ambition to imitate and perhaps even surpass the master.

In every full-time grandparent, every child has his own mentor. Unusually, children are not interested in *what* the

grandparent is doing. They are absorbed into the grandparent's world by a kind of emotional osmosis and *then*
learning takes place. Emotional attachment, therefore, is
the fixative which makes the grandparent's lesson stick forever in the child's mind. That's why in later years adults
usually cannot distinguish what they learned from their
grandparents from the experience of *being with* their
grandparents.

Grandparents teach out of the wisdom they have accu-
mulated through a lifetime of experience. Since this wisdom is personal rather than abstract, practical rather than
theoretical, it is never outmoded. A grandparent's curricu-
lum is limited only by the child's capacity to understand
and by the grandparent's interests. In the main, grandparents teach children ways of working with the basic materials of life: food, clothing, shelter, and transportation,
plus how to deal with the world outside the home. At their
mentor's knee, children learn how to cook this, mend that,
build this, put that in good working order. Since mentors
are usually of the same sex, the skills grandchildren learn
are normally sex-typed. These skills, such as baking and
building, are part of the lore of each sex. By making that
lore their own, children "become" women or men. Thus
grandmothers and grandfathers deepen the children's sexual identity and intensify their security in that identity.
The more secure that sexual identity becomes, the easier it
is in later life for men and women to cross culturally
defined sexual boundaries and do the work of the opposite
sex.

Most of today's grandparents were raised in an era when
"store-bought" was regarded as inferior to "home-made."
Here again, grandparents counter the passiveness of contemporary consumerism by emphasizing the virtues of well-
made things and the rewards of making things well. There

is an identifiable consciousness that accompanies any craft, whether it be the specialized practice of medicine, law or letters, or the "humbler" arts of cooking, carpentry or landscaping. This craft consciousness transcends mere technique or "tricks of the trade"; *it involves an emotional attachment to the work to be accomplished.* The closer the craftsman is to his materials and tools, the more his consciousness is shaped by the habits of mind they require.[8] These habits, as forms of consciousness, are what children "catch" rather than "learn" because when the grandparent is the mentor, the child is literally at play. In other words, grandparents teach in an ethos of being, where learning is play, while school personnel teach in an ethos of work, where learning is almost always work.

In a divergent society, where even parenting has become a specialized job, grandparents who have freed themselves from the ethos of work are true humanists. Grandparents are the only adults who have the time, commitment and playfulness to be full-time mentors to the young. In them, children find that work, play, love, and learning are fused into a single experience.

Role Model: Today's grandchildren can be grandparents for nearly half of their lives. The kind of grandparents they will be will depend upon the images of grandparents they carry inside of them. These images can come from three sources: a living grandparent, their parents' attitude toward their own parents (second-hand grandparents), or stereotypes created by the media. A living grandparent, therefore, is the only person in the world who can provide a real model of grandparenthood for children.

The image a child has of his grandparents does not change with age. Unlike parents, who change in the eyes of their children as each generation ages, grandparents are always "old" to a grandchild. They are old at forty no less than at sixty and unless their health fails they are no older at seventy or eighty. Although the relationship between grandchild and grandparent undergoes change with time, the grandparent as a constant object remains fixed forever in the child's mind.

The grandparent also serves as a role model for aging. The stronger the vital connection between grandparent and grandchild, the more immune the child becomes to socially induced stereotypes of the aged. Obviously, the more positive that connection is, the more positive will be the child's reactions to "old people." Conversely, a negative experience of grandparents encourages dislike and sometimes even violence toward the aged.

As a role model, grandparents are living examples of what the grandchildren expect to become. Once again, that example can be positive or negative, with corresponding effects on the child's future self-image as a grandparent. But a detached grandparent affords a grandchild no image at all of what his future self will be like. In the absence of vital connections, therefore, the child is vulnerable to false, prejudiced and condescending images of grandparents.

Grandchildren also notice grandparental attitudes toward the family and how grandparents continue to nurture their own children. If the parent-child relationship has survived the new social contract, the example of reciprocal love between the first and second generations has a profound influence on the image the child has of grandparenthood. Having preceded their parents in life, grandparents are also seen as being closer to death. How they adjust to the inevitable limitations of old age, and finally to death itself, powerfully influences the grandchild's sense of the last stages of life. Despite what some grandparents and parents feel about shielding the young from dying elders, those (above the age of five) who have enjoyed long vital connections to their grandparents often resent parental interference when it comes to saying good-bye to their beloved grandparents.

A special form of role modeling occurs when a child feels that he or she is a grandparent's "favorite grandchild." Frequently, this most favored status accrues automatically to the eldest child in each family. In other cases, the favored child is apt to be one who bears a strong physical or temperamental likeness to a grandparent. The more others call attention to these "chips off the old block," the more the child is likely to feel like and act like the grandparental model. More important, favorite grandchildren usually know by the grandparent's behavior that they have somehow been "chosen" and bask in their special status. Emotionally, this special status acts like a blessing which, in an almost biblical sense, solidifies the chosen child's sense of self-worth throughout life.

Powerful grandparents can also function as elders of the "tribe," embodying the attitudes, moral ideals, talents, and behavior of the family. In this role, the grandparents bequeath to every grandchild a family name which anchors them in a lineage and identifies them with the family's successes and failures.

Wizard: This is a grandparent's most undervalued role—by other adults. Grandparents enliven the child's world as an imaginative counterpoint to the purposeful world of parents and teachers. The latter are role-bound not to be arbitrary in their judgments or capricious in their behavior. Grandparents are free to be both. They are free to tell stories about their children's parents which playfully undermine—without necessarily destroying—parental authority. Indeed, they are delightfully free to burlesque all the powers that be because—like children—they are regarded as powerless by society.

To children, however, grandparents wear a mantle of magic. Like Don Juan, the mysterious Yaqui sorcerer celebrated in the books of Carlos Castaneda, grandparents can assume different forms because they have already been children, teenagers, and parents. At any moment, a grandparent can become one of these again. Similarly, most grandparents have been to far off places; on the tongue of a gifted storyteller, a grandchild can fly away too, with a grandparent. "Generation gaps" are really generational differences, not separations, and grandparents are more exciting for having lived in other times and places.

Because grandparents have lived a long time, they have learned to expect the unexpected. This knowledge often can inspire grandparents to stoke a child's imagination. A six-year-old revealed a secret he shares with his grandfather: "He is Santa Claus. Every year he makes himself small so he can fit down chimneys."

Being old is in itself a source of amazement to children. One child told us how she loves to sit on her grandfather's lap and stroke his wrinkles. She wondered how they got there. "Every wrinkle has a story," he said. Another youngster, age six, told us that his grandmother is magic when she knits a sweater from a ball of yarn. "My mother knits, too," he said, "but when Grandma does it, it seems to come out of her stomach." Even so stern a rationalist as philosopher Jean-Paul Sartre could marvel at his grandfather because the old man "magically" could recite what was written in any of the books in his library.

The role of grandparents as wizards can be found in every culture. Among the Tupian tribe of South America, the grandfather is a culture hero, associated with thunder. Every grandmother among the Yurok Indians has her own song, which she sings when someone is sick to drive the evil spirits away. In Western culture, the grandmother as wizard is disguised as the fairy godmother who watches over children and makes miracles happen. For grandfathers, the Wizard of Oz is almost an archetype. He is at once a fake—he has no "real" power as the world understands that term—yet he makes the seemingly impossible happen: he is a grandfather figure who knows the secrets of the heart and rewards those who dare believe that dreams really can come true.

Of course, parents and school teachers sometimes appear magical too. But their power as wizards is severely cramped by the press of practicality. Play is not their natural milieu; besides, their schedules do not allow much time for it. But grandparents and grandchildren, like artists and clowns, are attuned to a different ethos. Removed from the serious side of life, they laugh and joke together. And in those precious moments they lift the lid off the obvious and celebrate life's mysterious and mystical dimensions.

Nurturer: This is the most basic role grandparents play. It is also the role which society has most nearly succeeded in replacing with institutions. Children intuitively understand that nature has supplied them with two parents and four grandparents. When grandparents are not around, two adults are required to provide all of their children's nurturing needs, often without respite or support for themselves. This makes for an emotionally imploded family. With the rise of the new social contract, parents routinely rely on strangers for help in nurturing their children. Today, young grandchildren are likely to spend much more time in day-care centers, with baby sitters, alone in front of the television set or roaming unsupervised with peers than in the company of their grandparents. Only when a major family crisis occurs, it seems, are grandparents summoned to perform their traditional nurturing roles. The more detached grandparents have become, the less they are called upon for help and the less willing they are to respond.

When grandparents are functioning as Great Parents, they look after the physical and emotional needs of the grandchildren much as they did with their own children. They widen the womb of the family and increase geometrically the grandchild's life support system. Among other things, they are nurses and feeders, fixers and providers, caretakers and playmates. Love and safety, which a child normally expects from parents, is experienced as love in an incredible abundance when received from grandparents. Somehow, a grandparent's time and attention are regarded by a child as pure gifts, given without obligation—a boon.

When illness occurs, a close and living grandparent is the best family doctor a child and his parents can have. Grandparents come by their bedside manner naturally. As family counselors, grandparents can draw upon a large backlog of experience in receiving and giving nurture. When children are not getting along with their parents, a vitally connected grandparent is a natural negotiator who has the time and the place to listen, and the good of both sides at heart. At those times when children need advice but feel that they cannot go to their parents, grandparents are more knowledgeable and reliable confidants than the children's peers.

In sum, grandparents are the primary caretakers of grandchildren when the parents are absent, and the chief adjuncts to parents at all times. This is what it means to be a Great Parent, which is how children regard their grandparents. But this nurturing role readily disappears when grandparents allow themselves to be replaced by institutions. The Great Parent then becomes a mere totem figure —a titular grandparent to be ritually acknowledged and emotionally endured.

It must be emphasized that the roles grandparents play are not the same as developmental "life stages," nor do they appear according to a timetable in grandparent-grandchild relationships, as some researchers have suggested. On the contrary, the only fundamental variable, as we have repeatedly insisted, is the depth of the emotional attachment between grandparent and grandchild. The earlier in the life of the child that attachment is acknowledged and cemented, and the more time devoted to the growth of vital connections, the stronger are the bases upon which the grandparent-grandchild bond rests. On the other hand, the roles played by grandparents are not static. They shift and change as the child and the grandparent grow and change. At one point in their relationship, one role or set of roles predominate; later, one or more of these roles may recede as others become more pronounced. The point is, they are always there as long as the grandparent is there as a vital presence in the life of the grandchild.

For example, the grandparents' nurturing role predominates in the child's early years. The child experiences this care directly when the grandparental caretaker feeds, clothes, cuddles, and plays with him, and indirectly through the respite from child care and other emotional and financial support grandparents give to the parents. As might be expected, this nurturing role wanes in importance as the grandchild and his family become more self-sufficient. When adversity arises, however, as when the child becomes seriously ill or when parents have a serious falling out, the grandparents' caretaking role may be reactivated on a temporary or even permanent basis. The roles of wizard, mentor, and role model emerge when children are old enough to hear stories, imitate the grandparents' behavior and observe how grandparents interact with parents and society. The role of family historian is especially significant to children about the age of seven, when they become exceedingly curious about their family roots, and again during adolescence, when the search for identity causes them to reflect on the ways in which they are different from their peers.

How grandparents fulfill these roles depends upon a variety of personal factors: their health, financial means, emotional history and individual life goals, to mention only the most obvious. Today's grandparents, however, have options which their own grandparents never entertained. They can choose, for a variety of reasons, not to be grandparents at all; that is, they can accept the terms of the new social contract, as many have done, and elect to stay physically and emotionally removed from their grandchildren. They can also take advantage of the range of choices open to them by an increasingly age-irrelevant society. In such a society, says Bernice Neugarten, the expected ages at which people fill traditional social roles become scrambled. Thus, she observes: "Our society is becoming increasingly accustomed to the 28-year-old mayor, the 30-year-old college president, the 35-year-old grandmother, the 50-year-old retiree, the 65-year-old father of a pre-schooler, and the 70-year-old student, and even the 85-year-old mother caring for her 65-year-old son."[9] Under these evolving social circumstances, it is easy for grandparents to become confused over their emotional priorities. And if they are still healthy, attractive, leisure-oriented women and men in their forties and fifties, it is even easier to reject outmoded social stereotypes of rocker-bound grandmothers and grandfathers.

C. Assessing Yourself

Everyone who is a grandparent, or expects to become one, now faces these options. These choices seldom arise as clear alternatives; more often, they are experienced as "forces" which pull the individual this way, then that. Usually, what is most needed is unavailable—a structured opportunity to sort things out, assess priorities, get the feel of where one's emotional attachments really lie. On the following pages we have reproduced the questionnaire we used in talking with grandparents. We invite you to use it as a point of departure for your own self-assessment, to recall your own experiences as a child, a parent, and a grandparent. Use it to evaluate your current family relationships and to see how your own life story fits in—or diverges from —the emotional history we outlined in the last chapter. Talk it over with your spouse if you are married. Ask your grandchildren about their feelings. In any event, your personal response will be invaluable in addressing what we believe to be the agenda for the grandparents of today and tomorrow.

Do you reside:

  With your children?
  Within walking distance?
  Within daily driving distance?
  More than 100 miles from them?
  More than 1,000 miles from your children?

PERSONAL

Do you enjoy good health?
Do you feel "old"?
Do you find yourself thinking "old"?
Do others refer to you as an "old" person because of your
  appearance?
Do you allow people to treat you as if you are not there or
  do not count?
Do other people listen to what you have to say?

Do you make yourself heard when you disagree with
people?

Are you intimidated by the young, do you back off from
contact with them?

Are you intimidated by those with more education or
"book learning"?

Are you intimidated by those who are better off financially?

Do you feel free to use and express the wisdom and experience that you have learned by virtue of your age alone?

Do you have influence within your family?

Do you feel that your children "owe" you? If yes, what?

Do you feel that society "owes" you? If yes, what?

Do you "owe" your children? If yes, what?

Have you shared some of the skills that you have learned
along the course of your life with young people?

GRANDPARENTING:

Did you have a good relationship with your grandparents?

Did you have a good relationship with your parents?

Did you have a good relationship with your children?

Do you have a good relationship with your grandchildren?

How often do you see your grandchildren?

Does your relationship with your children affect your relationship with your grandchildren?

Do you have direct communication with your grandchildren when you wish to contact them?

Is your relationship with your grandchildren different from
your relationship with your children? If yes, in what
way?

Do you take your grandchildren alone on outings?

Do you know the ages of your grandchildren?

Do you know the favorite foods of your grandchildren?

Do you know your grandchildren's friends?

Do you celebrate your grandchildren's birthdays with them?

Do you celebrate holidays with them?

Do you feel that you are important to your grandchildren?

Do you feel that your grandchildren are an important part of your life?

Do your grandchildren need you? If yes, for what?

Do you feel that your grandchildren are part of you since they carry your blood in their veins?

Do you need your grandchildren?

Are you involved in the daily lives of your grandchildren?

Do you do "foster grandparenting" for other people's grandchildren?

Have you left your grandchildren to retire in another geographical location? If you have, was it a wise decision from an emotional and grandparenting point of view?

Would you do it over again if you had a choice?

Would you advise your children to do the same?

Do your children feel that you have abandoned them?

Do you feel that your children have abandoned you?

Do you feel that your children care for you?

Are you glad that you had children?

Would you do it over again if you had a choice?

Have you relinquished your role as head of the family to a younger person in the family?

Are you involved in decision making in your family?

Do friends and family seek out your advice?

Is your relationship with your own children different than your relationship with your grandchildren? How?

SOCIAL:

Do you participate in the life of the community or neighborhood in which you live?

Are you involved in any programs that offer help to the emotionally deprived children in day-care centers, orphanages, divorced families, etc.?

Do you use your emotional expertise?

Do you count in your community?

Do people in your community welcome your participation?

Do you have friends of different ages?

Do you live in an environment that is segregated by age?

Are you involved in any organizations that are concerned with child care?

Are you involved in any national organizations that deal with the problems of the older generations of our citizens?

Do you feel that the public's attitude is changing toward older people and their families?

Do you feel that you have achieved a stage in life where your personal experience, emotional maturity and factual knowledge have earned you the respect of others and above all, self-respect? Are you satisfied that you have been accorded a place as "elder" in the community in which you live?

Do you feel that you are an effective grandparent?

If you had it to do all over again what would you do differently, as a grandparent and as an elder?

What suggestions do you have to offer to people who would like to have a better relationship with their grandchildren?

Does the concept of ancestors have any meaning to you?

What have you learned from your grandparents? What legacy have they left you (material or otherwise)?

What legacy will you leave to your grandchildren?

What meaning does life hold for you at this time?

How would you like your grandchildren to remember you?

Using the same questionnaire, we found in our interviews that grandparents who had close bonds with their grandchildren shared the following characteristics:

—— They placed an emotional priority on their lives.

—— They valued their families highly and were committed to the well-being of each of its members.

—— They spent a great deal of time involved in the family, were available to the family, and family members knew where to find them. Even more, family members knew that they would respond if asked.

—— They appeared "by nature" to be altruistic people, highly sensitive to the feelings of others.

—— Relatively immune to social trends, they acted upon their intuition and feelings and had a strong sense that their actions were "right." This sense of "doing right" often placed them in conflict with the opinions of friends and made them skeptical of outside "experts."

—— They steadfastly defended the young.

—— They related well to people of all ages, even those who were "trendy."

—— As a group, they were generative people. They were active and made things happen within a circle of friends as well as within the family. People in the wider community knew them and spoke about them.

—— Although these people espoused "traditional" values, we found that they were able to relate to different types of people; in fact, people sought them out.

In a modest sense, they were "famous" in the world in which they traveled.

But, as we reported in Chapter 1, only fifteen of the 300 grandparents we visited could be described in this fashion—and, we suspect, it fits only a minority of our readers as well. The majority acknowledged upon reflection that they see their grandchildren intermittently and that their status as grandparent is more symbolic than real. They were, at best, part-time grandparents. Many regretted that they hadn't done more for their families and with their grandchildren. Some resolved to change their lives. Others felt helpless to do anything. Their children had moved away or they had retired to a home at a great distance from their children. A few, as we saw, shrugged their shoulders, insisting that detachment is the way "life goes." A few were adamantly opposed to doing anything at all.

Paradoxically, perhaps, the most difficult thing for disconnected grandparents to admit is that their grandchildren really need them. The second most difficult thing to imagine is that they can do anything to strengthen family relationships. Our own research, however, convinces us that both attitudes are wrong. To begin with, the new social contract tends to obscure a number of facts about grandchild-grandparent relationships which exist independent of any society's system of age relations. Secondly, the same forces which pry the generations apart in a divergent society actually intensify the attraction felt between grandparents and grandchildren. Thus grandparents who want to regain their vital connections have the following factors working in their favor:

1. Young children are naturally in awe of the old. At the same time they have the unique capacity to delight the old.

2. Both the young and the old inhabit the far margins of the ethos of work in so far as each is outside the productive mainstream of society and its attendant stresses. This means that they have more time to "be" and that what they do and mean to each other escapes the tyranny of measurement. Parents must "produce" and so must limit the time and attention they can give to children. Children, in turn, must produce and measure up to parental ex-

pectations. Significantly, as we have noted, neuroses are passed on to consecutive generations but not to alternate generations. This means that grandparent-grandchild relationships are notably free of emotional conflict. Thus the basis for the oft-heard parental lament: "I wish my mother had treated *me* the way she treats my children."

3. Similarly, attachments between grandparents and grandchildren circumvent the intense emotional environment of the isolated nuclear family. Normally, it is a "treat" for young children to visit a beloved grandparent and vice versa.

4. Grandparents are voices out of other times. So long as they do not remain locked in the past, they can assume considerable authority as critics of the present. They know, in their bones, that just because something is happening *now* does not make it right.

5. The old and the young are fascinated by one another. A grandmother can sit on a park bench for hours, transfixed, watching her grandchild at play. The child, aware of grandmother's undivided attention delights in performing for an audience of one. A grandchild, perched on a bathroom hamper, observing his grandfather preparing for bed, is at once mesmerized and astounded when grandfather removes his false teeth and places them in a water glass. Grandfather knows that he has just performed a minor miracle in the eyes of his grandchild.

6. Grandparents and grandchildren enter easily together into a world of fantasy and wonder. Grandparents are usually more tolerant than parents of the imaginative play of children: indeed, they often delight in it. Most children have imaginary playmates whom they hide from the adult world but feel free to introduce to close grandparents. Thus, grandparents give tacit permission for unique and imaginative expression by the child. Often this dimension

of the child's personality finds no encouragement in the "real" world.

7. There is a pronounced need for grandfathers as male figures in the lives of today's children. Most grandchildren are raised by women and, with more mothers working, by strangers. Note, for example, that there is a national organization of "Big Brothers," but no similar organization of "Big Sisters." Grandfathers are particularly well positioned therefore, to redress the pervasive lack of male influence in the lives of children.

D. Grandparents as the Foundation of the Family

The main function of today's grandparents is to rebuild the family pyramid. Look again at the pyramid Billy drew (frontispiece). The grandparents in Billy's pictures are not brittle, aging figures supported by the family. They are the very pillars on which the conjugal family rests. Every role grandparents perform derives from their function as the family foundation. Before grandparents can implement this function they must come to feel like strong family pillars. They have to recognize that they are essential to a sturdy family regardless of how unnecessary, redundant, or impotent society may make the aged feel. They have to see as well as feel that emotional attachments are deeper and stronger than the instrumental relationships defined by what people "do" for each other.

Billy's pryamid represents, better than any number of words can, how every child experiences the family as an emotional support system that nurtures every member. The pyramid is held together by the mortar of vital connections and rests upon the foundation of the grandparents. It makes visible the biological fact that one generation

emerges telescopically out of another. It shows that grandparents are the family's common denominators: in them,
each member of the family adheres to the other and is
rooted in a past which is uniquely his own. By superim-
posing the members of your own family on the pyramid
you can create for yourself a mental image of your own
family.

With this image firmly in mind, it is easy to see how
grandparents provide a cushion or buffer between the conjugal family and outside institutions. Imagine now that one
of the parents falls ill or dies. Grandparents are the next
echelon of support and, by the logic of the pyramid structure, they should move in to fill the gap. Would that happen in your family? Imagine now that both parents are removed from beneath the child, through death or divorce.
Would you be there to replace them, or at least to provide
emotional continuity and stability for your own grandchildren?

Unfortunately, the chances that a tragedy of this sort
will happen within your family are frighteningly high.
Every year, one million American children under the age of
eighteen suffer the divorce of their parents. Last year, there
were twelve million such children in the United States.
When the premature deaths of parents are included, esti-
mates are that forty-five percent of American children born
in any given year will live with only one parent before age
eighteen. Although there are some experts who argue that
divorce is easier on children than unhappily married parents, this is, we believe, a naive and insupportable position.
The overwhelming facts are that children of divorce experience rejection and abandonment, to which they react with
feelings of anger, fear, guilt, insecurity, and resentment.
They tend to devalue adults and mistrust the institution of
marriage itself. Far more than children of intact marriages,

children of divorce are more likely to become divorced themselves. Yet a recent study supports what the logic of the pyramid dictates; that mother-grandmother families are nearly as effective as normal mother-father families in sustaining the psychological well-being and social adaptability of children.[10]

The ability of grandparents to relieve marital stress has, we believe, been lost amid stereotypes of interfering in-laws. Among the children we visited was Russell, twelve, who is convinced that, "If my grandmother were alive today, I'd still have a family." Russell's parents divorced shortly after his grandmother died:

> She was different with me than my parents. She was tougher with them. In fact, I'm sure that they wouldn't be divorced if she were alive today. She just made things better for everybody. She would stay with us when my parents would take vacations and they would be happy and get along better after their vacations. Grandma would calm everyone down.
>
> She took care of me when I was young and my mother worked. My Grandma used to tell her that her place was home with me and that we didn't need the money, which is what my mother would say. Grandma was old-fashioned. Another time, my mother was complaining to her about my father and my Grandma said "Bullshit, Susan, you are just not trying hard enough." My mother got mad but the next day she kissed my grandmother and told her that she was right in what she said. My parents got along well for a time after that. I guess that my mother just didn't like to be home with us all of the time, she said it was boring. When my grandmother died she couldn't stand it anymore.

All too frequently, when parents divorce, the grandparents divorce their grandchildren. It jibes with the new social contract. Victor, eleven, lost his mother when she decided to move West to "be free," as he put it. Since his mother's departure, Victor has not had contact with his

maternal grandmother. She is his only living grandparent
and before his mother left Victor saw her often. He spent
every summer at his grandmother's house, a period which
he described as "the happiest time of the year." We visited
him in the late spring and up to that point he had heard
nothing from his grandmother:

> Grandma hasn't called since Mom left. Haven't heard from
> her at all. She used to call every Friday night. It's been four
> months and seventeen days since my mother left. You see,
> since my mother is so closely related to my grandmother it's
> possible that she doesn't love me anymore because my mother
> left. She may even hate me because I'm related to my father.
> I'm afraid to call her because I don't want to find out that
> maybe she has broken off with me. I couldn't stand that. It's
> bad enough losing a mother, but if I lose my grandmother too
> it's fatal.

Many grandparents are uncertain of their "rights" with
respect to grandchildren who have been separated from
them by divorce or remarriage. Since, as we have observed,
the new social contract is a kind of unwritten decree of divorce which determines the degree of intimacy that a
grandparent may enjoy with his or her own grandchildren,
grandparents who subscribe to that contract are likely to
write their grandchildren off along with their children's
failed marriage. However, U.S. jurisprudence is gradually,
grudgingly beginning to recognize the importance of grandparents to grandchildren and to support the pyramidal
structure of the family through law. According to one recent review of grandparents' legal status: "The visitation
rights of grandparents has been a problem since Little Red
Riding Hood made her famous trip to her grandmother's
condominium and found Mr. Lupine in bed and no grandmother anywhere. What might be called grandmother
clauses, if we were tempted to pun, have been enacted in

seventeen states in order to mitigate the severity and uncertainty of the legal status and standing of grandparents at common law to claim visitation privileges."[11]

In the absence of vital connections, however, grandparents have no power, legal or emotional, to affect their grandchildren's welfare. In all the public debate over abortion, for example, the nurturing role grandparents might play in such a controverted issue is never discussed—much less the grandparents' stake in the loss of a potential grandchild. When Mr. Watts, a fifty-five-year-old electrical engineer, heard that his married daughter had had an abortion because she wasn't ready yet to leave her job and be a mother, he literally got sick to his stomach:

> At first I thought it was a virus but then I realized that it was her abortion that got me upset. Who would ever think that I, as a man, would react like that? I still can't say anything about the abortion to her. It would only make her feel bad and there is nothing she can do about it anyway. My wife took it better than I did. I feel that a bit of me went with that child. It was a part of me, too—my grandchild. I didn't realize how much that means until I really thought about it.

Mr. Watts told us that he would have been willing to help raise the child and so allow his daughter to keep her job and the baby too. But that was in retrospect. Until he was told of the abortion, Mr. Watts had shown little interest in his daughter and son-in-law. He had abided by the new social contract and not "meddled" in their lives. But by virtue of his biological attachment to them, they had "meddled" in his. They had not only aborted their own child, they had aborted Mr. Watts as a grandfather.

Mr. Barnes, on the other hand, had been on hand when each of his three grandchildren were born. And, as he put it, he stayed close to them throughout their "early years." When his daughter and her husband began drinking heav-

ily and fighting at home, their children would call Mr.
Barnes surreptitiously and cry over the phone. Mr. Barnes,
still in middle age, tried to visit his grandchildren several
times but on each occasion his son-in-law wouldn't allow
him to talk to them. Finally he decided to take action:

> It was my feelings that got me to do something, my love for
> those children. It pained me to see them go through all that
> with their parents. Besides, I've got a responsibility to those
> young'uns. If I don't see to them who will, the welfare?
> I finally got so damn mad I called my daughter and told her
> that I was coming down to see the kids whether she liked it or
> not and that she could tell her bitchy husband not to get in
> my way—or else. I told her that as her father she'd damn well
> better listen to me or all hell would break loose. Well, after
> that they listened. I didn't ask anymore. I told them:
> "They're my grandchildren." It takes a grandfather to do that.

What Mr. Barnes did was to visit his grandchildren regularly and put them up in his own home at intervals until
his daughter and son-in-law could get the therapeutic help
they needed. He was on hand when his grandchildren
needed him because he had always been "there" in their
lives. The vital connections he had built up over the years
made him the natural person for the children to turn to for
help. Thus he was able to nurture and sustain his grandchildren until the family unit could regain its emotional
stability.

Detached grandparents must be prepared to be rebuffed
by the middle generation if they decide to establish themselves as the foundation of the family. Children who were
raised according to the new social contract do not regard
their parents as a family resource. On the contrary, they
normally think of their parents as having done their
"work" and therefore are "free" to live their own lives.
Among the families we visited we met a young father who

had recently lost his wife in an automobile accident. "I wouldn't think of asking my parents to move in with me," he told us. "They're comfortably retired and have their own lives to live." A thirty-five-year-old widow with a large family told us that she would never dream of asking her mother to help her out. "She needs a rest," she said.

On the surface it would appear that such parents are simply being "good children" by assuming full responsibility when adversity strikes. On a deeper level, however, they are merely honoring the new social contract which proscribes dependency between adult generations. But if grandparents do not insist on "interfering" they may lose all contact with their grandchildren. Shortly after Delores Rampoltz got divorced we talked to her about the role her widowed mother might play in the family. But she was adamant about not involving her mother:

> I don't want to be a burden to my mother. She's had a hard life and I don't want her to worry about me and my problems. I can't do that to her. Let her enjoy her old age in peace.

But Delores' mother does worry, even though she lives 600 miles away from her divorced daughter:

> I don't need peace, it's boring. I would much rather be with the children. But I'm not the pushy kind and I don't want to interfere. My grandchildren go to a day-care center after school when I could just as well be there for them after school. I haven't anything better to do. My daughter says that it would be too much for me, but I don't feel that way at all.

Mrs. Rampoltz and her mother are caught in a mutual bind created by the new social contract. The daughter looks upon raising her children as work and wants to spare her mother another round of it. Mrs. Rampoltz cannot accept at face value her mother's grandmotherly feelings. She is so absorbed by the work ethos that she cannot recognize that her mother's chief "function" is to "be" with her grandchildren. Conversely, Mrs. Mazurak lacks the self-assurance to insist upon the way she feels and demand her emotional rights as a Great Parent. She chafes at the thought of her grandchildren spending after school hours *among strangers* when they could be home with her. She does not want "peace" but involvement with her own family, but she lacks the will to prevail over her own daughter.

In some cases, even a vitally connected grandparent may encounter resentment from the middle generation. Mrs. Weiner, thirty-three, is delighted that her mother lives nearby and spends lots of time with her children. She has a daughter, four, and a one-year-old son. With her mother around, Mrs. Weiner is able to devote more attention to the baby than she could if she were alone in the house with both children. Moreover, Mrs. Weiner says, her mother is not the "bossy type" and never interferes with her and her husband as parents. Nonetheless, Mrs. Weiner confesses that she often feels threatened by the close bond that her mother has established with her daughter.

> When my mother's around I feel like I have to fight for my own daughter. In fact, my husband and I sort of fade into the background when my mother is around. My little girl gets one hundred percent attention from Grandma and she knows it. Sometimes I feel like *I'm* the one who is in the way, like my child knows who is really in charge around here. I do the housework and watch them have a good time together. When my mother's around, the only time my daughter bothers with me is at bedtime when she wants a story told and a kiss goodnight.

Grandparents who do not get along with their own children face the greatest obstacles in asserting their function as pillars of the family. Mrs. Potter, a widow with three children, spoke for many middle-generation parents when we visited her children: "If my mother or father tried to help me it would be more trouble than it would be worth." In these situations, however, parents usually fail to consider the effects of their emotional separation from their own parents on the grandchildren. When parents and grandparents do not get along, children either adopt at second hand their parents' negative attitude toward their grandparents or, if they know their grandparents directly, they suffer the tortures of divided loyalties. Jimmy, a sad-eyed ten-year-old, told us how it feels to be a victim of a dispute between his father and his grandparents:

> My father and my grandparents were mad at each other. I had a birthday party and my father didn't want my grandparents to come over. I asked my father three times and he got mad at me. He said, "No!" I was very upset. It's so stupid. My grandparents didn't come to the party. They sent over a dumb present instead. Everyone felt bad—especially me. My mother asked my father to call off the fight, at least for a little while, but he said no again. I don't know if my grandparents would have come anyway. It's so dumb. And their name is right under ours in the phone book.

Grandparents who have been rejected by their own children frequently look to their grandchildren for a second chance to be the kind of parents they wish they had been in the first place. And, since the emotional conflicts that occur between consecutive generations do not arise between alternate generations, the odds are that grandparents will indeed be better nurturers the second time around. However, grandparents who find themselves in this situation are more likely than others to experience anger, guilt, and frustration because children do not understand that their parents can be emotionally different people as grandparents.

We visited such a family in New Jersey. Mrs. Silver

works full-time as a nurse; her husband's job requires him to travel out of town quite frequently. The Silvers' three children are cared for by a housekeeper who told us that she "puts in my time" with the youngsters. In fact, she puts in so much time that the children mimic her Caribbean speech and mannerisms and in some ways are more like her than their own parents. Mrs. Silver's parents, the Fiellas live less than an hour's drive from her, yet she refuses to let them care for her children:

> I don't want them to have contact with my children. They did a lousy job with me and my brothers and I don't want them to screw up my kids too. I always get upset when I am around them. My husband agrees with me. I know they (the Fiellas) would like to do more for the grandchildren but I don't want them near them. Maybe I'm wrong but that's the way I feel. The housekeeper is not hurting the kids.

Mrs. Fiella did not hide the fallout that had occurred between her and her daughter and readily acknowledged the reason:

> It's true that we don't get along. We don't like the man she married and there is a lot of resentment between us. But it's a shame that we can't be with our grandchildren more. I would like to—I'd do anything for them.

Mr. Fiella was full of remorse for the way that he had raised his children. Now, he feels, he is being prevented from rectifying his mistakes:

> I'm a much better grandfather to my grandchildren than I was a father to my own children. I learned from my mistakes. But my relationship to my own children is so bad that I never get a chance to make amends or be with my grandchildren.

Mrs. Silver realizes how much her parents care for their grandchildren but she is only beginning to face up to the effects of her hands-off policy on her children.

> I know that my parents are crazy about the children and that the children enjoy them. I don't know . . . The children know that I don't like my parents and they don't like to hear me criticize them. In fact, the oldest asked me if he was going to feel like that about me when he grew up—hate me, I mean. One thing I wish, though, is that my parents would have treated me when I was young the same way that they treat my children.

The Silver children do not know which side to take. They love their parents *and* their grandparents and don't see why, therefore, they don't love each other. Ruth, twelve, summed up the children's emotional perplexity:

> I like to have my grandparents watch me but my parents fight with them and I get upset about it. My mother acts so weird. I really don't understand it. All of them are nice when I'm alone with them.

E. Special Cases: Adopted and Stepchildren

The mortar of the family is emotional attachments, which are primarily the expression of strong biological instincts. These instincts, however, are *not* aroused by the arrival of adopted or stepchildren. This does not mean that vital connections cannot be formed between grandparents and adopted or stepchildren. It means that vital connections are not forged as easily without the instinctual drive aroused by the birth of natural grandchildren. This is a fact of emotional life which grandparents—and parents—often find very difficult to understand and accept. Thus, the formation of vital connections can be very difficult to achieve unless grandparents do spend a great deal of time with their adopted grandchildren.

Some grandparents told us that they find it difficult to

relate to an adopted child with the same intimacy with which they welcome a grandchild-by-birth. Consciously or unconsciously, such grandparents are concerned about extending their own bloodline. And if grandparents discover that their children can give them no grandchildren except through adoption, they often accept this news as if they had lost their own claim to immortality. This is how Mrs. Bunch felt when she learned that her only son could not have children of his own:

> I became so upset when I learned that the kids couldn't have a baby. I became sorry for myself, too. I started thinking that I would never have a grandchild to take after me. I had all kinds of feelings, angry, sad, hurt, and feeling very sorry for myself, but mostly for the kids. They plan to adopt soon and I hope that God gives me the strength to love the child they adopt, even though it's not the same as having my own grandchild. Who knows, maybe I'll love the baby like it was my own grandchild—after all, you know the old saying, "Every baby brings its own love." But I don't know how I'd feel if they adopted a black or Korean baby like their friends did . . . But then in some ways it might be better. It wouldn't have to be a replacement. It wouldn't be the grandchild I didn't have, if it's a different color.

Emotional conflicts of this kind are understandable and can usually be overcome, as Mrs. Bunch put it, by letting the baby bring its own love. But grandparents are in certain respects more crucial to the needs of adopted children than to those of biological grandchildren. Adopted children need the extra love and attention that only grandparents can give them because deep down—and not without reason —they feel rejected. They long to know who their biological parents are and no matter how loving and understanding their adoptive parents may be, the specter of their "birth parents" never leaves their minds. It becomes particularly haunting during adolescence when the parent-child relationship is temporarily but often severely stressed. In his struggle to "grow up" and separate from his parents, the child may well reject them as being unauthentic, fearing all the more their rejection as the only parents he has ever known and loved. The overwhelmed parents, in turn, may temporarily come to doubt their decision to adopt a child and feel that they do not deserve the hassle after all they have done for the child.

During this very trying period, the roles of grandparent as family peacekeeper, negotiator, and confidant of the child are indispensable. Even though adopted children may be conflicted about accepting their parents as "real" parents, they have no such dilemma with grandparents, so long as the latter maintain their vital connections. We observed this extraordinary emotional phenomena many times. When we visited Robert, fifteen, he was right in the middle of a typical teenage battle with his adoptive parents:

> My parents boss me around too much, always giving orders. It's different with my grandparents. They are so easy-going and relaxed. I love to be with them, ever since I was a little child. I feel good around them. It's funny, I feel that they are my *real* grandparents. I never doubt that. But with my parents, when I get mad at them, I feel that I want to find my real parents. I never think about finding my real grandparents.

When stepchildren are introduced into the family, grandparents face a very difficult problem in sorting out their emotional priorities. Stepchildren bring their own grandparents with them into the "blended" family created by remarriage. When children have as many as four sets of grandparents, it is easy for all of them to ignore their grandchildren. By the same token, when grandparents find the ranks of their grandchildren swollen by the addition of several stepchildren, it is difficult for them not to give emotional priority to those who are theirs by birth. Indeed, in light of the fact that forty percent of second marriages also end in divorce, it is not surprising that millions of American children suffer the total loss of grandparental love and support.

F. Reconciliation and Reunion

There is no way that adults can truly understand what grandparents mean to children unless they learn to feel and see the world from the perspective of children. If we turn Billy's pyramid image upside-down we can enter emotionally into the world-view of the child. At birth, the child enters the postnatal world to join its parents. Behind them, it finds its grandparents. And behind them looms a large, anonymous world. Emotionally, the child's first steps beyond its parents are into the arms of its grandparents. They man the outposts of the young child's universe, familiar faces who mediate between the child and some of the strangeness, variety, and wonder of the adult world that the child will one day enter. When that day comes, the child must—if he or she is to achieve adult autonomy— temporarily separate from the parents. But a grandchild need never separate from grandparents, no matter how old or self-sufficient that grandchild becomes. Such is the stability of the emotional attachment between grandparents and grandchildren.

It is not enough, therefore, that grandparents support the conjugal family. They must also ensure that their grandchildren have direct, intimate, one-to-one experiences of them. This may require that grandparents reconcile their differences with their own children or at least prevent ill-will between the first two generations from blocking access of grandchildren to their grandparents. Reconciliation is seldom easy. It may require outside help in order to overcome some of the soured feelings and outright depression that can plague grandparents who find themselves, in later years, isolated from their jobs, homes, and offspring—classic victims of a divergent society. Mrs. Falks, when we first saw her, was as isolated as a grandparent can be. At seventy, she was living alone in a retirement community in South Carolina where she and her late husband had moved four years earlier. Her daughter, Mrs. Washaw, lives in Rhode Island with her husband and their three children. Mrs. Washaw said that she was worried about her mother but dreaded her visits and even her frequent phone calls:

> She always asks me why I don't contact *her*—but I'm the one who's busy. She would be better off if she'd died with my father. Not that I don't wish her well, but she is so useless. She doesn't do a damn thing except make me feel guilty. She sits down there in her apartment doing nothing. Nothing! One time, I asked her to invite the kids down for a visit and she said that they made her too nervous. My God! Her own grandchildren. She visits once in a while and I have to wait on her hand and foot. She is so self-centered and she's gotten worse since Dad died.

Mr. Washaw echoed his wife's assessment:

> She's out of the book, the stereotyped mother-in-law. It's like she is a child when she comes for a visit. Everything stops. I can hardly talk to my wife. She gets so uptight. If I say anything to her about her mother she gets defensive and we end up arguing with each other. You can cut the tension with a knife when my mother-in-law is around. I don't even want to come home. She just makes the kids nervous and runs my wife ragged.

Mrs. Falks' grandchildren see her as a distant, rather forlorn old woman from whom they try to keep their distance. Elston, eleven, told us how he and his brother and sister feel:

> Well, Grandma's O.K. Just old, I guess. She doesn't like kids much. She's kind of grouchy. She's nice on the telephone but she doesn't talk to us. She always wants to talk to Mom. I guess we make her uptight. She was nice with Grandpa—he was a lot of fun. Maybe she is just sad about Grandpa dying. We just stay away from her.

When we visited with Mrs. Falks we found that she agreed with what her family said about her. But she couldn't talk about her own feelings with them because they were still children to her:

> No one really wants me around. I should have died with my husband. My children are too busy for me, they have no time. When I'm ill they seem to be concerned. I was happier when my husband was around. We didn't get along sometimes but I felt more alive then. I have no purpose in life anymore.

Mrs. Falks was both emotionally and geographically isolated from her family. By herself she could do nothing to overcome her lingering depression at the loss of her husband and her feeling of being unloved by her children. She thought that her behavior was "normal" for a woman of her age and so did her children. She fit the stereotype of the self-centered widow who can do nothing for others. But their distance from her prevented the Washaws from recognizing that Mrs. Falks' continual complaining was really a cry for help. When grandmother did visit her family, her need to make up for lost time and the sudden closeness to so many people, in contrast to the isolation she lived in, made her tense. Her reaction was to withdraw from her family and be "on edge." She then felt guilty because she had expectations of a good visit. Thus, every visit from grandmother became an emotionally exhausting trial for her and for every member of the family.

With psychiatric treatment for her depression and family therapy for herself, her children and her grandchildren, Mrs. Falks' depression cleared rapidly. During the treatment she lived in a hotel room near the family and made new friends among people in the local church. With the help of a high school student, she moved into the Washaws' home and spent a week there caring for her grandchildren when the Washaws took a vacation by themselves. The children were surprised by the change in grandmother. "What happened to Grandma?" one of the daughters asked. "She laughs and plays with us." Once Mrs. Falks realized that she could make an emotional contribution to her family, she began to do more and more things with her grandchildren, even discipline them. Things improved to a point where her family insisted that she move nearer to them. She did and no longer feels that she "should have died with her husband."

Today's grandparents have many good reasons for becoming depressed. A society which overvalues work, undermines vital connections, encourages age segregation and emphasizes self-sufficiency is not an environment in which it is easy to grow old. In such a society it is often difficult for elders to acknowledge the physical or emotional problems that accompany advanced age. To do so, they would have to admit that they were old and apply to themselves the generally unrewarding images of the "Aged" held by society.

To a large degree the medical and other helping professions have in the past contributed unnecessarily to society's negative image of the aged. In physical medicine the stereotype of the complaining "old crock," constantly harassing the physician with complaints for which the physician had no remedy, was common. Psychologically, by the age of fifty or shortly thereafter, "old people are no longer educable," Freud thought, "[because] the elasticity of the mental processes is, as a rule, lacking."[12] In particular, Freud believed that the elderly are no longer capable of benefiting from psychoanalysis.[13] It has taken nearly a half century to prove that Freud's view in this matter is seriously flawed. First geriatric medicine, then social gerontology, and finally geriatric psychiatry have helped the aged discover that they have more power than experts imagined to induce change in their own lives—including changes wrought through therapies that have evolved from Freud's original psychoanalytic model. Most important, however, are the benefits that the aged are beginning to accrue from investigation of how emotional health affects physical health, and how both are affected by social factors.

Recent psychiatric research confirms what primitive societies have known all along: that the family, in its extended forms, is the best soil in which children have the opportunity to grow up to be emotionally healthy and altruistic adults. The aphorism, "One can only pass on to others what one has received," is especially appropriate to child-rearing. The ability to give and receive nurture is learned in early life and within a web of family attachments. The quality of family life also affects the character development of the young. An overly restrictive and authoritarian family can inhibit the creative and emotional growth of the child. Certainly the myriad neurotic problems which Freud found in his patients were aggravated, if not caused by, the strangulating intimacy and prohibition of expression within the Victorian family. By the same token, an overly permissive family can be equally destructive. Emotionally, children feel safe within a hierarchy of generations where lines are drawn between the behavior expected of grandparents, parents, and children. Although children usually chafe at the limits imposed by such boundaries, they respect adults who insist upon them. To many children, permissiveness is perceived as neglect and lack of interest on the part of adults. For adults, permissiveness is often an "easy out" for those who do not know what to expect from children, but children are more likely to feel it as an emotional abandonment. Adults who maintain family hierarchies must gauge the latter's development —in a phrase, they must "pay attention"—and respect their child's individual route to maturity. In sum, when the natural hierarchy within the family is blurred, children often suffer wounds in the structure of their character that endure throughout life.

Thus, the lack of intergenerational structure and nurture within the family lies at the base of what Christopher Lasch has castigated as "the culture of narcissism." Like many angry social critics, Lasch sees no solution to contemporary narcissism short of wholesale change in society. Lasch may be right. But our own analysis and prescription are at once more modest and more hopeful. We believe that narcissism can result when there is an impairment in the formation of vital connections, within the context of the three-generational family. Without a close family hierarchy in which the young, the middle generations, and the old act in emotional concert, each generation withdraws into narcissistic preoccupation with its own age-related concerns. Indeed, the growth in the field of family therapy indicates that the "helping professions" are rediscovering the indispensable roles that families play in the individual's adaptation to society and in the state of his well being. The fact that people who are detached from their families of origin tend to form "families" of friends and acquaintances attests to the natural instinct of man to bond to others. Unfortunately, bonds thus formed are rarely permanent and do not have the same lasting power or the ability to absorb great stress as do the bonds that are forged between members of the pyramidal family.

Therefore, it is clear that what is now needed is a strong emphasis upon the pyramidal family structure which offers the optimum environment for the healthy growth of children. Not only does this structure offer support to the conjugal family but it also facilitates the vital connections between grandparents and grandchildren. This structure, moreover, conforms to the natural order of things.

Today's grandparents are in a unique position. As a generation they are the last to have experienced, in childhood, the emotional security and plenitude of close family networks. They have also experienced the stifling effect when attachment to parents turns into oppressive emotional bondage. As parents, they forged a new social contract with their own children, freeing their children to pursue their fortune in a divergent society. As grandparents, they have seen their children form ties to the world of work which supercede their bonds to their families. They have seen their children's marriages buckle under the emotional burdens which they—often mothers alone—have tried to bear by themselves. They have seen their isolated daughters, as young mothers, place their grandchildren into the hands of institutions in order to enter the workplace. They have seen more and more of their grandchildren become emotional casualties of these events. And, in their later years, grandparents have felt the emotional desolation that follows upon the loss of family connections.

Many find themselves suspended in an emotional limbo, hard put to know where to go from there. In some ways their condition is not unlike that of an adolescent's as he seeks to "find" himself by freeing himself from the parental yoke. It is a pattern every human follows from conception; the drive to establish the "self." It unfolds in the following manner. Inside the mother's womb, the child and the mother are one. After birth, the child becomes dependent on the mother for physical survival, and a deep emotional attachment forms between them. At this point in his childhood, he cannot differentiate himself from his mother. As the child ages and renounces his physical dependency on his parents he becomes emotionally attached to others, friends, teachers and hopefully, grandparents, thus decreasing his emotional dependency on his parents and especially his mother. Once attached to others, he may in a flourish at adolescence reject, for a time, his parents and what they stand for. Often, this phase is accompanied by negative feelings. He turns to his peers for support, acceptance, and validation for his renunciation of the previous generation. Once maturity is reached, the child comes "home" to reaffirm his love and attachment to his parents, as an adult. He rejoins the family pyramid on the basis of a true mutuality, ready to take on the role of parent, as the cycle of life renews itself. In short, a mature person passes through three important stages of emotional development: symbiosis in infancy (attachment), narcissism in adolescence (separation and individuation), and reunion (mutuality).

The completion of this process ensures the ability of the individual to relate to other people on an intimate level, and to perpetuate the family. When this developmental progression is halted at the adolescent stage, reunion with the family is never achieved. The adolescent remains detached from the family and looks to the peer group for emotional sustenance. The family is no longer perpetuated. The generations remain isolated from one another.

Today's grandparents are in a state of detachment from the family similar to that of an adolescent who feels that he "can't go home again." They have achieved inde-

pendence from the family but are unable to reunite and resume their emotional attachments to the family—some
never will. Just as some adolescents never realize that they
can be emotionally attached without being controlled by,
or dependent upon, the object of the attachment, so many
of today's grandparents have failed to recognize that vital
connections do not require that they relinquish their self-
sufficiency. Fearful of dependency they hang back from
their families, aging victims of the new social contract.

Today's grandparents created the new social contract
and they can break it. The youngest among them will be
grandparents for thirty years—plenty of time to build up
the family pyramid. Already, today's grandparents are the
healthiest, best educated, and the most self-sufficient in history. But, as we have seen, these advantages are of little
value in a society that affords them no role.

Today's grandparents have a choice. As members of an
increasingly powerful group called the "Aged" they can
perpetuate the conditions of divergence which sustain the
new social contract. They can continue to ignore their vital
connections. Like aging actors, they can smooth back the
wrinkles, tan the flesh, tone the body, and repeat roles
learned in middle age. Like Mrs. Rutledge however, they
will inevitably see the curtain close, the lights go up and
discover that outside the theater there is no one waiting for
them.

Or today's grandparents can accept the unique opportunity they have to halt the segregation of young from old
and resume their natural function as foundation of the
family. To do this they will have to rebuild the family pyramid and roll back the influence of institutions which have
replaced them in the lives of their grandchildren.

These are tasks of enormous doing and undoing. Vitally
connected grandparents do not have to be told what to do;

they are doing it. But the majority are generationally impounded, all too ready to complain about feeling useless, left out, all too distracted by their narcissistic focus and much too hesitant to acknowledge their own part in dismantling the family pyramid. But this does not necessarily have to continue. Rebuilding the family pyramid can begin at almost any point: reconstruct. What follows are a few basic principles, a sort of primer for grandparents who don't know what to do.

G. *Primer for Grandparents*

First, establish a visual concept of your family as a pyramid, no matter how dispersed or detached its members may be, and locate your place in it. Imagine, for a moment, that you are at the top of the pyramid looking down at your descendants, and that your children and grandchildren are looking at you, the person they all have in common. In this position you occupy a symbolic role as oldest representative of the family and its titular leader. A strong and loving grandmother can be a matriarch without creating a matriarchy; similarly, a strong and loving grandfather can be a patriarch without creating a patriarchy. In divergent societies, however, families require matriarchs and patriarchs—not to dominate their lives—but to embody the sense of primordial unity. Much of the power that grandparents possess as family historians, mentors, and role models derives from their symbolic place as the head of the family. They have preceded everyone else in life and so take emotional precedence as the ones from whom everyone has biologically issued. This confers status and commands respect. One elderly woman who had recently become a great-grandmother told us of her notoriety among "the youngsters who were only grandmothers" when she heard of her great-grandchild's arrival. "I became the expert of experts on children," she told us.

But a grandparent's titular status means only temporary celebrity unless he or she is the foundation of the family as well. Indeed, without grandparents there is no family pyramid—only a fragile unit, increasingly dependent upon outside institutions and experts.

Second, grandparents must rebuild the family pyramid. There is only one way to do this: by establishing and maintaining vital connections to every family member. In many cases this will require a great deal of perseverance. The easiest approach is to begin at the beginning. When a grandchild is due to be born, prepare for the event. Anticipate what changes the child will make in your own lives and those of its parents. In your mind, relive the births of your own children: let your nurturing instincts come to life. Most important, be there when the baby is born. At that moment—one of the most precious that life has to offer—you are reborn as a grandparent. The event is a moment of celebration for all of the family. Whenever you can, hold the baby, feed it, and pamper the young mother so she has nothing else to do but enjoy her child in those important early days. Be gentle, supportive, but not "bossy" (even though you know more about children). This experience will inaugurate the vital connection between you and your grandchild. At the same time, the reknitting of the generations occurs. A new family pyramid, baby, parents, and grandparents is formed.

Third, remember that vital connections are the mortar of the family pyramid. In order to maintain vital connections, grandparents need only to spend generous amounts of time with their grandchildren. The roles we have described flow naturally out of shared time. Many of the old "feeling places" where grandparents held forth have disappeared. But love is a movable feast and today's grandparents have many options. Demographic studies show that the majority of grandparents still live within an hour's drive of at least one child. This means that most grandparents can still have direct access to at least some of their grandchildren. The grandparents' home should become a second home for the grandchild—a place to "get away" to, to explore, rummage through family memorabilia, encounter the unexpected; the place to celebrate holidays with the "whole" family and their friends. Thus, the grandparents' home can serve as the "center" of the family. From this center grandparents can keep family members in communication with each other, reaching out to distant kin.

Realistically, not every grandparent can be close to every grandchild. In a highly mobile society, grandparents must also be mobile if vital connections are to survive at all. Plan family vacations together so you can spend long days with the children. Make it a rule never to celebrate a major holiday by yourself. Visit your grandchildren often and regularly. If space is tight, put up at a local hotel. And while on your visit, get to know your grandchildren's friends; ask about them when you call. You might be surprised at their enthusiastic response. In between visits, write each grandchild individually; avoid the collective letter as the main means of communication. You may seldom get a letter in return but you may find yours tucked away in a child's dresser drawer or glued into a grandchild's scrapbook, as a keepsake. And whenever you can, send home-made gifts that your grandchildren can pass on to your great-grandchildren. Children understand that what you make for them is part of *you*, like heirlooms, and so are more valuable than "store bought" gifts.

Fourth, be the guardians of the young. Let everyone in

your family know that they have you to rely on in a family emergency. Insist on helping when adversity strikes. Above all, don't allow differences between you and your children to stand in the way of direct connections with your grandchildren. If you see that the children are suffering because of your problems within the family, don't stand idly by and wait to be asked to intervene. At all costs, protect the children from the effects of parental strife. If parents separate, be prepared to move in as surrogates. If the mother has to take a full-time job, move in as surrogates. If illness strikes, move in as surrogates. If you are not living in the same place as your family when adversity strikes, then go there. In this way, children can be protected and maintained in the bosom of the family. Don't let "strangers" in outside institutions, or experts (no matter how dedicated) do what you as a grandparent can do naturally. By supplying a strong foundation, you will strengthen the pyramidal family against the forces that would destroy it.

Fifth, follow your grandchildren into society. This is a radical departure for today's grandparents, who are accustomed to retreating from the mainstream of social activity. Viewed historically, however, elders have traditionally "peopled" the world of children, as kin, neighbors, or mentors to youthful apprentices. Even in the recent American past grandparents, sitting on millions of porches, were silent overseers of the "public" world of children. Such a social setting conformed to the world-view of the child, as seen from the inverted pyramid. In stepping beyond their parents, children moved into a world where grandparents occupied the interstices of the larger society outside the home.

Today, children are abruptly removed from the conjugal family—some even before they learn how to walk—and placed into caretaking institutions where too few adults tend too many children. During a crucial period in life, when children need deep, personal attachments in order to learn how to be close to people, most children enter age-segregated school systems where the few adults they do encounter are viewed as adversary "authority figures." This is a system that even the most inspired teacher cannot overcome. At best, a "teacher's pet" may establish a strong relationship with a teacher, all the more unfortunate because it is transient. Thus, for lack of available adults, children become prematurely attached only to their peers, which fosters generational stratification. Moreover, schools often ignore the emotional parameters of the child's development in the effort to accelerate their intellectual learning. This atmosphere of pressure, competition, and measurement heralds the child's entrance into the world of work.

In day-care centers, young children are warehoused. The younger the child, the more he suffers from the separation from his family. At an early age, he feels abandoned to the care of "strangers." At a time in life when he needs his own family to be with, he finds himself in a world peopled with many children and a few harried adults who are here today, gone tomorrow. This is not a system of child-rearing that teaches children to trust and respect adults. On the contrary, it teaches children that they are not important, or loved. Their capacity to form deep attachments may be impaired. Grandparents can change this by replacing day-care centers or working there.

Grandparents should follow their grandchildren into the schools. By their presence alone, grandparents disrupt the stratifying effects of segregation-by-age and provide an emotional climate in which learning can more readily take place. To be sure, some communities do sponsor foster-grandparent programs. But these services are principally directed at retarded children and others labeled as "needy."

These programs, commendable as they may be, are mere tokenism—giving the aged something to do.

In a divergent society, every child is emotionally "needy." Children from broken and highly stressed homes are very unhappy; often, they are so concerned with their emotional and physical survival that they find it impossible to learn in school. Thus, instead of finding school a sanctuary from an unhappy home life, the child encounters failure. These children are found in the classrooms of affluent as well as poor communities because these problems strike families indiscriminately. Indeed, contrary to the arguments of many experts and "child-advocates," poverty is not the major problem American children face. The major problem is the impairment of their emotional development by a paucity of caring adults (often a result of poverty).

Our own solution is to "people" schools and other institutions for the young with grandparents. Genetically, children enter the world with two parents and four grandparents—a potential of six caring adults (and more, if great-grandparents are alive). In schools this natural ratio is radically reversed. There is no structural reason why more adults of grandparental age and with a minimum of training—perhaps one for every five children—could people this nation's schools and thus provide a more caring environment. In such a program, under the teacher's direction, each child could enjoy the attention of a "class grandmother" who would get "promoted" with children from grade to grade and become, at one and the same time, a source of stability, a "constant object," for them; an advocate for each child; an ally of the parents, and a welcome help to the teacher. Such a program would humanize the school environment, structure the children's behavior, and impede student disorder and violence. Grandparents in the schools are a demonstration to children that adults care for them. No other program we can think of would do more to bring the generations closer together.

We have emphasized the need for grandparents in schools, but children are to be found everywhere. They are in hospitals and orphanages and—if one looks around— homes which house children yearning for a grandparental figure. There are millions of American children who have no grandparents anywhere at all. There are also millions of older Americans who have no grandchildren—those who never married, the childless, the homosexual, the grandparent who has lost his vital connections. Together, these millions of young and old represent the most isolated members of the generations apart. A few determined children, as we have seen, go out and find surrogates. Almost any older person can do the same. Vital connections are based on biology but they need not be limited to kin. Time, place, and undivided attention, given by an older person, can foster a close and enduring attachment with any child. Short-lived programs do not contain the right ingredients for the formation of deep attachments. Children need much more. They need a constant companion, a surrogate grandparent, who will serve as a constant object for life.

Experts often argue that there is no function for the aged in an industrialized society. Indeed, there is no function for the aged in any society where the ethos of work predominates. No doubt, as the ranks of the aged increase and "Ageism" becomes a social sin like sexism and racism, the status of the aged will improve—but not much. What the aged want is respect for themselves and for what they say and do. In a word, they want to be elders, with all the reverence for old age which that honorific title implies. Throughout this book we have stressed the functions of grandparents because it is the basis upon which nature itself pays respect to the old. Societies can and have ignored this function. But it is the only function, we believe, which supplies a pattern by which Americans can find a permanent role for elders in their midst. Elders do for society what grandparents do for the family. They nurture, teach, set examples, protect and provide continuity between past and future. And they tell stories. They tell us about the way things were, how things felt, and the way things might be. Mostly, they tell them to those who have ears to hear and eyes to see. They tell them to children. Because children readily understand.

5

Postscript: Requiem

At the beginning of this book we argued that "to exist is to be connected." This is as true of the last stage of life as it is of the first. Old age destroys whatever illusions of individual self-sufficiency a society may create. In old age we become physically dependent upon others, just as we were at birth. But whether those "others" are family or strangers depends upon the vital connections we have developed and maintained as grandparents.

In the course of our field work, we met numerous old people who were approaching death. A few were dying the death of grandparents; most were dying the death of the "Aged." That is, a few were dying in the womb of families they had nurtured while most were dying emotionally, spiritually, and sometimes physically alone. Among the latter was Mr. Sawyer, seventy, who was dying of liver disease when we met him and his family. Except for rare, ritualistic visits, Mr. Sawyer had ceased to involve himself with his children after they married. Whatever intergenerational contact did exist in his family had been maintained by Mrs. Sawyer, who had died seven years earlier. After his wife's death, Mr. Sawyer grew increasingly isolated and depressed. He made no effort to draw closer to his children and hardly knew his grandchildren.

When Mr. Sawyer began to die, his daughter put him in a hospital near her home so that she and her family could help nurse him through his final days. But much to her frustration she discovered that Mr. Sawyer did not want any of his children or grandchildren around him. The children, in turn, felt helpless and angry. Their father was depriving them of their last chance to show that they cared for him—and to make emotional restitution for the guilt that all children feel when they fail to maintain a close relationship with an aged parent. Mrs. Sawyer's daughter was quite candid about the hurt they all felt from her father's behavior:

> I don't understand. He doesn't really want us around. When he is sleeping, I go in and sponge off his face. But when he wakes he says he's all right. "Don't trouble yourself," he tells me. He's pushing us away like we don't count.
>
> We all feel so down about it. It's like his life was for nothing. He doesn't recognize us as being here. He takes no pleasure in us or in his grandchildren.

Only Mr. Sawyer's terminal helplessness allowed his family to stand watch over him in his final days. But they had to do so from an emotional distance. He had pushed them to the periphery of his life, and so of his death. They were unable to take leave of their father as they wanted to, unable to share the time and place of his death. For them it was the ultimate rejection, the last act of a detached father and grandfather. But that was the way Mr. Sawyer wanted it. Indeed, when we visited him he was quite emphatic about not wanting to burden his family:

> I want to be left alone to die in peace. I don't want anyone around. I've lived my life. I enjoyed my work. My wife is gone and that's it for me. The kids have got their own lives . . . I was never much to them. I raised them and they were off on their own. Now they are hovering around and I have to look at them. It makes me feel worse. I wish they would leave me alone and let me die in peace.
>
> I told them, "No funeral. Just cremate me and scatter my ashes and that's that." Life will go on without me. Being with me just takes them away from their work and their lives. All this sentimental stuff just isn't for me.

Mr. Sawyer was dying as he had lived—according to the new social contract. He preferred to die alone rather than experience the care and concern of his family. He was resisting to the end the pull of primordial emotional ties between himself and his family. He longed for a quick end to his life, an abrupt transition which would allow no gradual divestiture of his worldly goods, no reunion with his own flesh and blood. He wanted no tears, no mourning, no grave to remind his children of their origins in him. He simply wanted to disappear forever in a scattering of ashes.

In his terminal narcissism, Mr. Sawyer gave no thought to how his death would affect his grandchildren. His implicit message to them was this: "I am not important. You are not important. Life, apart from work, is not important." By denying his grandchildren the opportunity to share in his death, he denied their need to make death a part of their own on-going lives. Instead, he helped perpetuate the frightening fantasies that all children have of death as a great unknown that separates rather than unites one generation with the next. Through his example, they learned to fear death as something that must be experienced in isolation. In the end, Mr. Sawyer's grandchildren were unable to grieve for their grandfather because they did not know him.

He died alone.

By contrast, Mrs. Portos, eighty-one, died as she had always lived—at the center of her family. When we met Mrs. Portos she was living with her daughter's family. Mrs. Portos was bed-ridden and required the aid of a middle-aged "widow lady" who came by daily to look after her physical needs. It was, her daughter told us, the least she could do for her mother:

> I love my mother very much and so does my husband. As long as she doesn't need hospital care she belongs with us. She would do the same for me. She is very much a part of our family. Even though she rarely leaves her room, we can go to her.

Despite her advanced age and infirmity, Mrs. Portos continued to be a grandparent right to the end of her life. From her bed she read and told stories to her grandchildren. She even taught her grandsons how to knit their own sweaters. In turn, the grandchildren described their grandmother as "cute" and "fun—when she's feeling well." But what caught our attention was an observation by Paul, six, the youngest of her grandchildren:

> Grandma is here all of the time, but her body is shrinking. She seems to be getting smaller and smaller, a little bit every day. I mean, Grandma's *body* is getting smaller, but Grandma is not shrinking. Just her body.

In the oracular mode of young children, Paul told us precisely what was happening emotionally and spiritually between Mrs. Portos and her grandchildren. Grandmother's body was gradually shrinking but not grandmother herself. To the end of her life, she remained a full and constant object in her grandchildren's minds—a presence which will remain with them for the rest of their lives. Thus, through her vital connections Mrs. Portos gained a form of immortality which only functioning grandparents can achieve, and only grandchildren can confer.

Moreover, Mrs. Portos achieved an enviable completeness in her life which only close grandparents can experience. She ended her life as she began it, by receiving nurture from her own flesh and blood. At the same time, she never ceased nurturing her children and grandchildren. She told her grandchildren stories and taught them things, not the least of which was how to die. By allowing her children and grandchildren to nurse and nurture her in her dying days, she permitted them to rehearse their own deaths. Her grandchildren no longer had to fantasize about death because they were able to experience its reality through the death of their grandmother. By being "useful" to their dying grandmother, they gained a mastery over their own fears of death.

In sum, the death of Mrs. Portos was an experience shared, in time and place, by her entire family. When death came the generations were together, as at birth, sharing some of the most powerful emotions that life has to offer. Mrs. Portos died in full emotional communion with those she had brought into life. Her death completed the circle.

THE FOLLOWING DRAWINGS DEMONSTRATE THE DIFFERENCES IN THE WAY CHILDREN RELATE TO THEIR GRANDPARENTS

GROUP I

Children who have close contact with their grandparents portray them as large, active, fully viewed figures dominating the page, indicating their intimate knowledge of them.

Figs. 1–20

GROUP II

Children who have sporadic contact with their grandparents tend to draw them in a variety of ways that indicate a lack of intimate knowledge of them. Themes of abandonment and detachment predominate (i.e., scenes of leave takings are commonly drawn).

Figs. 21–38

GROUP III

Children who have minimum or no contact with their grandparents draw distorted, bizarre, and unrealistic images drawn primarily from their imaginations. They do not draw real people, indicating they have no knowledge at all of a real grandparent—it's like taking a test in a subject never studied.

Figs. 39–49

GROUP I

Fig. 1. A four-and-a-half-year-old drew this picture of her grandmother. The large sized, centrally placed figure represents the mental image that this child has of her grandmother, who lives in the same house and shares her daily life.

Fig. 2. A seven-year-old drew his grandmother. "My big Grandma." This child's grandmother has a full-time job, but finds time to see her grandson several times a week and to babysit often. In fact, "She tells my parents to go away so she can be alone with me."

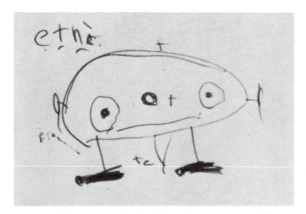

Fig. 3. This is a grandfather drawn by a youngster of three years and ten months. The large central figure demonstrates that grandfather is a very important person to the youngster. The figure dominates the page, is central, has a male appendage, and according to the child who waxed eloquently about his picture, "is watching what I'm doing and making sure that I don't get hurt."

Fig. 4. Mary's grandfather's stubble indicates her intimate knowledge of him.

Fig. 5. Mary accentuates her grandmother's mouth in this drawing because she perceives her as an opinionated and verbal person.

Fig. 6. Patty knows her grandmother is old and hobbles, but that is inconsequential to her. To Patty "She can't walk too well," but "I like to snuggle into her and smell her . . . And she is the best back-rubber in the world."

Fig. 7. Myra's family holiday shows her grandparents as large figures, creating a festive mood while nurturing the family.

Fig. 8. Doreen feels protected by her grandmother, who stands over her like a watchtower.

Fig. 9, LEFT. Joan's grandmother is concerned about her returning late from school.

Figs. 10, 11, BELOW. Michael, nine, drew large, realistic pictures of the "stern" side of his grandparents, indicating that they are major figures in his life.

Fig. 12. Peter has learned how to garden by watching his grandfather. The grandchild talks about sharing with his children what he learns with his grandfather.

Fig. 13. Jeff drew his grandfather watching the Yankees. Jeff says, "I'm a Yankee fan just like my grandfather. It's a tradition in my family."

Fig. 14, LEFT. Gail's grandmother, Big Ma, "holding the baby over her heart," demonstrates the nurturing of grandmothers.

Fig. 15, BELOW. Grandchildren who are close to their grandparents see them inextricably close to food, kitchen tables, and traditional dinners.

Fig. 16. Carmine's grandmother cooking the Sunday meal. This is still the central family experience for children close to their grandparents.

Fig. 17. Carmine's grandfather prepares to open the wine for the Sunday dinner—a traditional meal fast disappearing from the American family.

Fig. 18. Deborah's grandmother and grandfather preside over Sunday dinner like elders of the tribe.

Fig. 19, LEFT. Deborah drew her deceased grandfather "watching young children play." The image is large and full-faced, indicating that the relationship he established with Deborah in life was many-sided and close. *Fig. 20*, RIGHT. Deborah's aged grandmother reminiscing about the past and hoping that everything would stay the same after she was gone.

GROUP II

Figs. 21-23. Children with sporadic contact with their grandparents pictured them waving goodbye, as if leave-takings were the most emotionally significant moments between these grandchildren and their grandparents.

Fig. 21, RIGHT. A nine-year-old girl draws her grandmother waving goodbye. "I want you to stay with me," says the grandmother.

Fig. 22, BELOW. "Come back soon for another visit, dear! I get so lonely when you leave me! It's so long between visits!"

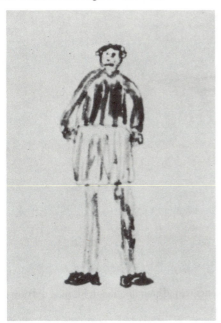

Fig. 23. "Here is my grandfather who lives in North Carolina. He is standing on the road to see if I am coming. He likes me a lot and I love him. We have a good time together but I never get to see him!" Grandfather looks puzzled.

Fig. 24. One eight-year-old, when asked to draw her retired grandmother in Florida, did not in fact draw her as a person but as an airplane.

Fig. 25, LEFT. Sheila's eyes began to tear when she thought of her grandmother, who had retired to a "far-off" place. She drew her slipping into the past. *Fig.* 26, RIGHT. Elizabeth's grandmother "turned her back on her" when Elizabeth's parents got divorced.

Fig. 27. Norma's Florida grandmother is portrayed as doll-like, which indicates a stereotyped relationship.

Fig. 28. Mark's grotesque portrayal of his grandmother indicates a great deal of anger. As he drew her he said. "It wouldn't bother me at all if I never saw my grandmother again . . . All I am to her is a prize on her charm bracelet."

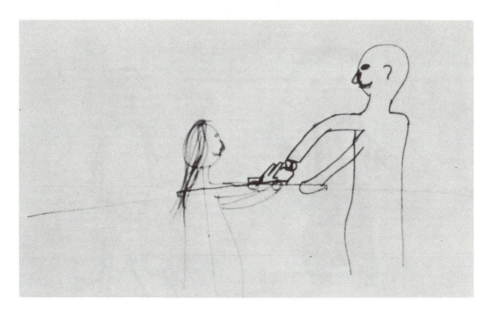

Fig. 29. Children with.intermittent grandparents feel detached from them and often draw them without substance.

Fig. 30. Grandparents known in a second-hand manner tend to be featureless specters. This child drew her absent grandmother as a ghostly figure in a family scene.

Figs. 31, 32, 33. Children who are not close to their grandparents portray them as specters, child-like dolls, puppets, or bizarre figures.

Fig. 34, LEFT. Mary drew her grandmother's face and her clothes inappropriately for any contemporary woman, suggesting that Mary has seen her grandmother only about five times, she guessed, and it demonstrated that she didn't know her grandmother.

Fig. 35, BELOW. Sean's hostile portrayal of his absent grandparents as clowns.

Fig. 36, LEFT. Jerry's satirical portrayal of his grandfather, whom he has seen only once. The drawing is an imitation of a grandfather Jerry saw in a television advertisement for a retirement village. *Fig.* 37, RIGHT. Jerry's media image of his grandmother is one of a decrepit old lady which he drew.

Fig. 38. Jerry's idea of a dinner table with his grandparents is as barren as his real life relationship to them.

GROUP III

Fig. 39. Melissa's drawing does not include her only living grandparent—whom she does not know—instead she draws a dreamy idealized family scene.

Figs. 40-43. Children without grandparents draw distorted images.

Fig. 40, LEFT. Wanda asked, "What's a grandparent like?" She drew a human form without human substance. *Figs. 41, 42,* MIDDLE and RIGHT. Grandparents drawn as expressionless faces floating in a sea of empty paper.

Fig. 43. A typical "puppet face" drawn by grandchildren without grandparents.

Fig. 44, LEFT. Tim portrays his grandfather who lives 1,500 miles away, and whom he has seen only twice in his life. The child's parents are close to his grandparents so the child is secondarily "connected." He envisions his grandparents as "old," which he depicts in his drawing. The grotesque quality of "deadness" of the grandparent is apparent. Fig. 45, RIGHT. Lynn, an eight-year-old girl with no grandparents, dutifully drew this "creature" when asked to draw a grand-parent. The child seemed as bewildered by what she drew as we were!

Fig. 46. Paul's phantom grandfather is an example of the form of a relationship without the substance.

Fig. 47. Terry, who has no grandparents, drew a picture of a family barbeque that included everything but people.

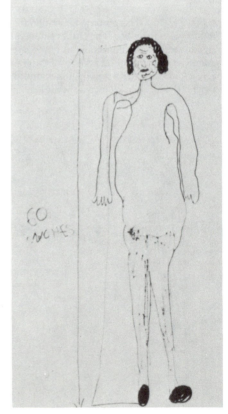

Fig. 48, ABOVE. Six-year-old Vinnie drew his dead grandfather as "Christ like." "He's saying that he's sorry that he died but that he couldn't help it." Vinnie hopes to see his grandfather again in heaven.

Fig. 49, RIGHT. Evelyn's grandmother, who is dead three years, looms large in her mind. She "is still alive" for her.

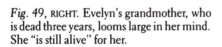

Grandchild Interview Format

Our study of how children perceived their grandparents was carried out in two different ways.

A broad survey was done in schools, day-care centers, etc., where (after parental permission was obtained) children were asked to draw their grandparents and then asked to fill out a brief questionnaire and to write a brief paragraph about their grandparents (anything that they would like to write). We obtained hundreds of drawings and comments which enabled us to formulate the technique and questionnaire which was the primary tool that we used to learn about the children's perceptions of their grandparents, the in-depth personal interview.

The in-depth personal interview was carried out by two investigators with over 300 children over the course of several years. This technique consisted of asking the child to draw a picture of a grandparent, then the grandparent of the opposite sex, to answer questions about the picture that they drew and then to draw a picture of their grandparent(s) doing something with their family. At the beginning of the study we asked the children to look at a stereotyped picture of a grandmother and grandfather and to tell us what they were thinking (projective technique). Although the comments of the children were interesting we soon found that this technique was superfluous and so we abandoned it after the first 100 interviews.

The interview was held in a quiet room, the interviewer and child were alone for a period of one hour. Although the environment was structured, the relationship between the child and the interviewer was unstructured and free floating. We went where the child would lead us. The examiner strove to meet the child at the child's cognitive level and to be spontaneous and as responsive to the child's language, needs, and method of communication as possible.

While the child was drawing, his spontaneous comments about the drawing were noted. After the drawing was completed the interviewer proceeded to ask the child the questions contained in the questionnaire.

Questionnaire (Fig. 1)

The questionnaire is divided into two parts. The first part contains concrete questions that explore the child's perceptions of the figure that he drew. His answers to these questions gave us an indication of his "first-hand" knowledge of his grandparent. The second part of the questionnaire contained questions designed to explore the abstract dimensions of the child's perceptions of his grandparents, allowing the child's thoughts to roam freely. The questions contained in the form are self-explanatory.

GRANDPARENT STUDY

Children's Drawings

CATEGORY _____   No. _____
                             Age _____
                             Sex _____
                             Date _____

Part I

Draw-A-Grandparent
Grandparent _____
  Saying? _____
  _____
  Doing? _____
  _____
  Feeling? _____
  _____

Thinking? _____

Live? _____

Best Thing? _____

Worst Thing? _____

Want Most? _____

Be With! Why? _____

Grandparent of Opposite Sex
Saying? _____

Doing? _____

Feeling? _____

Thinking? _____

Live? _____

Best Thing? _____

Worst Thing? _____

Want Most? _____

Be With! Why? _____

Part II

Draw grandparent doing something with family:
   (Kinetic Family Drawing)
Tell a story about picture.

Where do your grandparents live?

Maternal	*Father*
	Mother
Paternal	*Father*
	Mother

Other
What do they think about you?
How often do you see them?

Projective: Grandfather
              Grandmother

If your grandparents have moved away, how did that make you feel?

_____

If your grandparents died, how did you feel?

_____

Are your grandparents important to you? Do you need them, what
    for?

_____

What have you learned from your grandparents?

_____

Do you feel that you are important to your grandparents? Why?

_____

Do you "take after" them?

_____

How do you feel about grandparents in general?

_____

How are your grandparents different from your parents?

_____

What kind of a grandparent are you going to be when you grow up?

_____

Comments:

_____

_____

Grandchildren's Response

We found it most interesting to compare the responses of the children to the questionnaire and to divide the responses according to the group placement of the child (Group I, II, or III). The differences in their responses demonstrate their degree of intimate knowledge of their grandparents and the emotional tone of their relationship.

GROUP I Themes of Intimate Knowledge of the Person.

What the Grandparents Were Saying:

Hello, Sweetie Pie.
Where's my granddaughter, I don't see her enough, always in that darn school.
Don't worry dear, I won't let that bee sting you.
Christmas is coming and we'll have a wonderful holiday together.
Let me show you how to water the plants.
You look like the spittin' image of me.
Where's the doggone TV guide?
I wish that Grandpa would shave twice a day.

Out of the way dear, I've got to get to bed, I'm tired.
Stay out of the street.
I'm furious at your mother for smoking.

GROUP II These children put different words in their grandparents'
mouths: Themes of Separation.

Stay with me for a long time.
I must go now.
I'll see you next Christmas.
I'm going on a trip and I can't take you.
Boy! Are my new false teeth expensive.
I wish that I had more money.
I need a new car, will you buy me one when you grow up?
Can't you come and visit more often?

GROUP III Themes of Detachment.

I wonder what you look like, Grandson.
I got killed in the Second World War.
I'm tired.
Look, how big you are.
Here I am.

What Were the Grandparents Doing?

GROUP I (Grandparents were *with* the child—Closeness and
"being").

Smiling at me.
Hugging me.
Correcting my homework.
Building a kite with me.
Taking a walk with me.
Fishing with me.
Cooking with me.

GROUP II (Grandparents' world was separate from the child).

Talking to my parents all of the time and ignoring me.
Going on a trip.
Getting dressed up.
Giving me a present.
Having an argument with my mother.
Leaving again.

GROUP III (Grandparents were frozen).

Nothing.
Standing there.
Lonely (very frequent response).
Watching.
Looking.
I don't know.

What Were the Grandparents Feeling?

GROUP I (Emotional Priority).

I love you.
I'm proud of you.
Happy to be with me.
Happy when they look at me.
Angry that I want to go home.
Peaceful and serene.
Content.
Happy (very frequent).

GROUP II (Emotions were bland, tending toward the negative).

Lonely.
Bored.
Happy about the new coat that she bought.
Sad about being far from me.
Confused.

GROUP III (Emotional intensity was low, apathy prevailed).

Nothing.
Lonely.
Sad.
Silly.
Nothing because they are dead.
I don't know.
I have no idea.
How should I know? (Very common response).

What Were the Best and the Worst Things about their Grandparents?

GROUP I

BEST THINGS:

> Kind.
> Funny.
> Wise.
> Cheerful.
> Always nice.

WORST THINGS:

> Complains that his bones hurt too much.
> Too tired all the time.
> Compares herself with others too much.
> Critical too much, sometimes . . .
> Can't get away with a thing when she's around.

> These children displayed an intimate knowledge of the trials
> and tribulations of their grandparents.

GROUP II

BEST THINGS:

> Sometimes they give me money.
> Bought me a bicycle.
> Bought my mother a new car.
> Take me places sometimes.
> I like to visit them.

WORST THINGS:

> She ain't got no hair.
> Never lets us talk at night.
> Crabby all of the time.
> Afraid we'll break all the stuff in her house.
> Likes her cat more than me.
> She's all right, I guess, I don't know.
> Feels sorry for himself too much.
> He's too fat . . . Ugh.
> She's a crazy old lady. I'm glad that I don't have to see her that
> much.
> I'm glad when they go after their summer visit. When they
> come we have to wait on them. They are no fun.

> In Group II negatives prevailed. Age was singled out as a nega-
> tive factor. Positive factors were seen in terms of "things" and
> material gifts.

GROUP III

BEST THINGS:

I don't know.

WORST THINGS:

Never knew them.
They left me.
They never call or write to me.
They died.
I don't know.

> Detachment and devaluation of the importance of grandparents pervaded these responses.

This representative sample of the responses of the children enabled us to sort them into three major groups. An analysis of these responses is presented in the commentary following the section on children.

The Grandparent Survey

The grandparent survey was conducted in two stages.

At first, a preliminary questionnaire was constructed and used in personal interviews. As this questionnaire was refined it was circulated to many grandparents, personally and through mailings. When the forms were returned and examined a follow-up interview was held with grandparents in special situations or circumstances that offered us new insights and information. Eventually, we formulated the questionnaire that we used in our grandparent survey.

The grandparent survey was conducted over a period of three years by two interviewers. The questionnaire (Fig. 1) was used as the core of the interview. The interviewer allowed the grandparents ample time to express themselves in any way that they wished, about anything that they wished, concerning their experience as a grandparent, parent, or grandchild. Needless to say, many of these interviews were deeply moving emotional experiences for the grandparent and the interviewer.

Ours is not a "controlled study," it is a survey, an overview, and the questionnaire is a vehicle, that allows grandparents and elders to share their life experiences and their attitudes with us. Much of what we learned came from the spontaneous stories that grandparents shared with us about themselves and their lives. Often,

while responding to a question, the grandparent would at first answer briefly, yes or no, then reflect upon his answer and talk about
the issue in great depth. Since we recorded the interviews (with the
participants' permission) we were able to reflect upon the grandparents' answers long after the interview as we listened to the
tapes. Often, a question was confusing to the grandparent at first,
but upon reflection he or she was able to respond to an answer
with great insight and wisdom. By allowing the grandparent ample
time for reflection we were able to learn about things that grandparents "never thought about before in that way." Many of the
grandparents had never thought very seriously about their role as a
grandparent. Many responded that "I never thought of myself
in that way." This response revealed the "lacuna" in their perceptions of themselves as grandparents that we will discuss later on.

We allowed them enough time to reflect upon their state of
grandparenthood. The interviewers accepted the reflex answer of
the grandparents and coaxed them to discuss the question in greater
depth. Here, what the culture taught the grandparent was peeled
away and the grandparent was permitted to express his or her feelings about things. Thus we were able to ascertain what the grandparents "really" felt as opposed to what they thought they were
"supposed" to feel.

Most grandparents were intensely interested in, and greatly enjoyed the interview. We did not put "ideas" into the heads of
grandparents but rather assisted them to express thoughts and feelings that lay unexpressed within them. Of course, this method
would not bear rigid scientific scrutiny, but the information thus
gathered is useful in itself. We tried hard to guide the grandparents
and not to lead them.

Often, grandparents would change their original response to a
question after further reflection. This very consistent finding makes
us wary of the validity of the data on emotional issues collected by
national surveys. It is obvious that a survey asking a group of people about their favorite political candidate would yield accurate
data concerning the most popular political figure. *This does not
hold true in emotional issues.* This is illustrated in the following
segment that is excerpted from one of our interviews. (This grandfather moved south to retire, leaving his family in Chicago).

Time Spent In Interview

5 MINUTES.

Examiner: How do you feel about being retired?

Respondent: Fine, it's good. (This would be the answer recorded by a poll). I've waited for this a long time. I should be happy, right?

15 MINUTES.

Examiner: How does it feel not going to work?

Respondent: Fine, I can get up when I wish . . . it's relaxing. Although, sometimes I feel bored, don't do too much now, not much for me to do. Been put out to pasture, I guess.

30 MINUTES.

Examiner: What do you feel about retirement for yourself? Are you happy with your life now?

Respondent: To tell you the truth I really don't feel anything, don't think about it, just do it. But now that you asked, it's fine, I guess. I don't really feel too much. I miss the family a lot and the grandchildren. That makes me sad, and I get lonely for them at times, for the people I worked with. But I've looked forward to this a long time so I'd better like it. Not much I could do about it if I didn't.

45 MINUTES.

Examiner: How do you feel about being retired?

Respondent: I guess that answer is not as simple as I thought it was. It might be better to ask me how do I feel about the different aspects of retirement. If I added them all up I guess it wouldn't be so fine after all. It's a complicated question. I guess I feel fine about some things and bad about others.

In the following pages we present the responses of the grandparents to the questionnaire in terms of percentages responding to each question. Where appropriate, we add comment on the grandparents' responses.

PROXIMITY

Place of residence:
With grandchildren	5%
Within walking distance	10%
Within daily driving distance	40%
Over 100 miles	20%
Over 1,000 miles	25%

CONCEPT OF AGE

Personal Inventory:
Do you enjoy good health?

None of the time	5%
Most of the time	55%
All of the time	40%

(One grandparent had a serious visual problem)

Do you feel "old"?

None of the time	65%
Some of the time	25%
All of the time	10%

Do you think "old"?

None of the time	90%
Most of the time	10%

(This concerned loss of memory, slowness in thinking, decrease in mental alertness, lack of enthusiasm, etc.)

Do others refer to you as "old" because of your appearance?

None of the time	90%
Most of the time	10%

PERSONAL EFFECTIVENESS

Do you allow people to treat you as if you are not there or you do not count?

None of the time	45%
Some of the time	40%
All of the time	15%

Do other people listen to what you have to say?

Some of the time	10%
Most of the time	35%
All of the time	55%

Do you make yourself heard when you disagree with people?

Some of the time	35%
Most of the time	25%
All of the time	45%

(These questions assess the assertiveness of the respondents. Most of the respondents see themselves as relatively assertive; it would have been interesting to probe further to find out under what circumstances they are most assertive. Helplessness is evident in the nonassertive respondents.)

INTERPERSONAL RELATIONSHIPS

Are you intimidated by the young? Do you avoid contact with them?

None of the time	65%
Some of the time	15%
Most of the time	5%
All of the time	15%

Are you intimidated by those with more education or "book learning"?

None of the time	5%
Some of the time	85%
All of the time	10%

Are you intimidated by those who are better off financially?

None of the time	95%
All of the time	5%

Do you feel free to use and express the wisdom and experience that you have learned by virtue of your age alone?

None of the time	25%
Some of the time	10%
Most of the time	15%
All of the time	50%

(The above questions produced a most interesting reaction by many of the respondents. We have described this as a "Lacuna

Effect." We refer to the lacuna when the respondent has no concept of the principles of themselves as an "elder" and no conception of their importance or role in the world. The concept, for example, that age brings wisdom was completely foreign to those who demonstrate the "lacuna"—a vacuum in their self-concept.)

Do you have influence within your family?

None of the time	5%
Some of the time	35%
Most of the time	15%
All of the time	45%

(Several of the respondents who have influence within their family stated that their influence was purely financial. Again it would have been helpful to "fine tune" the question in order to learn the exact nature of the influence. We will do this in the more detailed studies that we plan to carry out.)

DEPENDENCE/INDEPENDENCE

Do you feel that your children "owe" you?

Yes	20%
No	80%

Do you feel that society "owes" you anything?

Yes	50%
No	50%

Do you "owe" your children anything?

None of the time	60%
Some of the time	10%
Most of the time	5%
All of the time	25%

(This group of questions was received with bewilderment by many of the respondents. We asked for a "reflex" response. We were attempting to explore the person's sense of continuity, of "connectedness" to the world. We were impressed with the amount of people and the degree to which their connections were severed in their minds. They had closed the door, "finished the job," "had enough." They had legislated the need for their children and society out of their cognitive sphere with denial and repression. This is a vivid demonstration of the "lacuna.")

Have you shared some of the skills that you have learned along the course of your life with young people?

None of the time	25%
Some of the time	30%
Most of the time	5%
All of the time	40%

PERCEPTIONS OF FAMILY AND GRANDPARENTING

Did you have a good relationship with your grandparents?

None of the time	20%
Most of the time	80%

Did you have a good relationship with your parents?

None of the time	10%
Some of the time	15%
Most of the time	20%
All of the time	55%

Did you have a good relationship with your children?

None of the time	5%
Some of the time	10%
Most of the time	25%
All of the time	60%

(The following questions were designed to appraise the ability of the grandparent to feel that the relationship to the grandchild was a direct one-to-one grandparent-grandchild interaction and not a grandparent-parent-grandchild system. Did they feel a direct rapport with the young?)

Do you take your grandchildren alone on outings?

None of the time	40%
Some of the time	10%
Most of the time	35%
All of the time	15%

(The frequency of outings were not tabulated.)

Do you know the ages of your grandchildren?

Yes	80%
No	20%

Do you know the favorite dishes (foods) of your grandchildren?

None of the time	20%
Some of the time	15%
Most of the time	10%
All of the time	40%

Do you know your grandchildren's friends?

None of the time	35%
Some of the time	25%
Most of the time	20%
All of the time	20%

(The social implications of this question concerning the separation of the generations is obvious.)

Do you celebrate your grandchildren's birthdays?

None of the time	20%
Some of the time	30%
All of the time	50%

Do you have a good relationship with your grandchildren?

Some of the time	10%
Most of the time	15%
All of the time	75%

(Here the lacuna was most evident. In the previous questions concerning "good relationships," we did not probe. The respondents did not understand that time and proximity were the basic foundation for a "good relationship." They confused spending a few pleasant moments together for a true relationship. They thought that they had a "good" relationship but upon deeper probing many expressed feelings that in reality, this relationship was not what they really wanted, that it had no relevance for them, that it wasn't enough.)

Do you see your grandchildren? How often?

None of the time	5%
Some of the time	70%
Most of the time	20%
All of the time	5%

(*Comments*: "As often as humanly possible." "Weekly." "Every other year." "Very seldom." It is of great significance that the emotional reactions of the respondents to this question were quite pronounced. The answers were accompanied with many "guilty and shameful"—the words of one grandparent—emotions. People offered excuses "why" even though it was not requested; some even thought about it and "promised to do better"; again the lacuna was in evidence.)

Does your relationship with your children affect your relationship with your grandchildren?

None of the time	45%
Some of the time	15%
All of the time	20%
No response	20%

Do you have direct communication with your grandchildren when you wish to communicate with them?

None of the time	20%
Most of the time	5%
Some of the time	75%

(We did not ask if the respondents were physically present or used the mail or telephone.)

Do you celebrate holidays with your grandchildren?

None of the time	15%
Some of the time	30%
Most of the time	55%

(Again we did not ask if these celebrations were at a distance or while the family was together. There seemed to be certain holidays in about 70% of the families that they would all try to celebrate together. These were described as times of great emotional impact, positive and negative. The coming together crammed a lot of emotional work into a short period of time.)

Do you feel that you are important to your grandchildren?

None of the time	20%
Some of the time	50%
All of the time	30%

(Again, the lacuna appeared. Many respondents did not understand and were incredulous that they were supposed to be important. They saw the children's parents as all important.)

Do you feel that your grandchildren are an important part of your life?

None of the time	10%
All of the time	90%

(Most of the respondents answered this question in the abstract as the lacuna effect appeared. Some answered: "What for?")

Do your grandchildren need you?

None of the time	20%
Some of the time	20%
All of the time	40%
No response	20%

(There were a considerable amount of respondents who were confused about answering this question. The concept that their grandchildren might need them was new to them. The lacuna was demonstrated. The emotional reactions to this query were quite strong in most every respondent. Several stated that they needed *their* grandparents.)

Do you feel that your grandchildren are part of you since they carry your blood in their veins—a so-called one-fourth of you? Is it important to you?

None of the time	5%
All of the time	75%
No response	20%

(The lacuna emerges again as many of these people have not thought along these very primitive lines of human survival and transmission of inherited factors, genetic traits, etc.)

Do you need your grandchildren?

None of the time	20%
Some of the time	5%
All of the time	75%

(This was a strong response especially since the behavior of most of the respondents was not consistent with the emotional reaction accompanying the response: "What a question! Of course!")

Are you involved in the daily life of your grandchildren?

None of the time	50%

Some of the time	35%
All of the time	15%

(A pattern emerges demonstrating that most of these people are *not doing what they are feeling.* The behavior toward their grandchildren is not determined by the way they feel.)

Do you do foster grandparenting for other people's grandchildren?

None of the time	100%

(Lacuna!)

Have you left your grandchildren to retire to another geographical area? If you have was it a wise decision from an emotional and grandparenting point of view?

Not moved	50%
Move sometimes	25%
Moved away	25%

Seventy percent of those who moved away said that they would not do it over again if they had a choice. They felt out of touch with the emotional life of their families. Much "help-lessness" was described, in an emotional manner. Many were very emphatic about having gone along with the crowd, not thinking about the implications of what they were doing: looking forward to retirement all of their lives and finding it a disappointment.

The respondents who moved away were unanimous in saying that they would not advise their children to do the same as they did.

Do your children feel that you have abandoned them?

None of the time	70%
No response	30%

(The people who could not give an answer seemed a bit bewildered by the context of the question as if they had never thought in these terms of "abandonment." Even the people who stated that their children did not feel abandoned experienced discomfort and uneasiness at the question.)

Do you feel as if your children have abandoned you?

None of the time	75%
Some of the time	25%

(This question elicited a considerable emotional response by the respondents. Almost all hesitated before answering. Many of the 75% were followed by a "but . . ." or "they can't help it.")

Do you feel that your children care for you?

None of the time	10%
Some of the time	10%
Most of the time	20%
All of the time	60%

(This was also a complicated question that elicited varied emotional responses by the grandparents. The "but . . ." following the answer was evident. The respondents went into long explanations evidencing the lacuna.)

Are you glad that you had children?

None of the time	5%
All of the time	95%

(People with unhappy family relationships responded "no." The rest of the people were unanimous in enthusiastically responding in the affirmative. Comments such as "I wish I had more," "I wish I could see them more," etc. were common.)

Would you do it over again, if you had the choice?

No	5%
All of the time	85%
Yes, but differently	10%

(The "differently" response was present with nearly all the respondents on further probing in the interviews.)

Have you relinquished your role as head of the family to a younger person?

None of the time	65%
Some of the time	5%
All of the time	25%
No response	5%

(The lacuna was very much in evidence here for many did not know that the job as "head of the family" existed in a titular or "elder"—"Emeritus" sense.)

Are you involved in decision making in your family?

None of the time	25%
Some of the time	20%
Most of the time	5%
All of the time	50%

Do friends and family seek your advice?

None of the time	0%
Some of the time	30%
Most of the time	20%
All of the time	50%

(These questions were designed to assess the degree that the grandparent was an effective counselor to the family and friends.)

COMMUNITY

Do you participate in the life of the community or the neighborhood in which you live?

None of the time	40%
Some of the time	10%
Most of the time	15%
All of the time	35%

Are you involved in any programs that offer help to the emotionally deprived children in day-care centers, orphanages, divorced families, etc.?

None of the time	65%
Some of the time	20%
All of the time	5%
No response	10%

(Lacuna: "Is that my job, to be involved in these functions?")

Do you use your emotional expertise?

None of the time	40%
Some of the time	10%
All of the time	10%
No response	40%

(To the nonresponders, the question of "emotional expertise" had little relevance. It was difficult to relate it to their own lives and their own value when a mature experienced person was needed in a difficult situation. Nowhere was the lacuna demonstrated more clearly than in this question.)

Do you count in your community?

None of the time	50%
Some of the time	10%
Most of the time	25%
All of the time	5%
No response	10%

(The lacuna was demonstrated again: "Why, am I supposed to be important in my community?" "No, I've done enough.")

Do people in your community welcome your participation?

None of the time	5%
Some of the time	25%
Most of the time	30%
No response	40%

(The answers were diverse and interesting. Many felt that they were rejected or ignored by the community. Many tried but did not get enough feedback or felt that they were shunted aside or patronized. Others felt that they were solicited for financial contributions. Many never tried to affect the community.)

Do you have friends of different ages?

None	30%
Most of the time	70%

(The intensity of the friendships was not examined. It was the consensus among the interviewers that upon closer questioning they meant acquaintances.)

Do you live in an environment that is segregated by age?

None of the time	55%
Some of the time	5%
All of the time	45%

(Most of the respondents felt a separation of the generations and were confused about how to get the generations together.)

Are you involved in organizations that are concerned with child care?

None of the time	90%
Some of the time	5%
All of the time	5%

(The disconnectedness factor is demonstrated in the respondents answer to this critical question.)

Are you involved in national organizations that deal with the problems of the older generations of our citizens?

None	60%
Some of the time	5%
All of the time	35%

Do you think that public attitudes are changing toward older people and their families?

None of the time	20%
Some of the time	15%
Yes	65%

(The respondents felt that the older generations were getting more media exposure than "say, ten years ago.")

Do you feel that you are an effective grandparent?

None of the time	15%
Some of the time	20%
Most of the time	50%
All of the time	15%

(Here the lacuna factor was in great evidence. Many of the respondents needed an explanation of what an effective grandparent was. "Effective in what way?" The people who were in close contact with their grandchildren answered "Yes" in a reflex fashion and needed no clarification of the question. They *felt* it.)

Do you feel that you have been accorded a place by society as elder?

None of the time	40%
Most of the time	50%
No response	10%

(Explanations of the term "elder" were needed in most cases. The concept and its explanation seemed unknown to the respondents, though they accepted it quickly, with enthusiasm, and identified it with their own developmental stage in life. The lacuna was present here.)

OTHER QUESTIONS: (Answers too complex to tabulate open-ended, for discussion)

–Do you have a favorite grandchild?

–What mistakes have you made as a grandparent?
–How did you feel when your first grandchild was born?
–What suggestions do you have to offer to grandparents who would like to improve their relationships with their grandchildren?
–What relevance does the concept of ancestors hold for you?
–What have you learned from your own grandparents. What legacy have they left you (material or otherwise)?
–What legacy are you leaving to your grandchildren?
–What importance does life hold for you now?
–How would you like your grandchildren to remember you?

Dear Grandparent,
    Thank you for your interest in our survey. We are conducting this survey so that we may learn more about how grandparents and grandchildren feel about each other. We are interested in learning about your thoughts and feelings concerning your role as a grandparent, and your relationship with your grandchildren. I would especially appreciate any of your own thoughts on the subject if it is not covered in the questionnaire. I am also interested in the role of the grandparent in society and how you see yourself as a member of society. Please feel free to write anything that comes to mind. All replies will be held in confidence. If you wish do not write your name on the questionnaire. Use as many extra pages as you wish.
    I thank you sincerely for your cooperation.

                                                    Arthur Kornhaber, M.D.

PERSONAL INFORMATION

Name and Address (optional)
Race   Religion   Age   Sex
Do you live alone   with someone   who
Place of residence   how long
        where did you move from
        why did you move
Are you retired   if so, what was your occupation
        do you keep in contact with former colleagues
Are you still working   if yes, what is your occupation
Please list the following information concerning your children
age   sex   residence   occupation

Please list the following concerning your grandchildren (use back of page)
age   sex   residence

Do you reside (circle one)   with your children   within walking distance
                    within daily driving distance   more than 100 miles
                    more than 1,000 miles from your children

Please answer the following by placing a number in the margin or a comment on the reverse side of the page.
(1=No, Never)   (2=Some of the time)   (3=Most of the time)   (4=Yes, Always)

Personal
Do you enjoy good health—
Do you feel "old"—
Do you find yourself thinking "old"—
Do others refer to you as an "old" person because of your appearance—
Do you allow people to treat you as if you are not there or do not count—
Do other people listen to what you have to say—
Do you make yourself heard when you disagree with people—
Are you intimidated by the young, do you back off from contact with them—
Are you intimidated by those with more education or "book learning"—
Are you intimidated by those who are better off financially—
Do you feel free to use and express the wisdom and experience that you have
    learned by virtue of your age alone—
Do you have influence within your family—
Do you feel that your children "owe" you—
Do you feel that society "owes" you—
Do you "owe" your children—
Have you shared some of the skills that you have learned along the course of
    your life with young people—

Grandparenting
Did you have a good relationship with your grandparents—
        "   "   "   parents—
        "   "   "   children—
Do   "   "   "   grandchildren—
You see your grandchildren (How often)—
Does your relationship with your children affect your relationship with your
    grandchildren—

Do you have direct communication with your grandchildren when you wish
  to contact them—
Do you take your grandchildren alone on outings—
Do you know the ages of your grandchildren—
Do you know the favorite foods of your grandchildren—
Do you know your grandchildren's friends—
Do you have a favorite grandchild—
How did you feel when your first grandchild was born—
Do you celebrate your grandchildren's birthdays with them—
Do you celebrate holidays with them—
Do you feel that you are important to your grandchildren—
Do you feel that your grandchildren are an important part of your life—
Do your grandchildren need you—
Do you feel that your grandchildren are PART of you (since they carry your
  blood in their veins)—   (heredity factors)—
Do you NEED your grandchildren—
Are you involved in the daily life of your grandchildren—
Do you do "foster grandparenting" for other people's grandchildren—
Have you left your grandchildren to retire in another geographical location—
  If you have, was it a wise decision from an emotional and grandparental
  point of view—
  Would you do it over again if you had a choice—
  Would you advise YOUR children to do the same—
Do your children feel that you have abandoned them—
Do you feel that your children have abandoned you—
Do you feel that your children care for you—
Are you glad that you had children—
  Would you do it over again if you had a choice—
Have you relinquished your role as head of the family to a younger person in
  the family—
Are you involved in decision making in your family—
Do friends and family seek out your advice—

Social
Do you participate in the life of the community or neighborhood in which
  you live—
Are you involved in any programs that offer help to the emotionally deprived
  children in day care centers, orphanages, divorced families, etc.—
Do you use your EMOTIONAL expertise—
Do you count in your community—
Do people in your community welcome your participation—
Do you have friends of different ages—
Do you live in an environment that is segregated by age—

Is your relationship with your grandchildren different from your relationship to your own children. If yes, in what way—

Are you involved in organizations that are concerned with child care—

Are you involved in any national organizations that deal with the problems of the older generations of our citizens—

Do you feel that the public's attitude is changing toward older people and their families—

Do you feel that you are an effective grandparent—

If you had it to do over again, as a grandparent and an elder, what would you do differently—

What suggestions do you have to offer to people that would like to have a better relationship with their grandchildren—

Do you feel that you have achieved a stage in life where your personal experience, emotional maturity and factual knowledge have earned you the respect of others and above all, self respect. Are you satisfied that you have been accorded a place as "elder" in the community in which you live—

What meaning, or importance, does life hold for you now—

What does the idea of ANCESTORS mean to you. Does this concept have any relevance to your own life and experience—

What have you learned from your own grandparents. What legacy have they left you (material or otherwise)—

What legacy are you leaving to your children or grandchildren (material or otherwise)—

How would you like your grandchildren to remember you—

Please add any additional comments that you could offer concerning your feelings about grandparenting and your own place as "elder" in society. What could we do that would be of help.

Many thanks for your kind cooperation

Notes

1. Our inquiry into what was already known about grandparents and grandchildren led us into diverse academic territories.

A review of the classic work of Margaret Mead, Erik Erikson, and Robert Coles was especially helpful. In the "primitive" or "basic" cultures that they described, grandparents had a place, a role and were a vital force in the culture. Thus, we learned that what was industrially primitive, was not necessarily emotionally primitive. Indeed, these cultures seemed to have an ethos that balanced emotional and work needs: people were together in time and place, children flourished, grandparents were celebrated.

This substantiated our observation that the disconnection of the generations occurred with the rise of industrialization. To confirm this, we inquired of colleagues all over the world about the status of grandparents in their countries. Sure enough, when we reviewed their responses we found that the degree of dismemberment of the family was proportional to the pace of industrialization of the country. It is happening at the present time in different degrees in many of the Third World countries. Our colleagues expressed dismay that this was happening. They also felt helpless to do anything about it.

The helping professions have virtually ignored the role of grandparents in the family. We learned little from the psychoanalytic literature. This is understandable because the primary focus of psychoanalysis has been on parent-child relationships in the formation of personality.

For the most part, family therapy has limited itself to dealing with the nuclear family. This is all the more surprising since pioneers in the field, such as Murray Bowen, M.D., have stressed the importance of extended family attachments. Indeed, he has linked the resolution of these attachments to the individual's well-being. Fortunately, a few therapists have taken notice of grandparents. Salvador Minuchin, M.D. describes three subsystems within the family (spouse, parenting, sibling). He observes that the parenting system "may include a grandmother." Phillip Guerin, M.D. has called attention to both the positive and pathogenic roles of grandparents in the family. Carl Whittaker, M.D. has taken an active role in recruiting grandparents to assist their troubled families. He frequently invites grandparents into family sessions and has stated that he "grows more and more convinced that it is always helpful." He advises therapists to invite the grandparents to family sessions when therapy has reached an impasse.

It is our profound hope that grandparents will be included as an integral part of family research and therapy. They should be routinely included in the treatment of troubled children and adolescents. They offer a plausible answer to one of the greatest problems that plague our young and our society—the lack of caring adults.

Social scientists have talked about grandparents in different ways: some negatively, some disdainfully, some nostalgically. There are few systematic studies that examine the relationship between grandparents and grandchildren. The following studies are among the most important: In 1964, Bernice Neugarten and Karol Weinstein described the "Changing American Grandparent."* In this study of seventy grandparent couples, inquiring into the symbolic meaning of the grandchild to the grandparent, they found that:

> Sixty percent were comfortable in the role of either grandmother (59%) or grandfather (61%). Thirty-six percent of grandmothers and twenty-nine percent of grandfathers experienced displeasure or discomfort.
> To grandparents, the role meant: biological renewal, emotional

self-fulfillment, being a better grandparent than parent, resource person, accomplishing vicariously through the grandchild, or little effect
(grandparent feels remote from grandchild).

The styles of grandparenting they described included: formal, fun-
seeker, surrogate parent, reservoir of family wisdom, the distant
figure.

At the end of this study the authors stated that their information was not conclusive and recommended further lines of inquiry.

In 1970 Kahana and Kahana published their findings of their
study on "Grandparenthood from the Perspective of the Developing
Grandchild."† They explored the changing meaning of the grandparent for children of different ages (4–5, 8–9, 11–12). They
stated:

> Children's views of grandparents paralleled developmental cogni-
> tive changes ranging from concrete perceptions of physical characteris-
> tics by the youngest children, through functional views of behavior
> in the middle group and finally to the emergence of an abstract inter-
> personal orientation among the oldest children. Major differences in
> the quality of perception occurred between the youngest and middle-
> aged groups. Young children valued grandparents mainly for their in-
> dulgent qualities, the middle group preferred the fun-sharing active
> grandparent, and the oldest group reflected distance from their grand-
> parents.

Their study was conducted with eighty-five children. "The
youngest were interviewed in their homes. Questions were adminis-
tered in groups during a class period to the older children." The
findings of their study suggested that "the meaning of the grandparental role for the aging grandparent must be understood in the
context of the changing needs of the developing grandchild." They
concluded that further research was necessary and suggested "a
most fruitful approach of future investigations would be a simultaneous consideration of the changing needs of grandchildren and of
their grandparents and their perceptions of one another."

Robertson and Wood‡ studied the meaning and significance of
grandparenthood to middle-aged and older adults in a predomi-
nantly stable working-class area in Wisconsin. They interviewed
257 grandparents. They examined (1) the individual's evaluation
and description of the role, and (2) the way the person enacts the
role. They found that "more involved grandparents did tend to
have slightly higher levels of life satisfaction, involvement with the
role appears to stem from personal forces within the individual and
meet his needs." They concluded with suggestions for further research.

Our own work confirms and amplifies the findings of these excellent studies and, we hope, links them together in a useful pattern. Our section on "roles" includes many of the same observations made by Neugarten and Weinstein. The "kinetic" factor of the shifting and changing relationship between grandparents and grandchildren was observed by Kahana and Kahana. We would add however, that although the relationship changes according to the cognitive style of the youngster, it also changes according to the needs of the youngster. We asserted that *all* of the roles of the grandparent are available to the child at any time. The earlier "caretaking" roles of grandparents are reactivated when the child is in danger. Our study confirms the observation of Robertson and Wood that "personal" factors are important in grandparenting. We have noted the immunity of some grandparents to the "nonrole" designated them by society. We noted that they place an emotional priority on their lives. We further postulate that the reason they are able to do this is because they have had a close relationship to a grandparent of their own when they were children, or, by nature, are exceptionally altruistic and compassionate people, or both.

* Neugarten, Bernice and Weinstein, Karol, "The Changing American Grandparent." *Journal of Marriage and the Family*, Vol. 26, No. 2, May 1964.

† Kahana, Boaz and Kahana, Eva, "Grandparenthood from the Perspective of the Developing Grandchild," *Developmental Psychology*, 1970, Vol. 3, No. 1, 98–105.

‡ Wood, Vivian and Robertson, Joan F., *The Significance of Grandparenthood Time, Roles and Self in Old Age*, Gubrium J. Human Sciences Press, 1976, 278–304.

2. Jones, Ernest, *The Life and Work of Sigmund Freud* (New York: Basic Books, 1957), pp. 91–92.

3. Neugarten, Bernice L., "The Rise of the Young-Old," The New York *Times*, January 18, 1975, reprinted in Gross, Ronald, Gross, Beatrice, and Seidman, Sylvia, eds. *The New Old: Struggling for Decent Aging* (New York: Anchor Press/Doubleday, 1978).

4. Fischer, David Hackett, in *The New Republic*, December 2, 1978, p. 34. For a fuller view of Fischer's position, see Fischer, David Hackett, *Growing Old in America* (New York: Oxford University Press, 1978).

5. *The Older Woman: Continuities and Discontinuities.* Report of the National Institute on Aging and the National Institute of Mental Health Workshop. September 14–16, 1978. National Institutes Publication No. 79–1897, October 1979.

6. Flanagan, John C. and Russ-Eft, Darlene, "Identifying Opportunities for Improving the Quality of Life of Older Age Groups." *Program Report*, January 1978.

7. Butler, Robert N., M.D., *Why Survive? Being Old in America* (New York: Harper & Row, 1975, 1977), pp. ix–x.

8. Mead, Margaret, *Blackberry Winter* (New York: William Morrow & Co., 1972), p. 45, 54.

9. Sartre, Jean-Paul, *The Words*, trans. by Bernard Frechtman (New York: Fawcett World Library, 1977), p. 14.

10. Lowell, Robert, *Selected Poems* (New York: Farrar, Straus & Giroux, 1976), p. 74.

CHAPTER 1

1. "You know, there are a lot of myths about young children. Many people think of them as cute, simple, and rather dumb—'childish.' But I've found that they're surprisingly good social diagnosticians. I mean, they're quite alert and sensitive to what's happening around and to them. They know about and react to their parents' frustration and inadequacies." Kessen, William, "Family Survival: The Carnegie Report," in *Today in Psychology*, Vol. 5, No. 2, February 1979, p. 2.

2. "Many children do not need toys with which to construe a play situation. They can express themselves by means of drawings. The mere drawing of a house sometimes gives clues to the child's feelings, especially when he begins to talk about it and its inhabitants. He can depict drabness and brightness, draw a doorless and windowless jail, or crayon smilingly his version of

a colorful mansion. He can eliminate from its occupancy a resented sibling or rival. He can bring himself meaningfully into relation to the house and the family who lives in it . . ." Kanner, Leo, M.D., *Child Psychiatry*, 4th edition (Springfield, Ill.: Charles C. Thomas, 1979), p. 219.

3. Freud, Sigmund, "The Occurrence in Dreams of Material in Fairy Tales," 1913 in *Collected Papers*, Vol. 4, trans. under the supervision of Joan Riviere (New York: Basic Books, 1959), p. 253.

4. Levy, Sidney, "Projective Figure Drawing," in *The Clinical Application of Projective Drawings*, Hammer, Emanuel F., Ph.D., ed. (Springfield, Ill.: Charles C. Thomas, 1978), p. 85.

5. "When an individual attempts to solve the problem of the directive to Draw a Person, he is compelled to draw from some sources. External figures are too varied in their body attributes to lend themselves to a spontaneous, composite, objective representation of a person. Some process of selection involving identification through projection and introjection enters at some point. The individual must draw consciously and no doubt unconsciously upon his whole system of psychic values." Machover, Karen, *Personality Projection in The Drawing of the Human Figure* (Springfield, Ill.: Charles C. Thomas, 1949), p. 5.

6. For detailed discussion of protest, despair and detachment, see Bowlby, John, *Attachment and Loss*, Vols. 1–3 (New York: Basic Books, 1969, 1973, 1980).

7. "The loss of the mother figure or of the love object is responded to by the infant with grief. A study concerned with the effects of continuous institutional care of infants under one year of age for reasons other than sickness. The subjects were children in a foundling home, those in a nursery for children of juvenile delinquent mothers and noninstitutionalized children of deprived and disadvantaged backgrounds. A comparison of developmental quotients at the age of four and twelve months showed a severe deterioration in the foundling children . . . as opposed to the nursery home children who were cared for by their own mothers." Spitz, Rene A., "Hospitalism," *Psychoanalytic Study of the Child*, Vol. 1 (New York: International Universities Press, 1945), pp. 53–74.

CHAPTER 2

1. Erikson, Erik H., *Childhood and Society* (New York: W. W. Norton & Co., 1964), p. 267. For fuller treatment of the concept of generativity, see also *Insight and Responsibility* (New York: W. W. Norton & Co., 1964); *Gandhi's Truth* (New York: W. W. Norton & Co., 1970) and "Reflections on Dr. Borg's Life Cycle" in Erikson, Erik H., ed., *Adulthood* (W. W. Norton & Co., 1978).

2. Ibid.

CHAPTER 3

1. For the concepts of life story, turning points and standpoints, we are indebted to the work of John S. Dunne, C.S.C. See especially his *A Search for God in Time and Memory* (New York: Macmillan, 1969). Also, *Time and Myth: A Meditation on Storytelling as an Exploration of Life and Death* (New York: Doubleday, 1973). Also, Woodward, Kenneth L. in conversation with John Dunne, "The Emergence of a New Theology," *Psychology Today*, Vol. 11, No. 8, January 1978, pp. 47–92.

2. For a discussion of the new class see Bruce-Briggs, B., ed., *The New Class?* (New Brunswick, N.J.: Transaction Books, 1978). Also Gouldner, Alvin W., *The Future of Intellectuals and the Rise of the New Class* (New York: Seabury Press, 1979). For a brief summary of new class discussion, see Woodward, Kenneth L. with Mark, Rachael, "America's New Class," *Newsweek*, May 21, 1979, pp. 91–93b.

3. Pritchett, V. S., "Finite Variety," *The New York Review of Books*, November 8, 1979, p. 7.

4. Pifer, Alan, "Perceptions of Childhood and Youth," *Annual Report of the Carnegie Corporation of New York*, 1978.

5. Cited in Neugarten, Bernice L., "Time, Age, and the Life Cycle," *American Journal of Psychiatry*, Vol. 139, July 1979, p. 890.

6. Hareven, Tamara K., "The Last Stage: Historical Adulthood and Old Age," in Van Tassel, David D., ed., *Aging, Death and the Completion of Being* (Philadelphia: University of Pennsylvania Press, 1979), p. 175.

7. Mead, Margaret, *Culture and Commitment,* revised and updated edition (New York: Anchor/Doubleday, 1978), pp. 75, 76.

8. Bakan, David, *And They Took Themselves Wives: The Emergence of Patriarchy in Western Civilization* (San Francisco: Harper & Row, 1979), p. 11.

9. For a representative sample of diverse viewpoints among historians of the family regarding intergenerational relationships in previous periods of American history, see the following: Fischer, David Hackett, op. cit.; Rossi, Alice S., Kagan, Jerome and Hareven, Tamara K., eds., *The Family* (New York: W. W. Norton & Co., 1978); Van Tassel, David D., ed., op. cit.; Erikson, Erik, ed., op. cit.; Achenbaum, W. Andrew, *Old Age in the New Land: The American Experience Since 1790* (Baltimore: Johns Hopkins Press, 1979); Achenbaum, W. Andrew, "From Womb Through Bloom to Tomb: The Birth of a New Area of Historical Research," *Reviews in American History,* June 1978, pp. 178–183; Stone, Lawrence, "Walking Over Grandma," *The New York Review of Books,* May 12, 1977.

10. "During periods of economic constraint, families thus balanced their resources through the allocation of tasks and responsibilities among their members. In this setting, the old could also continue to perform valuable services. After they were too old to work, they took care of the children of working mothers, helped with the housekeeping and, if necessary, shared housing space with younger family members in exchange for economic support . . . The system often placed considerable constraint on individual careers and generated tension and conflicts between aging parents and their children. Nevertheless, in the absence of institutional buttresses, instrumental relationships were a pervasive and realistic response to the pressures that economic exigencies imposed on individual families . . . Such interdependence also exposed children and youth to greater responsibility toward older people than is common among them today." Hareven, Tamara K., "The Last Stage," pp. 180–181.

11. Freud, Sigmund, *Civilization and Its Discontents*, trans. by James Strachey (New York: W. W. Norton & Co., 1962, 1963), pp. 26–27.

12. Inholder, Anne, "The Language and Thought of the Child: The Work of Jean Piaget," lecture delivered at the University of Florida, 1969.

13. For a detailed elucidation of the ethos of being, see: Pieper, Josef, *Leisure the Basis of Culture* (New York: Pantheon, 1964); *Happiness and Contemplation* (New York: Pantheon, 1958) and *In Tune with the World: A Theory of Festivity* (New York: Harcourt, Brace & World, 1963).

CHAPTER 4

1. Neugarten, Bernice L., "The Rise of the Young-Old," The New York *Times*, p. 49.

2. Butler, Robert, *Why Survive?* pp. ix–x.

3. Bronfenbrenner, Urie, *Two Worlds of Children: U.S. AND U.S.S.R.* (New York: Russell Sage, 1970), p. 116–117.

4. Bronfenbrenner, Urie, quoted in Woodward, Kenneth L. with Malamud, Phyllis, "The Parent Gap," *Newsweek*, September 22, 1975, p. 48.

5. Rossi, Alice S., "A Biosocial Perspective on Parenting," in *The Family*, p. 1.

6. Ibid.

7. Mumford, Lewis, *The City in History* (New York: Harcourt, Brace & World, 1961), p. 7.

8. Bensman, Joseph and Lilienfeld, Robert, *Craft and Consciousness* (New York: John Wiley & Sons, 1973), pp. 1–5.

9. Neugarten, Bernice L., "Time, Age, and the Life Cycle," *American Journal of Psychiatry*, p. 889.

10. Kellam, S. G., Ensminger, M. E., and Thurner, R. J., "Family Structures and the Mental Health of Children," *Archives of General Psychiatry*, September 1977, Vol. 34, No. 9, p. 1012.

11. Forster, H. H. and Freed, D. J., "Law and the Family," *New York Law Journal*, January 2, 1978, p. 1.

12. Freud, Sigmund.

13. Quoted in Shainess, N. S., M.D., Address to the Annual Meeting of the American Academy of Psychoanalysis, 1979.

Bibliography

BOOKS

1. Achenbaum, W. Andrew. *Old Age in the New Land: The American Experience Since 1790*. Baltimore: The Johns Hopkins University Press, 1979.
2. Anastasi, Anne. *Psychological Testing*, 4th edition. New York: Macmillan, 1976.
3. Bakan, David. *And They Took Themselves Wives: The Emergence of Patriarchy in Western Civilization*. San Francisco: Harper & Row, 1979.
4. Bensman, Joseph and Lilienfeld, Robert. *Craft and Consciousness*. New York: John Wiley & Sons, 1973.
5. Blythe, Ronald. *The View in Winter: Reflections on Old Age*. New York: Harcourt Brace Jovanovich, 1979.
6. Bowlby, John. *Attachment and Loss*, 3 vols. New York: Basic Books, 1969, 1973, 1980.
7. Bronfenbrenner, Urie. *Two Worlds of Children*. New York: Russell Sage, 1970.
8. Bruce-Briggs, B., ed. *The New Class?* New Brunswick, N.J.: Transaction Books, 1978.

9. Castaneda, Carlos. *Journey to Ixtlan*. New York: Simon and Schuster, 1972.
10. Coles, Robert. *Eskimos, Chicanos, Indians*. Vol. 4 of Children in Crisis. Boston: Little, Brown & Co., 1978.
11. Coles, Robert. *The Old Ones of New Mexico*. Albuquerque: University of New Mexico Press, 1973.
12. Curtin, Sharon R. *Nobody Ever Died of Old Age*. Boston: Little, Brown & Co., 1973.
13. de Beauvoir, Simone. *The Coming of Age*. New York: Warner Books, 1973.
14. Deutsch, Helene. *The Psychology of Women*, 2 vols. New York: Grune & Stratton, 1944, 1945.
15. Dunne, John C.S.C. *A Search for God in Time and Memory*. New York: Macmillan, 1969.
16. Dunne, John C.S.C. *Time and Myth: A Meditation on Storytelling as an Exploration of Life and Death*. New York: Doubleday, 1973.
17. Erikson, Erik. *Childhood and Society*. New York: W. W. Norton & Co., 1964.
18. Erikson, Erik. *Insight and Responsibility*. New York: W. W. Norton & Co., 1964.
19. Erikson, Erik, ed. *Adulthood*. New York: W. W. Norton & Co., 1978.
20. Fischer, David Hackett. *Growing Old in America*. New York: Oxford University Press, 1976, 1978.
21. Freud, Sigmund. *Collected Papers*. Vol. 4, trans. under the supervision of Joan Riviere. New York: Basic Books, 1959.
22. Freud, Sigmund. *Civilization and Its Discontents*, trans. by James Strachey. New York: W. W. Norton & Co., 1962, 1963.
23. Gaylin, Willard. *Feelings: Our Vital Signs*. New York: Harper & Row, 1979.
24. Gouldner, Alvin W. *The Future of Intellectuals and the Rise of the New Class*. New York: Seabury Press, 1979.
25. Gross, Ronald, Gross, Beatrice and Seidman, Sylvia, eds. *The New Old: Struggling for Decent Aging*. New York: Anchor Press/Doubleday, 1973.
26. Hammer, Emanuel F., Ph.D., ed. *The Clinical Application of Projective Drawings*. Springfield, Ill.: Charles C. Thomas, 1978.
27. Josephy, Alvin M., Jr. *The Indian Heritage of America*. New York: Alfred A. Knopf, 1968.

28. Jung, Carl G. *Memories, Dreams, Reflections*. New York: Random House, 1961, 1965.
29. Kanner, Leo, M.D. *Child Psychiatry*, 4th edition. Springfield, Ill.: Charles C. Thomas, 1979.
30. Kenniston, Kenneth and The Carnegie Council on Children. *All Our Children: The American Family Under Pressure*. New York: Harcourt Brace Jovanovich, 1977.
31. Lasch, Christopher. *Haven in a Heartless World: The Family Besieged*. New York: Basic Books, 1979.
32. Lasch, Christopher. *The Culture of Narcissism*. New York: W. W. Norton & Co., 1979.
33. Levinson, Daniel J. *The Seasons of a Man's Life*. New York: Alfred A. Knopf, 1978.
34. Lorenz, Konrad. *On Aggression*. New York: Harcourt, Brace & World, 1966.
35. Lowell, Robert. *Selected Poems*. New York: Farrar, Straus and Giroux, 1976.
36. Machover, Karen. *Personality Projection in the Drawing of the Human Figure*. Springfield, Ill.: Charles C. Thomas, 1949.
37. Mead, Margaret. *Blackberry Winter*. New York: William Morrow & Co., 1972.
38. Mead, Margaret. *Culture and Commitment*. New York: Natural History Press/Doubleday & Co., 1978.
39. Mumford, Lewis. *The City in History*. New York: Harcourt, Brace & World, 1961.
40. Paulme, Denise. *Women of Tropical Africa*. Berkeley, Calif.: University of California Press, 1963.
41. Pieper, Josef. *Happiness and Contemplation*. New York: Pantheon, 1958.
42. Pieper, Josef. *In Tune with the World: A Theory of Festivity*. New York: Harcourt, Brace & World, 1963.
43. Pieper, Josef. *Leisure the Basis of Culture*. New York: New American Library, 1964.
44. Rossi, Alice S., Kagan, Jerome and Hareven, Tamara K., eds. *The Family*. New York: W. W. Norton & Co., 1978.
45. Sartre, Jean-Paul. *The Words*, trans. by Bernard Frechtman. New York: Fawcett World Library, 1977.
46. Sheehy, Gail. *Passages*. New York: E. P. Dutton & Co., 1976.
47. Soloman, Robert C. *The Passions*. New York: Anchor Press/Doubleday, 1977.
48. Spitz, Rene A. *Psychoanalytic Study of the Child*. Vol. 1. New York: International Universities Press, 1945.

49. Storr, Anthony. *Jung*. New York: Viking Press, 1973.
50. Tournier, Paul. *Learn To Grow Old*. New York: Harper & Row, 1973.
51. Van Tassel, David D., ed. *Aging, Death and the Completion of Being*. Philadelphia: University of Pennsylvania Press, 1979.
52. Wigginton, Eliot. *The Foxfire Book*. Anchor Press/Doubleday, 1972.
53. Wilson, Edward O. *On Human Nature*. Harvard University Press, 1978.

ARTICLES, ADDRESSES, REPORTS

1. Achenbaum, W. Andrew. "From Womb Through Bloom to Tomb: The Birth of a New Area of Historical Research," *Reviews in American History*. June, 1978.
2. "America's New Class," *Newsweek*. May 21, 1979.
3. Fischer, David Hackett. *The New Republic*. December 2, 1978.
4. *The Older Woman: Continuities and Discontinuities*. Report of the National Institute on Aging and the National Institute of Mental Health Workshop. September 14–16, 1978. National Institutes Publication No. 79–1897, October 1979.
5. Forester, H. H., and Freed, D. J. "The Law and the Family," *New York Law Journal*, January 2, 1978.
6. Inholder, Anne. "The Language and Thought of the Child: The Work of Jean Piaget," lecture delivered at the University of Florida, 1969.
7. Kellam, S. G., Ensminger, M. E., and Thurner, R. J. "Family Structures and the Mental Health of Children," *Archives of General Psychiatry*. September 1977.
8. Kessen, William. "Family Survival: The Carnegie Report," *Today in Psychology*. Vol. 5. No. 2. February 1979.
9. Neugarten, Bernice L. "Time, Age, and the Life Cycle," *American Journal of Psychiatry*. Vol. 139. July 1979.
10. Pifer, Alan. "Perceptions of Childhood and Youth," *Annual Report of the Carnegie Corporation of New York*. 1978.
11. Pritchett, V. S. "Finite Variety," *The New York Review of Books*. November 8, 1979.
12. Shainess, N. S., M.D. Address to the Annual Meeting of the American Academy of Psychoanalysis, 1979.
13. Stone, Lawrence. "Walking Over Grandma," *The New York Review of Books*. May 12, 1977.
14. "The Parent Gap," *Newsweek*. September 22, 1975.

Index

About the Authors

ARTHUR KORNHABER, M.D., is a member of the American Academy of Child Psychiatry and the American Association for Geriatric Psychiatry. A clinician, medical writer and researcher, he is presently medical director of a Pediatric Neuropsychiatric Group that treats children and their families. He is also a member of the American Medical Association and the American Psychiatric Association and has received numerous awards for medical research. He lives in Westchester County with his wife and four children.

KENNETH L. WOODWARD is a Senior Writer for *Newsweek* magazine and a contributor to numerous other publications. Among his more than two dozen cover stories for *Newsweek* are "Saving the Family," "Who's Raising the Kids?" "The Graying of America," "The Quest for Identity," and "Living With Dying." In eighteen years as a journalist, Mr. Woodward has won numerous awards, including the National Media Award from the American Psychological Foundation and the National Magazine Award. A native of Cleveland, Ohio, and a graduate of the University of Notre Dame and the University of Iowa, Mr. Woodward lives in Briarcliff Manor, New York, with his wife, Betty and three children.